A Merry Xmas
and A Happy
New Year.
To Floyd
From Edith & Leigh

THE IMPOSSIBLE BOY

"I shall come when the violets are in bloom."

THE IMPOSSIBLE BOY

By

NINA WILCOX PUTNAM

Author of
IN SEARCH OF ARCADY

Illustrated by
ARTHUR I. KELLER

INDIANAPOLIS
THE BOBBS-MERRILL COMPANY
PUBLISHERS

COPYRIGHT 1913
THE BOBBS-MERRILL COMPANY

PRESS OF
BRAUNWORTH & CO.
BOOKBINDERS AND PRINTERS
BROOKLYN, N. Y.

To
R. F. P.

CONTENTS

Chapter		Page
I	OF INTRODUCTIONS	1
II	A BELIEF IN SIGNS	18
III	A LOSS AND A FIND	40
IV	THAT WHICH IS NO ROBBERY	57
V	TWO MEETINGS	80
VI	THE PEOPLE DOWN-STAIRS	102
VII	A PARTY IN THE ALLEY	112
VIII	OF REVOLUTIONARY SAVOR	136
IX	THE LADY OF MYSTERY	158
X	CONCERNING BOHEMIA	185
XI	SUNDRY ADVENTURES	213
XII	A COMPROMISE	250
XIII	SOME ADVENTURES WITH VARIATIONS	268
XIV	TO THE RESCUE	300
XV	SNOW AND DOGS AND THINGS	314
XVI	A BYZANTINE PRINCESS	326
XVII	PLOTS	345
XVIII	AND COUNTERPLOTS	359
XIX	A MOMENTOUS EVENING	373
XX	THE BEGINNING	386

THE IMPOSSIBLE BOY

THE IMPOSSIBLE BOY

CHAPTER I

OF INTRODUCTIONS

"YOU see, Mr. Jones, so many people are introduced, who never really meet," said Pedro, "that it seems a pity those who could meet have to wait for an introduction, eh?"

Mr. Jones stopped licking his front paws, and raised his head, the tip of his nose twitching attentively. For several moments he looked at Pedro with an unwavering stare, and then, as though suddenly remembering what he had been about, resumed the lavatorial process. It might be mentioned in passing that Mr. Jones was a small brown bear, fat, young, and intelligent.

Pedro rolled over in the dried yellow grass, luxuriating in its warmth, and in the poignant odor of autumn foliage turned to flame by long absorption of the summer sun. On either hand the meadow rolled away in golden brown waves; here to a skyline topped by silhouetted corn-stacks; there to where, distantly, a scarlet trolley-car was speeding along the dusty highway. Still farther off lay Long Island Sound, seen dimly through the haze. The day was one of those, filled with a spirit of yearning, which stirs the imagination, encourages tender melancholy, and gives impetus to the search after the indefinable—that search which lurks forever fugitive in the human consciousness. The pale blue sky seemed closer than usual, and the soft cool air stirred the very heart of suggestion. To the youth lying in the stubby grass, life seemed just now to hold all too many possibilities, and he was filled with a sort of self-pity, because he could not grasp them all.

Although it was only mid-afternoon, he had already stolen away from Beau-Jean, Rico, and the others, in order to fight out the battle of an important decision in privacy. But now that he was alone with his problem and his bear, he found himself afraid of the former, and to put off the evil moment when he must think in good earnest, he talked to the animal. Mr. Jones, having satisfied himself that his paws were immaculate (as bear-paws go), had fallen to biting his chain in a meditative manner, which was not indicative of resentment induced by the sign of his captivity, but merely a sort of ruminative habit he had. The lad reached out a slim brown hand and took up one of the newly laved paws.

"How do you do, Mr. Jones?" said he solemnly. "I am delighted to meet you!—That's how they do it, eh? Now, I call it silly that some one has to say a charm before two others are permitted to make an inquiry after the health! What do you think, Mr. Jones?"

The bear gave a little grunt and thrust his nose into the boy's palm.

"Ah! I knew you would agree," exclaimed Pedro. He gave the creature's ear an affectionate tweak and then spread his slender length upon the ground again.

"I liked that girl," he continued aloud, "you should have seen her, Mr. Jones; she had red hair. Not horrid red, but red-gold like,—like *joy!* All crisp and curling it was. And such a beautiful pale face. She looked at me, you must know, but I did not dare to speak, because she would not have answered, and that would have been a tragedy. Why should she speak to a ragged young man to whom she had never been introduced? Of course, she would not! I wish she had, though, because I liked her . . . But I could look at her. That was something!"

The bear cocked its head to one side and smiled moistly.

"It was this morning, while I was persuading that shoemaker beyond to exchange good leather for an indifferent song," continued Pedro, "she walked past the shop with her head in the air, stepping daintily across the dust to a great automobile of exceeding redness. There was a line, *amigo mio,* from her chin to the base of her throat—ah!"

He rolled over again, burying his face in his folded arms. One long sigh escaped him, and then a second, for the mention of that beautiful line from breast to chin had reawakened his subdominant problem—the problem of his future, and of his life-work. Happy as he was, he could no longer put off a decision regarding it. The craving to get at the occupation nearest his heart had been gathering strength these many months past and was now straining at the leashes of his will, tearing him from one dearly loved way of life to another, scarcely tried, yet which called him ceaselessly. Was he to continue free—(a mere dancer of bears) but *free?* Or should he at last become a painter, chained to his work by ties as strong as those which held his bear, for all they would be invisible?

Before his mental vision arose the phantom of what he would fain interpret and depict . . . The spires of cities, smoke from the altars of commerce, teeming multitudes of men and women. Shops' lights, color, movement, broad boulevards adorned by the equipages of the rich; narrow alleys where the poor jostled and bartered at push-carts in the murky flare of lamps; visions of broad roof-tops, spreading acre on acre, mile on mile—a veritable ocean of roofs stretching far as eye could see, covering more pain and passion than the heart could know, more colored with joy than the hand could depict. And the boats of travel, of trade, on errands of pleasure or of war. Gleaming, they slipped through the night with music; portentous, they loomed through the fog, speaking hoarsely their warning to each other. Again a stretch of roof-tops —giants, on whose heads the sky seemed to rest: pinnacles of faith, diversified and of many creeds; and still taller pinnacles, reared to Mammon. Wet streets gleaming beneath a million lamps. Like the black shadows cast of clouds, the people, massing, separating, remassing upon the pavements. For an instant he seemed to hold the Empire City, its life, its very soul, in his two hands, and of it molded a presentation of Truth. With a start he knelt upright, stretching his arms wide in ecstasy.

The bear, who had fallen asleep, was disturbed by the sudden movement of his master, and when no apology was forthcoming, and no attention paid him, thrust an affectionate inquiring snout into the youth's side. With an incoherent exclamation, Pedro dropped his visioning, and looking upon the bear, the dear familiarity of every-day things swept over him with an emotion that was no less poignant for being narrower than the one that had preceded it.

"Oh, Mr. Jones!" he cried, throwing his arms about the animal and hugging it to him.

How could he let go the infinite variety of every day? Ah! he could not; it was impossible! Renounce the long white road that led to nowhere, yet which brought one to a new place each hour? Renounce the nights spent beneath the open heavens: the sweet summer nights among the meadow flowers; the winter twilights, when he and the bear cowered down together in the hay of a lonely barn, or if they were rich, procured the privilege of a tavern kitchen with the spoils of the evening's performance! Oh, blessed days of journeying among simple adventures, tramping all through the noon, or loafing long hours and dreaming! Now, it was a group of children, laughing for glee at Mr. Jones' dancing, then a curious crowd in a sordid village street, enticed into merriment and self-forgetfulness by his antics. At another time, Mr. Jones, sedate and full of decorous tricks, was solemnly exhibited to the inhabitants of a great country house, where the governess gave him money gingerly and kept her charges at a safe distance, while in the background giggling maids, white aprons fluttering in the breeze, watched half-afraid. And there were the road houses at night, where laborers of the district came, and others, too —coachmen, and men servants and delinquent husbands of the townswomen. Here he and the bear would dance the "coquette" (learned in Paris), to the accompaniment of uproarious applause; and the harvest was rich, thrown clinking into the apron of Old Nita, one of the little troupe to which he belonged. Ah! those were the gay nights!

Past the last few months his thoughts flew back to journeyings far and wide: white roads of Lorraine, a theatrical little village near Naples, where Mr. Jones had worsted a rival in combat for honors on a market day; Holland, where the bear had stolen the little wooden shoe from the tulip-selling girl, and where they met the gigantic Beau-Jean, and he, with his wife, Guneviere, and the great grizzly Koko, had joined them. That made a company of six, for already there was Rico, his bear and his Anna, and Nita—that wicked Old Nita, who danced the "coquette" herself when they, bears and all, went late one night to the Bal Bodin in Montmartre. How funny she had looked, dancing, with her shapeless old mouth a-smiling!

Tramp steamers! The smell of them came sharply across the autumn wind. How horrible they were, yet how delightful, for they meant getting to new places! Weeks of motion, stowed in a little space with your fellow-creatures and with the bears, till you yourself became like an animal. Weeks of motion and of stench, and then at last the dying of the engine-throb, the crowding and the jostling, and the great rush out upon the shore of some new land. On such a voyage it was that

OF INTRODUCTIONS

Carlos and Hermania had joined them, bringing a cinnamon bear, who they said could "sing," though from that day to this no one had heard him do it.

Where had not these eight been—what roads they had traveled together under sun or moon! Down among the palms of Florida, tramping the long beaches, dancing for human puppets, trim as dolls, unreal, exquisite, who had thrown gold to them in the sand. Or up in Maine, in the hard bleak country, where the farmers, looking at them askance, would scarcely render a night's lodging. It had proved a barren land, devoid of all that nourishes performing bears, and a lean party had turned southward at close of summer.

How they had tramped along the Road to Nowhere, the Road to Maybe! First, Beau-Jean, chained to Koko, the great grizzly; Beau-Jean with his great head bent beneath the pack upon his back, and beside him his wife Guneviere, a Roumanian woman, squat and of sturdy build. Then Anna, hastening southward two steps ahead of her mate, in eager discontent. Next Rico, chained to their bear, both of them sullen, and at times dangerous. After them came Carlos and Hermania, solicitous of their animal, which they fed before they themselves ate. And Nita then, who went along mumbling, usually with a rosary in her hand, a constant saying of which she hoped would save her from the devil, which her old eyes betrayed. Lastly, himself, Pedro, who often lagged behind to examine some wonder of the roadway, or to gaze down a vista, opened suddenly by a turn of the path. Sometimes he ran ahead, sometimes trod slowly beside Old Nita, listening to her murmured tales of a wild youth, her fear of hell, and her fierce pride in her evil achievements. And always there was Mr. Jones, the well-beloved, shambling at his heels.

This host of memories Pedro felt in their essence, in a single breath, as it were, bereft of detail save for some picture—of a small incident or two, trivial, but never to be forgot. The heart of that past life he held for a moment in his own. No! no! he could not give it up. And yet, this other call, which had been with him, it would seem, since birth, was now grown too strong for resistance. Before his eyes he must see the thought of his heart depicted by the labor of his brain and hand. He *must* paint! He was an artist, an *artist!*

With a gesture he released the patient bear and looked wildly about him as though looking his last upon liberty. The thought was appalling, but to buy his soul he must sell his body into the bondage of routine.

Dusk was falling and the haze had quite obscured the distant water. The evening was very still.

"I will go!" said Pedro shudderingly. Then, as if shedding the past, he squared his shoulders.

"Come!" said he to the animal. "We shall return to camp and tell them what we are going to do."

Slowly he picked up the tall staff to which, as a rule, the bear's collar was fastened by a long iron chain, but which was now detached, and, hat in hand, climbed the hill to the yellow corn-stacks. There he paused on the windy summit, the staff like an alpenstock, held at arm's length, his well-worn coat of green blowing about him,—a slim young figure, quick with energy, his small head thrown back courageously.

"*Adios!*" said Pedro, as though to something incarnate, making a sweeping bow as he spoke. Then he covered his crisp brown hair with his wide-brimmed, weather-stained hat of felt and marched into the valley, the bear bounding along before him.

Not until he was within a hundred yards of the

road did Pedro realize that he had been trespassing on what now evinced itself to be a country estate of some pretensions: and at this point the fact was made manifest by the sight of a cedar and fir hedge, well planted and cared for, that, growing to some twenty feet in height, marked the frontage of the property. Near by was a closed gate, flanked by pillars of old brick and soapstone, giving access to a narrow foot-path which wound along at the base of the hill he had just crossed.

Apparently he had been dreaming away the afternoon upon the farming section of the place. The sloping ground which lay between him and the hedge was smooth and soft, and tempted by it, Mr. Jones lay down and rolled a little way. Then he got up and trotted on some distance in advance of his master. The road was very near now, and there came a sound of pattering footsteps from it and the swish of light garments. Through the somber evergreens Pedro could see a gleam of white, moving swiftly. Then came the noise of heavier tramping —a man's step this time—a man in haste at that. Then a woman screamed, her frightened cry ringing out sharply.

The bear, moved to curiosity by the sound,

plunged through the hedge and disappeared, and Pedro, grasping his staff like a cudgel, set off down the slope at a run, reaching the hedge only a moment later than the bear. The fragrant branches whipped across the boy's face as he rushed past, emerging breathless upon the highway. A dramatic scene awaited him.

Down the road a thoroughly frightened tramp was speeding from the terrifying and wholly unexpected apparition of the bear, a cloud of dust enveloping his horrified retreat. Close to the gateway, her purse clasped frantically to her bosom, stood a girl, bewildered and alarmed—a girl whom the last sunbeams bathed in glory, gleaming on her hair that was "red-gold, like joy." And to complete the picture, there stood Mr. Jones, erect upon his hind legs, his tongue lolling out and his clumsy paws waving from her to Pedro.

It was an introduction.

That she was the lady of the morning there was not a doubt. That she was almost as much frightened by the bear as by the tramp, whose attempted robbery the animal's sudden appearance had frustrated, was equally clear. At sight of Pedro she screamed again.

"Oh! the bear! Help, help! Oh, take him away!" she cried.

"*Abas!*" said Pedro sharply, addressing his pet. But Mr. Jones did not obey immediately, and for a moment the three stood as if transfixed. Then the bear dropped to all fours, and the spell of the tableau was broken. Still they did not speak, however, each waiting for the other to begin; the girl's breath still coming short from her recent fright; the youth fairly paralyzed by her beauty. She was very young—not more than nineteen or twenty, and the ivory of her skin was flushed now, and her eyes were like stars. Her head was held aloft in a way she had that was all her own; a delicate pose, and quite unconscious. Pedro's eyes were upon that beautiful line from chin to breast as she spoke, timidly breaking the silence.

"Oh, how fortunate that you were near!" she began breathlessly. "It was a tramp. He wanted my little silk purse . . . but the bear frightened him away; he came so suddenly—the bear did, that is. In another instant that dreadful man would have had my bag. Not that I would have cared so much about the money, you know," she added a trifle apologetically, "but I have registered letters

It was an introduction.

in it for my father. I have just come from the post-office, and if they had been lost . . . but, perhaps, you do not understand English?"

"Oh, yes!" said Pedro, taking his eyes from her slender throat and flashing a brilliant smile at her. "Oh, yes, indeed, I understand you!"

"Then please let me thank you," said she, her interest in him growing every moment.

"But there is nothing for which I may receive thanks!" he protested.

Her fingers, which, in the recess of her rescued purse, were fumbling some coins, relaxed, and she closed the receptacle with a snap. His words and tone were unusual, and he was looking at her strangely. Perhaps it was better not to offer money.

As a matter of fact, he had not noticed her gesture, being obsessed by the wonderful fact that she was speaking. Actually, she seemed to consider the bear's introduction sufficient. Delighted, he moved his lips to reply, but even as he did so he became aware of the growing intensity of her gaze, and an overwhelming nervousness came upon him. Fumblingly he removed his wide soft hat and clasped it upon his heart with both hands. How she stared! Waiting for him to speak again, she gave her chin a tilt which accentuated that heavenly line. Involuntarily he pictured drapery behind it, his artist's soul longing to depict it. Like a Madonna.

"It should be blue!" he said aloud in a queer choked voice.

"What did you say?" asked the girl with a puzzled expression.

At realization of his speech his confusion became complete, and suddenly his one idea was to escape her watchful eyes.

"I—that is to say, er—it was Mr. Jones entirely," he stammered, "I—I did nothing, *nada!* It was all the bear."

"But he is your bear, evidently," she replied, "and I insist that he share the thanks with you."

"Thank *you!*" said Pedro eagerly. "You do not know the exquisite delight—er—ah—oh!" Gasping, he sought to extricate himself from the awkwardness of the impulsive compliment he had half-blurted out.

"Forgive me, gracious lady, er—er—I must go now!" he finished lamely.

"Well, I give you my most grateful thanks,

whether you take them or not," said she with a smile.

But he was now too embarrassed to rally and did what one often does upon attaining a desired situation: became suddenly panicky and ran away from it.

"I shall hold your words in my heart," said he, and then, with a gesture half beseeching, half apologetic, and wholly graceful, he swept his hat upon his head, and calling the bear, set off down the road.

The wording of his speech was odd and unexpected, and the manner of his departure so precipitant that it looked like a retreat. For as long as he remained in sight she stood gazing after him, her interest in him cemented by his flight. Through the dappling shadows he passed, over the fallen leaves. Then a crimson maple hid him, and the sound of his footsteps died away. With a sigh she was scarcely conscious of uttering, so faint it was, she reluctantly turned in at the gate in the hedge and went slowly along the little winding path.

CHAPTER II

A BELIEF IN SIGNS

BUT Pedro walked rapidly, so that the bear had difficulty in imitating the pace. The youth had now definitely made up his mind to take the new course of action, for this second vision of the beautiful lady had confirmed his resolution, and he felt he must get back to the others quickly, in order to tell them before he had time to change his mind. As he walked he kept muttering "blue, blue!" and his brows were knit furiously.

He had to pass some villas with a semi-suburban look about them, and then an elm-shaded street, where commerce and conservatism rubbed shoulders. Next, by switching off from this thoroughfare, he passed between rows of frame houses, which diminished in their appearance of importance and prosperity the farther he went, until finally the street, if such it could properly be called at this point, was fringed only by shacks that leaned inquisitively over the gutters, or braced themselves at a fearsome angle against the slanting little gardens at their backs.

Where these humble habitations came to an end there stood an old barn amid a stony field, scattered over with paper, rubbish and discarded cans. In the lee of the dilapidated building a fire was burning upon the ground, and about it a group of people had gathered. Over the blaze a kettle had been hung, into which an old woman was throwing greens from her apron. Near her, his back against the barn, lay a giant of a man, with a patch over one eye. This was Beau-Jean, the mighty Provençal, who at this moment was engaged in carving an elaborate design upon the base of a bear-stave; while beside him lay the great animal whom he ruled, asleep with its nose tucked under its paws. Two younger women—Gunny, Beau-Jean's wife, and sturdy Hermania, wife of Carlos (who lay asleep near by)—were mending their shoes. They performed this task in company, one holding a flap of leather against the sole while the other pulled a cord through the holes and knotted it. At a little distance, Anna, the pretty and irresponsible, was weaving a garland of bright golden maple leaves, Rico watching adoringly, the while he pretended to be busy nursing the wounded paw of their animal. The thickening mist from an alder swamp beyond enclosed the picture like a screen, and the dancing firelight threw weird silhouettes against the tall black wall of the barn. An odor, bitter yet appetizing, came from the steaming kettle, and Old Nita muttered while she stirred its contents, as though some witch-broth were bubbling there. At sight and smell of his familiars, Mr. Jones trotted up, eagerly sniffing as he came. Old Nita aroused herself at his approach.

"Pedro, you have let him loose again, oh, careless one!" she cried; "some day he will betray you and be off! or worse yet, stolen."

"Cross Old Nita!" replied Pedro, stepping into the lighted circle and smiling at her. "He is too fond of me to run away—aren't you, old fellow, eh?"

"Chain him! Chain him!" shrieked Hermania. "He is eating my shoe."

Pedro ran to the rescue, and snapping the chain to Mr. Jones' collar, thrust the pointed end of the heavy staff, to which it was attached, into the ground, and the animal considered himself secured. As a matter of fact he could have uprooted the stake with very little effort; but such is a habit of mind.

"What's to eat?" inquired Pedro, stooping over the kettle. "Greens! Is that all?"

"There is rye bread—a single loaf," responded Nita. "Thanks to your going off by yourself, we have only taken in a few *pesetas* all day!"

"You know very well, Aged One," responded Pedro, "that you take in as much alone as with me, or very nearly. And as for going off! . . . Well, I have something to tell you, but all must hear. Let us gather together first, and eat."

So far the conversation had been in Spanish, the native tongue of these two. Now, as the conversation became general, they fell into a patois English, the language of the road, sometimes slipping into French, sometimes back into Spanish, their talk being as polyglot as their origin.

Beau-Jean closed his great knife with a snap, and without arising hitched himself lazily a little nearer to the fire. The women opposite had finished their task and now brought out tin plates and a bouquet of dried garlic. The drowsy Carlos was aroused and sent to the nearest house for water, which he brought in a clean new pail, dripping diamonds from its brimming edge. Anna flung her garland about her Rico's head, and as ever, hand in hand, they came to eat when all the work was done. Then, crowding close to the glowing embers (for the night was chill), they sat and ate until the greens had vanished and the bread and garlic were consumed to the last morsel.

From the town, at first, came muffled sounds, made melodious by distance; but gradually these died away, while nearer at hand came echoes of evening life from the huts. Somewhere a woman was singing a nasal plaintive refrain, which broke off abruptly when the protesting wail of a child, dragged reluctantly from his play, arose shrilly. The late autumn night fell swift and black. Overhead a few frosty stars began to gleam. Gradually quiet came upon the neighboring hovels, and one by one their feeble lights were being extinguished. Around the first bend of that shabby street the open door of a low saloon shed a flare of light across the dusty road, and from its dubious back room came the tortured strains of a concertina. But all this seemed afar, unreal, like a setting for a play. Pedro drew the thin blanket from his knapsack, flung it

A BELIEF IN SIGNS 23

about him and, underneath it, fastened his old coat of green up closer.

"Now, do you want to hear, eh?" he asked, addressing the company. "If so, I shall tell my plan."

Beau-Jean replied first, in his deep husky voice.

"Let the little one tell his notion. The plans of Pedro have brought many a laugh, and so, many a coin from the crowd on the market street."

"My shoes will not stand another mending," said Hermania. "If Pedro can tell a plan to get others, I will heed."

"The lad has wit; did he not conceive the praying trick for Koko?" mumbled Old Nita. "Come, child, what has thy brain devised now to help us?"

"Pedro is beautiful; that is reason enough for my listening!" cried Anna, laughing. Whereat Rico said nothing, but looked sullenly into the fire until she slipped her hand back into his. Then he smiled.

"Pedro is a good fellow," he said slowly. "What should we do without him?"

"Oh, don't, don't!" cried Pedro. "Why do you say these things on this night of all nights? I can not endure it! Call me evil names, and abuse me, rather! Please! It is almost too hard for me to do, and yet I must! *Amigos!* It is for myself only that I am planning—my notion will not help you, alas!"

He buried his face in his hands, and for a moment there was an astonished silence. Such an outburst of emotion on the part of their joyous Pedro was a thing undreamed of by any of them.

Into the silence the voice of Old Nita broke tremblingly.

"Hast thou sinned, even as I, that thou weepest so? What is it, Pedro of my heart?"

"No, no!" he cried, raising his head. "I have not sinned, but I have seen a line—an exquisite curve from an oval chin to the base of a white throat."

"Ah! In love!" exclaimed Rico and Anna simultaneously.

"No; again no!" cried Pedro. "I do not love it, *but I've got to paint it!*"

There was another interval of puzzled silence, broken this time by Beau-Jean.

"Oh, little Pedro," said he, "what do you mean by *'paint it?'*"

"Just that," said Pedro, striving to conquer his emotion. "I am going to be an artist, a *painter*. Don't you understand?"

The little group stirred relievedly. This was nothing so terrible, after all. Then for a few moments all spoke at once, voicing their relief. Hermania's query made itself evident above the clamor of the rest.

"But why does this distress you so? Always, always you have made pictures. Pictures of us all, of everywhere, of everybody; always, always scribbling little pictures upon bits of paper! Where is the trouble?"

"The trouble comes because I shall have to leave you all," said Pedro sadly. "I must go to the city, where I can have the right things to work with, and colors—colors—*colors!* I must learn about them. It will be hard, but I can do it."

"*Go away! Leave them!*" Such a clangor as they raised! It was beyond human power to quiet them, and he was obliged to wait in silence until the first violence of their emotion had subsided before he could make himself heard.

"I have tried not to do this," he said as soon as they let him speak, "but I can't help it. The art— it bosses *me* now!"

"But where shall you go?" asked Nita.

"To New York; it is nearest," replied Pedro.

"And how will you live?" from Carlos.

"I do not know."

"Who will teach you?" queried Hermania.

"I do not know."

"And those colors, where will you get them?" asked Anna.

"I do not know."

"And knowing nothing, you are yet determined to go?" Beau-Jean demanded.

"Yes," answered Pedro stubbornly.

"Then," said Beau-Jean with a sigh, "it is our plain duty to help you."

"How will you do so?" asked Pedro eagerly.

"I do not know that, either," responded Beau-Jean.

Next morning the eight set out together for the city. Whatever strange undertaking Pedro was considering, they would all go along and assist if possible. And so, without any idea save that of action, they set forth, determined though indefinite.

The coppers of yesterday were all expended for breakfast, and the first step toward the beginning of a day being accomplished, they betook themselves to the railroad track, and walked beside it. But

A BELIEF IN SIGNS

noon came and passed, and still no granite towers loomed before their expectant eyes. Finally, to rest themselves, they turned from the wearying shining vista of rails, and seated themselves upon the dead grass beside the mile-post that bore the discouraging legend:

N. Y. 25 M.—Harrison 1 M.

By this time all were tired and hungry. Worse yet, the bears were hungry—a condition to be reckoned with before the need of the masters.

"Let us go," suggested Pedro, "into the town which this dusty road leads to, and dance the bears, pass the hat, and eat, eh?"

The suggestion needed no seconding. With groans and complaints they got to their feet again, and set off for the village.

But fate was not smiling upon them just then. The town was almost deserted at this hour. Besides which, near the end of the performance, Toto, who was supposed to "sing," raised his voice from his usual growling monotone to a hungry howl. That sent the watchers running off in all directions. Ruefully Old Nita counted the earnings.

"Only seven pennies in all," she complained.

"Better to have rested beside the railroad."

"It is not enough to feed one bear even," remarked Beau-Jean, "and I am as hungry as two."

Meanwhile, Pedro was talking to himself. "You got them into this; otherwise they would have traveled the regular way. Now you get them out." And his eyes swept the grimy little square in search of a solution for the immediate difficulty. The place was sufficiently down-at-heel to discourage anybody. On one side was the low-roofed station building of dirty bricks, a row of billboards filled the space to the right, and to the left a bridge crossed the railroad. Then Pedro noticed a dingy lunch-wagon by the broken curb, some fifty feet away. At the entrance to it stood a fat man with a dismal flabby face. His hands were tucked beneath an apron whose immaculate whiteness shone out conspicuously among the gray surroundings. The man was motionless, as though he had become petrified while waiting for customers who never came.

"Ah!" said Pedro aloud, "I have an idea!"

"You have had enough ideas for the present," grumbled Nita.

"But it is good! Wait, you shall see!" cried

Pedro. "Stay where you are, all of you, until I beckon."

Then, thrusting his hands into his pockets, he strolled nonchalantly away in the direction of the lunch-wagon.

It was a dingy affair, as has been said, and upon its tawdry sides the lettering had grown dim. Still, it was easy enough to make out the inscription:

—The Elite—
Pies, Coffee, Milk, Frankfurters

By the doorway hung a battered canvas sign marked:

Special for To-Day—Egg Sandwich

Over the doorway was an invitation to "walk in", and underneath this the owner's name—"Isaac Lovejoy, Prop."—had been printed small. Pedro sidled up to the individual who, it would seem, bore this name and title.

"Business thriving 'bout here?" asked Pedro conversationally, by way of an opening.

The man gave him a glance, but without moving to do so.

"Nope!" he replied.

"What! In a place where travelers must pass so often?" Pedro exclaimed, lifting his eyebrows.

"Yep!" said the man, still motionless.

"What is the trouble? Are there no travelers?"

"Travelers, all right," said the fat man, "but no *customers!* No one stops here! Why, look at this!"

Without changing his position, he reached behind him with one hand, and brought forth a large sandwich.

"Look at this!" he repeated, flapping the bread and meat at Pedro, "that's a fresh sandwich, that is; but it might as well be a *rubber* sandwich for all it has a chance of bein' eat! *That's* how good custom is around here."

He slapped the edge of the door with it, and replaced it inside the wagon, Pedro's eyes following it greedily.

"What's the trouble, do you think?" Pedro inquired.

"The lunch-wagon trust!" exclaimed the man. "I'm an independent, I am; but everywhere I go where there might be good business doin'—say a corner near a factory, or any such real wide-awake place—one of them trust wagons is there before me,

A BELIEF IN SIGNS 31

all shined up an' covered with gold paint an' plate-glass! A fellow like me ain't got no show."

"Why don't you spruce up a little then, eh?" asked Pedro.

"Why don't you buy somethin' so's I'll get the money for to buy the gold paint with?" retorted the other.

"Because I have no money," Pedro replied.

"Same reason here, in answer to your first," cried the fat man triumphantly.

"Oh!" said Pedro.

"Works in circles, don't it?" said Mr. Lovejoy.

There was a pause which Pedro ended, glancing sidelong at the lunch-wagon. His manner was very tentative.

"Supposing, now," said he, "that I could put you on the right track to competing with those trusts, eh?"

"What d'yer mean?" demanded the man.

"Those wagons of the trust—they are all alike?"

"Yes," said Mr. Lovejoy, "all the same; and *very* slick and fancy."

"Aha! Then what you want is something entirely different from them; something to make people *notice* you."

"Sure, but what?"

"That," replied Pedro, "is just what I can tell you. I have a proposition to make."

The man scowled at him for a moment, as though wondering at the imprudence of this whipper-snapper's offering to deal with him. Then Pedro looked at him, and smiled one of those vivid startling smiles that were peculiar to him, and usually took people unawares, making them smile back at him before they really knew what they were doing. Nor did it fail this time. The flaccid face of the lunch-wagon man expanded into a broad grin.

"That's it!" exclaimed Pedro.

"That's what?" asked the man, growing serious again.

"Oh, don't spoil it!" cried the lad, "that smile is just what you need to attract customers!"

This time the man laughed.

"Well," said he, "what is your proposition, young one?"

"I have some friends with me," began Pedro; "all those over there and the bears. We are all hungry, see? Now I will paint you a picture on the side of your wagon, and also I will paint for you a new sign; and if, when I have finished, you agree that the sign and the picture will bring you customers in the future, you will feed us all, not forgetting the bears, eh?"

The fat man considered a long time before replying, and Pedro watched him anxiously. With one large pale hand the man stroked his chin several times, as though caressing an imaginary beard. Then he looked at the group upon the opposite corner and counted them up upon his stubby fingers. Then he looked at Pedro and the lunch-wagon by turn.

"Well," he said at last, "the old dog-wagon couldn't look no worse'n it do now; an' my stock what I have laid in will get spoiled if it don't get eat. You can have a try, young one, if you like."

"Hurrah!" said Pedro, and hurried over to tell Nita and the others.

A musty hardware store that also sold grain and lumber, furnished a few crude materials. Pedro looked at the paints dubiously, but accepted them, as there was nothing else to do. The fat man paid for them, and Pedro carried them over to the cart and set to work.

"Please, one thing," he begged of its proprietor, "don't you look till all is finished."

"All right," agreed the man, "I'll set here, just inside the door, and read outer the paper till you're done."

Pedro answered nothing, but gave a glance at a little mirror that hung just opposite to where the unconscious Mr. Lovejoy sat, whipped off the old green coat, and began working frantically.

The proprietor settled himself on the little stool near the door, and faithful to his promise, unfolded a pink evening paper. Cautiously, and speaking not at all, Old Nita drew near, leading Mr. Jones. They sat down in the dust beside the step, and watched Pedro in silence. Then came Beau-Jean and Koko, followed by Gunny, who settled themselves beside the old woman. The sight of this drew Anna and Rico, who came slowly to join the group, because Toto still limped. And lastly, Carlos and Hermania laid aside an ancient dispute which they had unearthed to keep ennui at arm's length, and led their animal into the interested circle. After a few minutes two hack-drivers strolled over to jeer, and remained to watch in fascinated silence. They were joined before long by several of their fellows. No train being due just then, the station master turned the key in the lock of his cubby-hole, and emerged to see what was going forward. He rubbed elbows with the hardware-store keeper, who was keen to find out the use to which his wares were being put. From the neighboring saloon came the red-faced, white-aproned bartender. He looked twice, wiped his face upon a bandana handkerchief, muttered, "Holy mother," and stood rooted to the spot. Women from the dismal flats above the little shops joined the crowd, babies in arm, and about their skirts the younger ones clung, noisy and wondering. A handful of gamins, all that the town boasted, darted in and out, and fought for front seats. In short, before half an hour was gone, all the town, for the first time in the lunch-wagon's history, had clustered before its door. As for Pedro, he had forgotten that there was a world which might come to gape and criticize. He was working.

But if the painter was unconscious of the crowd, the proprietor was not. Twice he wanted to move, but dared not; and as the crowd increased, so did his impatience. Finally he began to read aloud from the newspaper, to relieve his feelings.

" 'Wife shoots husband; both may die'. Hum, ain't that awful, now? 'Girl missing'—something fierce the way girls act nowadays. Here's two fellers broke into a house an' took all the lead-pipe. Dear! dear! they got three months for it. 'May be trouble in Venezuela'—ah! Them South Americans are all the time makin' trouble. 'May be trouble in Venezuela over asphalt' . . . Oh! I read that once already."

"I come from there," said Old Nita suddenly.

"From where?" asked the fat man.

"Venezuela," said Nita.

This was too much for Mr. Lovejoy. He could not resist taking a glance at her, even though it involved breaking his promise not to move.

"You don't say!" he exclaimed, looking her over as though seeing her for the first time and finding her very strange, "you don't say!"

"I do!" she replied, her eyes fixed upon Pedro in a peculiar way.

"Please!" exclaimed Pedro, waving his brush at the fat man, who guiltily resumed his former position.

For half an hour longer, or more, Pedro worked, glancing now and then at the little mirror just inside the door, in which Mr. Lovejoy's unconscious face was reflected. There began to be an occasional tittering from the crowd, and then, later, spontaneous bursts of laughter.

"When kin I come out?" cried Mr. Lovejoy at intervals, and—

"Wait," commanded Pedro. Feverishly he added the finishing touches to his production, and then at length stood back and invited his patron to descend. As the fat man came down the steps there was a little burst of applause which he was at a loss to understand until he stood before his transformed place of business.

All the old lettering, already faint, had been obliterated, and in the center of the largest space was a portrait-head of himself—a large laughing portrait, just like him, yet irresistibly merry. It was a face at which one instantly smiled in sympathy; indeed it wore the very "smile to attract customers" as Pedro had said. Withal it was a remarkable piece of work, though coarsely laid in (not that its original was critic enough to know this), but the least knowing could not have failed to be attracted by it. Its possibilities as a magnet for trade were undeniable. Over this extraordinary production Pedro had painted in neat black letters:

I. Lovejoy
Eating is Joyful
Come In and Eat—
I Love to See You Do It

Then underneath:

Lovejoy's Luscious Lunches

After a moment of spellbound silence, the fat man drew a long breath.

"You win!" he said to Pedro, a smile like that in the picture overspreading his large countenance.

In a second the square was in an uproar, the crowd expressing its delight noisily. Small boys set up a hooting and yelling, and three hackmen, who had never before patronized the place, purchased sandwiches upon the spot. In a circle sat Old Nita, Pedro and the rest, a bear between each couple, and Mr. Lovejoy fed them all generously. Then, just as the weary Pedro was accepting a cup of coffee and a gigantic plateful of doughnuts from the hand of his patron, the whir of an automobile caused him to look around. All unperceived it had been standing near for some time, and now bestirred itself at the approach of the train it had come to meet. As it moved away, a girl in the rear seat stood up for a last backward look at the little crowd, and then, against the clear blue of the sky, Pedro beheld a fleeting vision of red-gold hair.

CHAPTER III

A LOSS AND A FIND

"I AM sure that there must be color in our souls," said Iris Vanderpool.

"At this moment," replied Mr. Samuel Hill, "my soul is the exact hue of tea with lemon in it, shading off to the color of a jam sandwich."

With a petulant little gesture, Iris turned from the window out of which she had been gazing at the slowly darkening city.

"You always spoil my best ideas!" she said. "Why can't you reply sympathetically? But you shall have tea, of course."

The room in which the two were talking was a curious one: all gray and green, and quite unlike anything one would have been led to expect by the exterior of the house, which was large, old-fashioned, and situated in the aristocratic section of Fifth Avenue which lies below Fourteenth Street. All along one side of the room ran a Japanese screen of gray silk, upon which were embroidered great white birds. This was the most conspicuous of the furnishings, and the rest seemed to have been chosen with the sole idea of subordinating them to it. The furniture was all of gray, and scarcely noticeable, except in a far corner, where upon a teak-wood sacrifice-table there blazed a blue jar, like a gem.

The impression was of elimination; of striving after an effect which was not quite sincere. Still, it was very beautiful in its way, and set off the red-haired girl, who was its mistress, to great advantage. Now, as she came away from the window, her graceful figure was silhouetted curiously against the wonderful old screen; while her hair was thrown into relief upon the gray, so that the red-gold of it seemed like a halo. Her features were cameo-like. The pose into which she dropped as she pressed the almost invisible bell was so naive that the man watching her laughed a little, the while he was inwardly thrilled by her beauty.

"Oh, yes! you *do* look awfully well there!" he said teasingly.

Again the girl was vexed at his failure to play up to her little scene. As she crossed over to seat herself beside him, he noted the shade that clouded her eyes. She settled herself in her corner of the sofa, and he leaned over, taking both her hands in his.

"You mustn't be cross," he said tenderly. "You looked simply corking, posing there. Honestly, you did!"

But she was not to be appeased, and withdrew her hands impatiently.

"*Simply corking!*" she quoted in a tone of disgust. "What an expression! Why don't you learn to use the sort of language one would expect a painter—a real painter—to use? You are never in the least poetical. It is so disappointing to me. At least, you needn't use slang when you are making love to me!"

"But Iris—"

"What is more," she continued, ignoring his interruption, "I think you owe it to me to be a little more—more romantic! No! That is a poor word to express my meaning. A little more *poetic!* Why, you don't even *look* like an artist any more!"

"Don't I?" said he, slowly rising and regarding himself in a mirror opposite.

It must be granted that her accusation in regard to this last item was a just one, for the reflection which faced him did not in the least resemble the traditional or stage-manager type of artist. It was a man of moderate height who stared back at Sam Hill from the mirror; a well-set-up man of perhaps thirty-one or two. His features were good but ordinary, and the trim little brown mustache above the well-cut upper lip lent him the appearance of a far more foppish type than that to which he honestly belonged. His eyes were gray and humorous, well set, with deep markings of blue at the inner corners. His hair was brown, and brushed in the latest fashion, and his clothes were remarkably well cut and immaculate. On the whole his appearance was that of a well-groomed, well—but not too well-fed, dapper, prosperous citizen, whose calling might be anything from the stock market to the manufacturing of commodities; anything, indeed, except a painter.

"Iris," said he after a moment of silent inspection, "must a fellow really have long hair in order to be a good painter, do you think?"

"Don't be absurd!" she answered; "it isn't that, of course! But it is something deeper, something more important, far. Why, if I did not see the lovely things you do with your brush, I could not believe you were an artist. You *never* give out your temperament in any other way, and I am hungry for it."

"For what?" he asked. "A lot of silly talk about the color of your soul? Lord! girlie, can't you learn to live those things instead of talking about them? Can't you see that they lose in value if expressed in any but the highest way? One has to keep one's mouth shut in order that all the strength be left for one's hand."

"And apply none of it to daily life?" she cried.

"Live it; don't apply it," he answered dryly.

"One grows by expression!" she declared; "by expression of every sort. My father's friends, lots of the people who come here, are living splendidly inside themselves, and they give it out, and consequently they are interesting. When I became engaged to you, I thought I was going to find the same sort of intercourse, only intensified. But you are not what I thought you were, and my soul is unsatisfied."

At this dramatic juncture tea arrived, and for a few moments there was silence while she inspected it and dismissed the servant. Hill strolled about, humming under his breath. When the door had shut, he stopped his pacing and resumed his place beside her.

"Look here, dearest," said he lightly, "don't go for me the first day you get home. It's a long while—two entire weeks—since we have been together, and here we go, off the handle, first thing. Let's cut it out, and be sweet to each other instead. Tell me, did you motor down from Stamford? And did your father come with you?"

"We only came as far as Harrison in the car," she answered sullenly. Then a picture which she had seen at recurring intervals for the last twenty-four hours came before her mental vision again. It was of a curious group gathered about a slender young figure of a man who worked at the decoration of a lunch-wagon. She could see the handsome earnest face with startling vividness.

"And your father, dear," persisted Hill, ignoring although noting her abstraction, "when are you going to let me speak to him about you? I want him to know, and every one to know of our engagement. Did he come down?"

"Yes, but on the train," she replied still absently.

"Then I'll talk to him to-night," exclaimed Hill.

"Now tell me about the last couple of weeks. You're not a very satisfactory correspondent, you know. What did you do at the farm?"

For a moment she was about to tell him of Pedro and the bear, but as she looked at her lover the certainty was borne in upon her that if she did so, the incident would lose its glamour. So she said nothing of it.

"I walked, and rode horseback, as usual," she replied. "There was time for once for me to learn to know myself; to commune with my inner consciousness. I read Swinburne. Do you know, I think his aura must have been blue, like mine?"

Sam Hill helped himself to a fifth jam sandwich before replying.

"That must have been great; especially the riding," he exclaimed. "And that reminds me, Iris, there is a wonderful house at the Winter Garden. I'll get seats for to-morrow, if you say so. You'll like it, I'm sure. There are some bully acrobats, too."

With the air of a tragedy queen, Miss Vanderpool arose and swept to the center of the room, her gray gown coiling about her feet like clouds of smoke. Very young she looked, and quite like a

A LOSS AND A FIND

child dressed up and acting a play. But to her own mind, she was a woman hurt in her sensitive soul. Withal, she had a certain dignity despite her youth, consequent, perhaps, on the position which had been hers since the death of the mother she could scarcely remember.

"Why, what on earth is the matter?" cried Hill, admiring her immensely, unspeakably.

"Matter?" she cried tragically; "you ask me that? I tell you that my soul is hungry—starved! and you retort with an invitation to a music-hall! It is unthinkable! How *can* you? You have no sympathy, no understanding. I *hate* you. There!"

She turned from him abruptly.

"Iris!" he cried, springing to her side and putting his arm about her. "You must not say such things, you silly child. When I leave my work, I want to play—just to play like a child—and a trained horse amuses me; frankly and truly, I do like it. *You* hardly ever laugh for sheer merriment. It's most neurotic, I'm darned if it isn't!"

"I'm *not* a silly child," cried Iris hotly, disengaging herself from his embrace. "I'm not neurotic! My soul is torn."

"Oh, marry me right away, and let your soul go

hang!" exclaimed Hill. "All you need is a taste of life! Honestly I understand about this feeling of yours, dear. Believe me, work and living in earnest, are the answers and the cure."

"You *don't* understand!" she cried; "every word you utter makes that plainer. You never have any great emotional experiences—at least, that I can see —and so, of course, you can't recognize them as real in others. You may be an artist on canvas, but you are not an artist of life, and that is far more important! I suppose you will go on leading your ordered existence forever. I shall stifle if I have to share it! And I thought you were a romantic figure. Why, you work as regularly as any business man, and as hard!"

"A curious complaint," said he, the half-smile dying upon his lips. "You know little, dear, of life, or you would not talk like this. Control is the password to success. It is a bitter fact, perhaps, but one we all have to learn."

The atmosphere of the strange gray room had become tense, for the dispute that had arisen almost banteringly, had changed to a crucial thing, and both persons concerned were suddenly aware of it.

"That is a theory which I do not intend to live by," she said rather breathlessly.

"How am I to take that?" said the man.

"As you see fit," she replied. "I mean to live by expression. I used to think that you did so. You have changed."

"For your sake!" he expostulated, suddenly angry. "If I have whipped myself into some semblance of a human being, it has been—I was going to say, for you; but it is more than that. It has been for the work's own sake. And now you are ready to repudiate me because of that very accomplishment. You are unfair, unreasonable."

"Oh, don't be so logical, or I shall go mad!" she cried. "I hate your reasonableness!"

"Very well, then," said he, trying to smile, "I'll be unreasonable."

"And don't be facetious! Oh, go away, I can't endure you!"

"Look here, Iris," he said hoarsely, "I'm not joking. God forbid! This is getting too serious. Am I really to go?"

"Or let your spirit out of its cage," she said.

For the third time, Hill committed his greatest mistake.

"You are a foolish child!" he said angrily. "Very well, then, I'll go. But I warn you, if you send me off, I'll not come back."

For a moment he waited, hoping that she would speak, but she said nothing, merely standing there and trembling a little, though white and silent. Suddenly Hill turned on his heel.

"Confound all women!" he muttered, and without a single backward glance, flung himself out of the room in a fury.

For a moment or two longer she stood motionless, and then throwing her arms out wildly, she cried his name aloud.

"Oh, Sam!" she called, "come back—please come back!"

Running out into the upper hall, she arrived at the stair-head just in time to hear the front door close after him, and was instantly obliged to flee the mildly-inquiring gaze of the footman, who came in to remove the tea-tray. When he was gone, however, she cast herself face downward among the gray cushions of the sofa and cried bitterly, a cold horror clutching at her heart as she slowly came to see the reality of what she had done.

For Hill had spoken the truth when he implied

that she was merely a child bored with luxurious surroundings and striving after she knew not what. Her father adored her, and gave her absolute liberty. The people whom she knew by inheritance meant little to her; she found them introspective, self-absorbed, and amateurs at the arts they affected, many of them simply hangers-on of her beauty-loving father, who with the years had become less the man of affairs, and more the man of letters and patron of the arts. As she grew up, her discontent increased, until finally, within the last two years, she had stumbled upon a group of people with whom brains meant aristocracy. Here she had met Hill, and after about a year, he had persuaded her to become engaged to him. She had consented on condition that it remain a secret for the time being. There had been no reason for concealment but the girl's innate love of romance and mystification. And so no one had been told of the engagement, although it was a well-known and widely-discussed subject among their friends.

And it was all over! Well, possibly it was for the best.

She buried her face deeper in the esthetic gray cushions. Her soul must have expression! It *must!*

If only he would do something really great for his art! But there was no hope of that. She felt bereft, weary, yet tried hard to remain unrepentant. For (she told herself) no matter how it hurt, it was better to break with him than to continue with him, since he stifled her so, and yet—

Desperately unhappy, but not without a certain enjoyment of her own misery, she arose with the determination to find her father, and extract what comfort she could from him, without telling him her trouble. Perhaps he was in his library now. She would go and see. Slowly she descended the wide stairs. At the street entrance stood her father, evidently on the point of leaving the house.

Vanderpool was a handsome man, and had retained an intangible atmosphere of youth, despite the responsibilities of his wealth, and despite the obvious fact that he had lived intensely in the emotional side of his nature. Peculiarly graceful in every movement, alert, his hair, which was nearly white, was the only indication of age about him; and by contrast to the thick mass of it, his face looked the fresher, and his eyes more blue. He was truly a romantic figure, and despite his extremely fashionable clothing he would have appeared to be poet or actor, rather than

A LOSS AND A FIND

practical man of affairs. At sight of Iris he smiled, the habitual melancholy vanishing from his face as fog before sunshine. Then he ran his gloved fingers down the length of black ribbon that secured his eye-glasses, found them, and regarded his daughter.

"Hello, little Iris!" he said. "You seem a bit pale, my dear! Were you looking for me?"

"Yes, father!" replied Iris, "but I—you are going out, I see, so—"

"I've an appointment that is rather pressing," said he, a little anxious pucker gathering between his eyes, "but if your business can't wait, mine will have to."

"Oh! mine is nothing, *nothing!*" said Iris, with what seemed to her divine submission to fate.

"Then we'll have a fine talk at breakfast," returned her father. "I'm dining out. Good night, my dear!"

The door closed behind him, and Iris turned into the library.

Through the high windows of stained glass a dull light still filtered; upon a broad table of gleaming oak, black with age, a shaded lamp burned dimly. Lured by the somber quiet of the place, she curled herself up in a large armchair, and leaned her tired little head against its cushioned back.

The room spoke strongly of her father. It was large and fine and romantic, like him; it was dignified, too, containing several almost priceless treasures. Over the mantel-shelf hung a world-famous Madonna, the plain-faced peasant girl who had posed for it, cuddling her child and smiling down the long vista of centuries from beneath her hood of blue. Below the window ran a low chest, framed from what had once been the altar of a Spanish church, while on either hand, row upon row, up to the vaulted ceiling rose the ranks of books, well worn or in new covers: thousands of them—a rare and well-loved collection. But perhaps the most unique feature of the apartment was the great low desk. It was a Flemish piece, unusual in shape and construction, and covered with a multitude of intricate ornaments, carved deep into its heavy surface. It was a massive hand that produced it. Upon its broad surface lay a few letters addressed to her father, carefully placed by the precise hand of his secretary. There were also a calendar of a practical sort and the usual writing implements, neatly arranged.

Vanderpool had never been a very light-hearted person, but he had a subtle charm which was more fascinating than any gaiety could be, and his rare smile was a thing to be remembered. Of her mother, Iris had no recollection, but from her earliest childhood she had seen her father as an individual, instead of merely as "father", a being from whom came the luxuries of material existence; and she had always adored him. There was a cloud over his existence, she knew, and she assumed it to be the loss of her mother. But this explanation was not sufficient to account for the depression which had come upon him lately. The difficulty with which he was obviously struggling could scarcely be financial, she reasoned, since he was certain to warn her against any excessive expenditure; and although their mode of living was lavish in the extreme, he had given no hint that its curtailment was desirable. What could the trouble be? Had it to do with those letters which came by registered mail, with foreign stamps, some of which the tramp by the wayside at Stamford had so nearly stolen from her? Stamford! If only she had stayed in the free innocent air of the country, among the crimson maples, where troubles slipped from one so easily. Her thoughts flew to her erstwhile lover, and bitter regret welled up afresh in her heart.

"Oh, Sam!" she wailed aloud, and cast herself across the desk-board, grasping the carvings opposite with agonized white fingers.

Then suddenly an utterly unexpected, astonishing thing happened. The carved ornament beneath her right hand flew outward with a spring. Iris raised her tear-stained face in amazement, and there before her lay open a secret compartment, responsive to her unwitting touch. It was a shallow drawer, about six by ten inches in diameter, and was filled with papers, written out in Spanish (to her an unintelligible language), the script being that fine close one of which she had just been thinking. There were a number of these, but stranger still, on top of them lay a miniature in a frame of brilliants. At this she stared long, with fascinated incredulous eyes, for the face was that of the youth who had sung before the cobbler's shop; the youth who, with his bear, had saved her from the tramp; the youth who, later, she had watched paint the wagon in the grimy suburban square!

CHAPTER IV

THAT WHICH IS NO ROBBERY

MEANWHILE Sam Hill had flung himself into the street, and into a state of mind which was the reverse of enviable. Reason was suddenly impossible. The arguments which he had advanced to Iris but a moment since now failed him, and his one mastering, overwhelming thought was that he had lost her. The idea had nothing of the element of incredulity in it; it was horribly, terribly real, overshadowing the possibility of any other thought. Lost! He had lost her! She had sent him away!

It had all happened so suddenly that the shock left him gasping. Probably she had never really cared from the first, he thought, for had she ever been in love with him she could not have dismissed him on so flimsy a pretext. That his lack of "artistic" atmosphere was really what she felt the need of so bitterly, he did not for a moment believe. The only alternative, however, appeared to be that she had never really known him for what he was, seeing him through a glamour which she had created around his profession. Could a few trappings, a velvet coat, long hair, soft ties and such things be sufficient to hold her? Were they really more important in her mind than what a fellow actually was? Incredible!

The only aspect of the situation that held a ray of light for him, was that she had found out her mistake before it was too late. He loved her so well that for a moment the burden of his grief at losing her was lifted by the realization that she had escaped the irreparable misfortune of marrying him. Poor child! he thought, she should not be made to suffer because of his continued presence, either. He would go away, to some far place where she would never see him. The awful possibility of their being obliged to meet under the inquisitorial eyes of their friends could be eliminated. He would hide himself in order that she might be free to go about. That her outburst had been merely because of her youth, he fully understood. There was nothing fundamentally unfair or unwomanly about her. She was simply the victim of the unreal atmosphere in which she had lived. If only he could take her out of it! Poor little girl, how young she looked, how frail, as she stood there with her beautiful angry face! A black misery filled his soul, a hatred of himself, and a wretched sense of failure in the thing most vital to him in life.

While this passed through his brain, he had been walking rapidly, and after a few moments, coming upon Washington Square, he flung himself upon one of the benches near the center, stretching his legs out straight in front of him, folding his arms, and, frowning under the tilted brim of his hat, he sat moodily staring into space.

Darkness had not quite fallen yet, and all about him poured the homeward-bound crowds from the neighboring shops, factories, and offices:—an unceasing stream, varied as the nations of the earth. From the north side the generous old houses of mellow brick looked on in dignified somnolence. From the south stared the wide windows of a row of buildings, motley as the crowd they faced, and as scarred with the throes of living. Here dwelt and strove with agonized souls many who fell or merely struggled on in the cause of an art which the north side, in idle moments, sometimes condescended to patronize, lorgnette to nose, always without enthusiasm, always with a sense of bestowing a favor. To the west a few semi-modern apartment-houses rubbed shoulders with their more ancient neighbors, the spacious low-roofed residences of two generations past. Here and there, up the bulging façades of the former, lights were beginning to flower forth.

At the eastern end of the park tall buildings massed, lowering, the advance bulwarks of commerce spreading octopus-like beyond.

Between such boundaries then, lay the Square, a pitiful scrap of nature's handiwork, snatched from the country and imprisoned here, to be mauled into ugliness by the eager multitudes who came to use it; a shamefully inadequate little handkerchief of green, cast down amid a parched waste of stone and mortar; yet precious, and valued, too. In its center arose the white rainbow of the Washington Arch, spanning a stream of clumsy vehicles of trade. And around it, down the paths, across the intersecting and boundary roads, went the people, newly released from toil, hurrying to such a variety of habitations as the mind can scarcely grasp or, grasping, believe.

Here one saw cheaply clad shop-girls, singly or in little groups, their silhouettes outlining the sharpest cut of the latest fashion. In the same wave

THAT WHICH IS NO ROBBERY 61

with them were the younger members of their sex, who followed the same trade,—pale-faced little girls, half-women, half-children, whose garments were a curious garbling of both. Their laughter was shrill from sheer relief at their release from the tediousness of tying up endless parcels. Following these, the elder and younger alike, were lean youths who seemed mere match-board marionettes inside their exaggerated clothes, calloused young men with blotched faces and bad eyes, following, following ever, hats a-tilt and cigarettes dangling from loose lips.

Jews with long beards went by, and stumpy Jews and Russians and Poles, stunted in mind and body by long service in factories where white foamy garments are made in their thousands, at the cost of immortal souls. Through the park came laborers with slouching gait; a group of them chattered in Italian about the misdoings of some padrone. In a side street, just glimpsed, a second gang piled their picks into the yawning blue tool-chest, standing in line to do it, and then came filing across the Square, leaving a little garden of red lights where they had been toiling. From the Little Club a knot of laughing art students came racing. Arm in arm they sang as they crossed to the French restaurant which furnished them a dinner of mystery for little more than the song itself. Up Fifth Avenue the double string of glowing pearls, which illuminates it, had been strung. The crowd was lessening now.

One by one the noises began to subside. Only an occasional late worker scurried past, and the Square was gradually emptying of all save its habitués. The number of these was increased by shabby figures who drifted in at random, blown there by some whirlwind of the city, like atoms in a dust cloud.

It grew darker.

Infrequently, a dray, with great, heavy, fringed-hoofed Flanders horses, clattered past, their drivers little needing to urge the homeward-bound beasts. How they rumbled and swayed, towering loads deposited afar, laths and poles rattling loosely. Into the surrounding gloom they vanished, roaring, squeaking, jolting over the cobblestones.

Quieter and yet more quiet grew the Square. At this hour the virtuous were eating in their homes, while the wicked fed in luxury over there to the northwest, where already the white flare of middle Broadway was flung against the darkened sky. Over all hung the indefinable yet definite spirit of the

THAT WHICH IS NO ROBBERY 63

city; intricate, throbbing, fraught with the joys and horrors of civilization.

And Sam Hill still sat glowering out upon the scene.

"Oh, the wonder of it!" said a low voice at his elbow.

With an effort Hill aroused himself, the aching trouble in his heart pulsing painfully at the return to consciousness of his own personality. Had some one spoken to him? It was only his fancy, perhaps! Suddenly something cool and damp and unmistakably alive thrust itself into the relaxed palm of his hand, causing him to start up. Then the cool thing shot forward, leaving his hand upon a rough coat of fur. An animal! What could it be?

"Great Scott!" he exclaimed, all alert. In the darkness beside him crouched a shapeless mass, which grunted softly.

"It's only Mr. Jones," said the voice that had spoken before. "He just woke up. It's only my bear!"

Then Sam Hill realized that the creature at which he was staring in the dimness was a small bear, to which was attached a chain that clanked upon the asphalt walk.

"Mr. Jones, is it?" snapped Hill. "And who the devil are you?"

"I am Pedro," replied the animal's custodian. And even in the gloom Hill could see the white gleam of a smile. The slender figure straightened up on the bench beside him.

"What Pedro? Pedro who?" demanded Hill, interested in spite of himself.

"Only just Pedro," came the answer. Then followed a laugh—a wonderful rippling laugh, ending abruptly, as though a door had been closed upon music.

"Well, Pedro, whoever you are," replied Hill, "you seem to be in as ill straits as myself, else you would not be sitting in the Square at such an hour."

"Are you hungry, too?" Pedro inquired.

Hill laughed, a short laugh, not so pleasant to hear as the other's.

"In a way," said he.

"Ah!" said Pedro pityingly, and by the tone Hill knew that the youth had guessed at a hidden meaning in his words.

"Why do you come to the city?" asked the latter, after a pause. "Your brotherhood usually keep to the open road."

"I come because I am an artist, and here I shall have more opportunity to paint," replied Pedro.

"You speak as though you were a genius," said Hill bitingly.

"Perhaps I am," Pedro returned.

"Surely every one knows how it feels to be a genius," remarked Hill; "we all have the potential qualities that are necessary. To prove you're a genius to some one else is quite another matter. Can you do it?"

"As to that, I am quite indifferent," Pedro responded. "I want to paint; that is enough for me."

"Hum!" said Sam, "how are you going about it? Have you friends here?"

"Several, who came with me," the other answered, "but they can not help me to begin."

"Too bad!" commented Hill. "We all have our troubles."

There was a silence, during which Mr. Jones fumbled the hand of his new acquaintance affectionately. Then said Pedro:

"What is your trouble?"

Somehow Hill was not in the least offended by the question. For a moment he considered it, then:

"I must go away and hide myself," he said.

"And you don't want to go away?"

"Yes—or rather, I want to go, although it is a duty I take a bitter pleasure in discharging. But I must go, because I must hide."

"Oh!" said Pedro. "Why go off to hide? A good way to get out of sight is to remain where you are, and tell no one about it. People so promptly forget about you."

Hill peered at the youthful face to see if the bear-trainer was joking; but no trace of mirth could he discover.

"Perhaps!" said he. Then to change the subject, "When did you arrive in the city?"

"This afternoon."

"And what, exactly, do you expect to do?"

"To find a master, and to study; to find a studio, and to paint," was the terse reply.

"And meanwhile you are hungry! Are you saving all your money for the ends you mention?"

"I have no money," explained Pedro cheerfully.

"Then how do you plan to get your studio?"

"I do not know yet," Pedro told him. "But there must be a great many in so large a city."

"They are filled, for the most part."

THAT WHICH IS NO ROBBERY 67

"But by worse artists," remarked the youth, as though that solved everything.

Hill laughed—a better laugh this time.

"Unfortunately it is not so simple to be rid of these inferior fellows," said he. "You will have to think of some other plan than ejecting them, or expecting them to turn out on your criticism."

"Perhaps I shall find a patron," suggested Pedro with a vague gesture.

"I would not depend on that," Hill advised him. "This is not the Renaissance."

"No, it is New York!" the youth flashed back. And again Hill could not quite determine whether he was being laughed at, or doing the laughing himself.

"So you are not daunted by the somewhat uncertain future before you," remarked Hill, "even though you are unfed?"

"I have been that before," retorted Pedro dryly.

"Well," said Hill, "the most immediate of our troubles can be mended. I, too, am hungry. Will you dine with me?"

"We shall be glad to," said Pedro.

Hill had forgotten the bear, but when Pedro said

"we," he realized that there were three hungry beings.

"All right," he said, making a rapid mental inventory of the restaurants he knew. Hitting at last on the right one, he got to his feet with a jerk. "Come along, we'll go over to Galotti's."

Pedro obeyed with alacrity, hauling Mr. Jones to attention, and the three of them set off briskly in the direction of Sixth Avenue.

Past the dark houses they strode, house after house with curtains drawn closely so that no ray of light stole out to the passer-by. Farther on, under the arc-lights, children swarmed over the littered pavement. Sam and his companions turned up-town, hugging the lighted fronts of the shops. Overhead, the railway thundered, making conversation impossible. Loungers stared after them in momentary curiosity as they passed, and a little crowd of children attached themselves to Mr. Jones. At Tenth Street they turned eastward again, and coming to a halt before a low iron gateway, Hill dispersed the children with a handful of coppers.

The house before which they had paused was an old-fashioned brownstone building, five stories high, with barred and shuttered windows which

THAT WHICH IS NO ROBBERY 69

gave no sign that food and cheer might be obtained within. Only against the basement window-blinds, drawn tightly down, with gleaming cracks upon them, shadows moved swiftly, abnormal in bulk, as though a race of giants served the guests. Pushing open the little gate, Hill made his way down the steps and through the accumulation of ash-cans and wooden crates that littered the area-way, Pedro and the bear following. Then all three waited in the cavernous gloom of an archway under the front-door steps, at what was apparently the tradesman's entrance. After a moment a dark shape appeared upon the ground glass of the door, and Signorina Galotti opened to them: a plump little woman with a scarlet apron, and heavy gold rings in her ears.

"Santa Maria!" she gasped, at sight of the company in which Hill presented himself, "what now?"

"This is Pedro," said Hill, "and his bear, Mr. Jones." Then turning to Pedro, he remarked that an introduction by a habitué was necessary before the signorina would admit a new patron to the joys of her abundant table. Then he entered, motioning them to do likewise.

"But the bear?" objected the hostess.

"It is less a bear than many of your friends here,"

said Hill, waving a hand toward the inner room. The witticism was lost upon Signorina Galotti, being far beyond the boundaries of her English.

"But I can not, even for the signor," she began.

Then Pedro smiled at her, and without warning, sailed into a sea of voluble Italian which Hill found it impossible to follow. Not so the *restaurateure*. She beamed upon him before he had half finished, and without further difficulties, they were admitted.

"What a smile! *Che bel dentin'!*" she purred.

From the front basement room several guests craned inquiring heads, only to withdraw indifferently after a glance. Anything might happen at Galotti's, and a well-behaved bear which showed no indication of performing, was, therefore, of only the slightest interest. But it was not into this first room that Hill went. Down a narrow corridor they groped and thence into a kitchen full of activity and color, picturesquely disordered, not to say untidy. Three waiters in decrepit evening-dress clothes, bustled in and out from the room beyond, to which the kitchen was the only passage. On the whole, it was a reassuring atmosphere. However things may be cooked at Galotti's, they always taste divinely.

Passing through this place, they emerged into

what had once been the back yard, the brick fence of which had since been carried up to the height of the second story, and roofed in with glass. Around all four sides ran a wooden balcony with tables upon it, and to this a narrow staircase gave access. On the ledge were plants in pots and boxes, and between them, at one corner, reposed a huge yellow cat with a short tail, asleep amid all the clatter and talk. Below were more little tables, so close together that it was hard to avoid jostling your neighbor's elbow. In the corner of this strange room grew large trees whose tops vanished through the roof, which in summer could be removed, leaving only their feathery branches to protect the diners below.

All along both sides of the apartment were indentures, where once the windows of the houses next had looked into this one-time garden. These spaces were now filled by paintings, obviously contributed by the habitués, in some cases, perhaps, in lieu of payment for a score. From one a life-sized horse gazed in upon the assembled company; through another a young lady could be descried struggling with Signorina Galotti's famous spaghetti, and so on, according to the fancy of the decorator. The upper walls had drawings on them, too, some executed directly upon the brick; and even the posts supporting the balcony boasted pencil drawings and sketches in colored chalk.

The company was large and varied: respectable Italian bourgeois of the neighborhood, voluble and greedy, artists, music students from the neighboring institute, lonely men in search of amusement, two prim maiden ladies on an intellectual spree, professional models, and socialists out of employment. Hill selected a table in a corner, and after persuading Mr. Jones to lie down beneath it, they seated themselves. No need to order here. There is what there is, and the waiter brings it to you. In a few moments a generous bowl of soup was put before them, and the long crisp loaf had been given to the bear, to keep him occupied. With a sigh at the thought of Old Nita, and the others who were doubtless hungry also, Pedro fell to.

"So you are an Italian?" remarked Hill by way of renewing conversation.

"No," replied Pedro, adding nothing to the information.

"But you speak it, I observe," said Hill.

"Yes," said Pedro, eating busily.

"But you are surely a foreigner?"

THAT WHICH IS NO ROBBERY 73

Pedro waved his spoon vaguely.

"I am an *everywhere*," he explained.

"Oh!" said Hill, "a cosmopolitan, I see!"

They ate the entire menu with very little conversation. Tomato with garlic; *potage,* slab of unrecognizable fish, mysterious entrée, the leg of a chicken, lettuce *vinegette,* tiny lobster, pink spaghetti, an infinitesimal lozenge of ice-cream, ancient Camembert, and thick coffee in heavy cups; dubious fruit, and sour wine of Sicily [California] to wash it down withal. Then they pushed back their chairs a little, and talked. Hill tossed a package of cigarettes upon the table, lighting one himself. Pedro followed suit, inhaling the fumes with a long sigh of contentment.

"You are fond of that bear?" asked Hill.

"I am," replied Pedro. "He is my good friend; he is the thing I love most of all."

"How did you come to give him his name?"

"Mr. Jones?" said the boy. "Oh! that is not his real name. His real name is Michael-Angelo-Goya-Rodin-Rembrandt. I only call him Mr. Jones for short."

Hill laughed.

"Tell me of your wanderings with him," he asked.

And Pedro told him. The elder man sat very still

as he listened, his chair tilted back against the brick wall, his eyes narrowed to mere slits of light as he watched the young raconteur through the blue haze of smoke. What tales these were to which he listened; how they stirred the *wanderlust* in him. Their possibilities how many, their adventures how varied! Simply told, and without affectation, they were yet replete with dramatic interest, full of color, of suggestion. This boy had a marvelous personality. He made you see things without describing them to you. A look, a gesture, did it. Dreamily Sam listened, yet intently. Those companions of whom the boy spoke, what of them? Again he listened, having put the question, and again his interest responded immediately. And all the time his first favorable impression of Pedro grew in strength, and was the more solidly confirmed.

The ingenuousness of the youth, the simplicity, the wit, the direct decent look of him, the understanding that he displayed, were remarkable. Then, too, his honesty seemed obvious. Furthermore, he was unquestionably without the desire to impress Hill, or to befool him. Of himself and his origin the boy said little or nothing, but even this failed to trouble his listener. More and more he

THAT WHICH IS NO ROBBERY 75

liked this youth whom chance had thrown his way at such an unwelcome moment, and as he watched the eager young face, animated by talking of the things he loved, Hill felt that here was one of the exceptional people who bring into contact with their fellow creatures the selves that they really are, unshielded by a mask of pretense, because unafraid and unashamed of their own hearts.

Then, too, the fascination of the ancient and honorable profession of bear-dancing had taken hold on Hill. But though he listened well, every little while came the thought of his lost love, and with it, a wave of depression swept over him. With a desperate effort to pull away from it, he asked another question.

"Where are your companions?"

"Very near the public garden from which we have just come," responded Pedro. "Down the little cobbly street to where the air-railway turns; then in a little door, through a court, to an old house with wooden balconies. They await me there."

"How fitting!" murmured Hill. "How I should like to see them! Would they receive me well?"

"Without a doubt," said Pedro; "they recognize a friend at once, even as a dog or a bear does!"

"I've a mind to go back with you," said Hill jokingly. "They must be corkers. That Old Nita, now—what does she look like?"

"She—why she looks—she looks like Time himself," responded the boy. "See, I will show you."

Saying which, he brought out a stump of a pencil and a small pad from some recess of his old coat of green.

"This is Nita," said he, turning over several pages, and handing the open book to Hill. "Old Nita, and that next is Beau-Jean, scolding Koko."

Hill took the proffered papers idly; gave one glance at them, whistled a little, and suddenly sat very erect, examining them intently.

"Who drew these?" he inquired after a moment.

"Why, me, of course," said Pedro.

For another little space Hill was silent, turning over the sheets in his hand. There were perhaps twenty sketches in the pad. From his scrutiny of them, he raised his eyes to Pedro. Could the boy be telling the truth? Had he actually drawn these things? They were remarkable. Surely, such a one as had done them would be famous, for work like this was not to be hid easily. Indeed, it was amazingly good. It was the work of a born draftsman. But

Pedro's face showed no signs of uneasiness. On the contrary, his eyes were alight as he explained who the people were.

"That is Rico and Anna, who are kissing," said he. "Has she not a beautiful long thigh? And the way her back bends—*so!* The fine old gentleman is a farmer, though he looks so like a Jewish patriarch. See, Nita dancing the 'coquette.' Ha! ha! here is another pose of that! And if you will turn that sheet, you will see a whole page of Mr. Jones."

"It's—It's—Gee!" said Hill.

"Do you like my drawings?" asked Pedro, suddenly self-conscious, a deep flush spreading over his face and neck.

"*Like* them!" was all Hill replied, but at the tone of his voice Pedro's eyes sparkled.

"When did you do all this?" Hill added.

Pedro told him. Again there came to Hill a vision of that wonderful irresponsible life, and again the overwhelming sense of his loss of Iris.

"You see, I can do them very quickly," Pedro was saying. And indeed, while he had been speaking, the profile of the man at the next table had appeared upon the pad, a masterly piece of drawing in which the subject's most salient characteristics seemed to have been caught. "I love to draw people, and lots of people together, and places. And I love to draw Mr. Jones."

"Who taught you?" asked Hill.

"Long ago, when I was small, some one taught me every day," said Pedro. "Then I have painted a little here, and a little there. Once at Barbizon, Rodin, the great one, was there in the woods, idling, and although it was of modeling he talked, he taught me infinitely much."

"How did you come to know him?"

"I spoke to him."

"Ah!"

"But I have yet so much, so much, to learn! That is why I came here to find a studio, that I might really learn."

Privately, Hill was convinced that what Pedro needed was the opportunity. That was all. It was remarkable, but true. Suddenly he leaned across the little table.

"I suppose you love that bear tremendously?" he asked.

"Yes," said Pedro, instantly aware of an impending development.

"More than your art?"

Pedro laughed. Then he sobered.

"No," he said, "of course not. I suppose I would even give him up if need be—and yet he is like my own brother."

The boy's eyes were bright with excitement, and the warm color had crept into his face as he spoke. Across the mouth of the man opposite to him was the stamp of a new-born decision.

"Then give him up!" cried Hill. "I am a painter. Give him to me in exchange for my studio and all that is in it!"

CHAPTER V

TWO MEETINGS

NEXT morning, Pedro awoke with a sense of strangeness upon him, and instinctively stretched out his hand to touch Mr. Jones, who always slept beside him. But the bear was missing. Instead of a rough warm coat that heaved sleepily beneath his hand, he touched a coverlet soft as silk. At this, his sense of uneasiness increased, and with an effort he opened his eyes and sat up. Ah, yes! He remembered now. Mr. Jones was gone. Gone with the sanction of his master, gone perhaps never to return! One by one the events of the preceding evening came back to his mind. His hesitancy, Hill's arguing with him, the details of their compact, and his final agreement to the extraordinary proposal. Ah, yes! and Hill's writing of the two letters, one of which gave him, Pedro, possession of the apartment in which he now found himself. The other to a friend of Hill's, to be delivered on the morrow— that was to-day—to-day.

Still more clearly the events of the night just past crept into his memory. He recollected his own inability to realize the magical good fortune that had befallen him, his dazed acceptance, his vague wondering if it were really possible to carry out such a plan! All had appeared unreal, until it came to parting with his bear, when he had almost wept. He recalled now his introduction of Hill (who had decided to begin his new life instanter) to the other bear-dancers, and his own explanation to them of what was to happen. Their cries of protest and congratulation still rang in his ears. He remembered pleading that Hill be kind to Old Nita when she was penitent, and firm with her when she drank. Poor Old Nita! She would still have some one to lean on; he was glad of that!

He remembered his lonely entrance into the studio, too, awestricken by its height and luminous darkness. How he had entered, clutching the money that Hill had loaned him, a twenty-dollar bill, crumpled tightly!

Slowly he let his gaze travel about the comfortable little bedroom in which he lay. Its furnishings were simple in the extreme, yet adequate. Opposite him stood a chest of drawers, mahogany, and old.

There were brushes on it and a few simple ebony toilet necessities. On a rack above it hung several neckties in quiet silks, all good and new. Higher still swung a small three-sided mirror for shaving, and for some reason Pedro smiled as he looked at it. An ample closet occupied one end of the room, and beside the bed-head was a little table with an electric reading lamp and several books upon it,—Whitman, R. L. S., Gautier, a catholic assortment. Through the single window, opening out to the leads, the sun was shining merrily. At the foot of the bed was a door, half closed. *The studio was in there!* At the thought he sprang up and flung the door wide to discover if his memory of the night was a vision or a reality.

As he stood upon the threshold he seemed for an instant to see, not the room before him, but the upright, fashionably clad figure of Hill, leading a bear off into the dark regions beyond Washington Square. Then throwing back his head, he laughed, and stepped into the studio.

Once it had been the attic covering the upper floors of two adjoining houses. In every sense the place was a workshop, replete with the most perfect tools for the trade of the brush, and the only spot conducive to idling was the chimney corner. Upon the smaller easel stood the half-finished portrait of a man, while against one wall a pile of canvases was standing, their faces hidden.

Pedro drew a long breath of delight. Then it was true; it had not been a dream, after all! He thought of Mr. Jones again, and for a moment the pang of that dear remembrance was bitter. How was Hill getting on with Old Nita? he wondered. If only it were possible to be with them, and here at the same time! Ah, well! one could not serve two masters, and he had chosen and did not regret.

On the mantel-shelf stood a letter that Pedro had placed there on the previous evening. Hill had given it to him with the injunction to deliver it at the earliest possible moment. He read the superscription with interest:

Abraham Lincoln Leigh.

An address on Tenth Street followed. Pedro determined to deliver it at once, and, accordingly, hastened with his dressing. But the sense of possession was too much for him. Once, flinging his arms wide, he made as if to embrace the great bare chamber and its contents; and then, as suddenly, sank down upon the model throne and burst into sobs, great strangling sobs that shook his entire frame. For several moments he lay so, and when at last he raised himself, he was smiling through his tears.

"*Dios!*" he said aloud. "Such happiness! Ah! such happiness."

He took up his sketching-pad and slipped it into his pocket. Again he tried to leave, and this time a bit of color, yellow, vivid, magnetic, called him back. He crossed to where it lay upon a palette and carefully closed the tube. A little got upon his hand, and in turn upon the letter that he held, making a tiny yellow sun around which spread an aura of oil.

"I must go," said Pedro.

But still he lingered. The light was all wrong. If one were working on that portrait now, it would have to be changed! Not until he had adjusted each of the shades to suit his fancy, did he finally leave, reluctantly, dragged away only by the letter in his hand. Even at the door he turned for one last look. Then he latched it after him and ran down-stairs.

It was still very early as New York reckons time, being not quite eight o'clock. To Pedro this seemed late to be starting on any errand, and he was surprised at the comparative quiet into which he emerged. The house, or rather houses, in which Hill's studio was situated, were the last two of what had once been a terrace of considerable pretensions, and they ran bias to the streets that had demolished all the others like them. Consequently, these decaying aristocrats of buildings did not stand upon any avenue or street, but upon a queer little triangular court of their own, shut in at the front by Sixth Avenue, and bounded on either side by Eighth and Ninth Streets. At the rear loomed one of the city prisons, terra-cotta, ungainly, ugly as the sins that necessitated its existence. The little court thus formed was paved with flagging, and within it the two old houses huddled in dignified, rather sad seclusion.

In the courtyard Pedro paused again to gaze up the mellow brick fronts where his skylight glittered in the sun. The floors below were occupied by apartments of a makeshift sort, and of these most had the windows closed and the blinds drawn. On the floor next the top, however, one was flung wide, and the befrilled muslin curtains that guarded it bellied in the breeze. There was a little bunch of violets upon this window's sill, and each advance of the sail-like muslin seemed to threaten them with precipitation on to the stones below. A charming place, truly, and all about it hung an atmosphere hard to describe, keen to feel as the things that happened there; and more—infinitely more—*might* happen! The very tilt of the leads, a little aslant and rakish, was suggestive, different, peculiar to the place. But delightful as it all was, the winking, flashing, northern skylight that topped it, held the lad most strongly. He gazed up at it wraptly, and then, once more his emotional nature got the best of him.

"I love you!" he cried to the studio window, and he threw it a kiss.

There was a laugh—a silvery laugh—the laugh of a young woman, of a girl pleased by a gallantry—and it rang out from behind the billowing white curtains. For an instant Pedro stood transfixed, while a golden head was thrust out quickly, and as quickly withdrawn. Then a bare white arm flashed between the ruffles, and the violets flew to his feet. Picking the flowers up, he swept off his old felt hat in that magnificent bow of his, and looked up again, but there was nothing further to be seen, and the window had been shut against the chill wine of the morning air. Holding the little purple blossoms against his heart, Pedro turned away, and passing beneath the old brick arch with its bracket-lantern and its sign, Muldoon Place, went out into the awakening city.

· · · · · ·

The house in which Abraham Lincoln Leigh lived, was, like almost every other building in this neighborhood, now being put to a use other than that for which it was originally intended, for once it had been a warehouse for the storage of paper.

"Yep!" said the hall-boy, in response to Pedro's inquiry as to whether Mr. Leigh was in. "Third to your right. Last door!"

So Pedro mounted and knocked.

"Come!" said a resonant voice, which was like the booming of a great bell. And Pedro, rejoicing at the music of it, promptly obeyed.

It was a large studio which he entered, large and crowded and disordered beyond belief. Several corners had been screened off for uses other than those of sculpture, which was the self-evident occupation of the proprietor. The walls were crowded with casts, the room was filled with figures, and the damp odor of plasterline was in the air. Upon a sea-chest against the far wall books were stacked, and books lay about everywhere, most of them stained and worn, as though handled by the fingers of toil. From behind one screened corner peered a crockery-laden shelf, while another screen partially concealed a shower-bath. At the end of the room, a door stood ajar, and the foot of a rumpled bed, which nearly filled the tiny chamber, could be seen. One instantly felt that the prime reason for this admixture of living and working was that the two were so intersected in the mind of the sculptor that he would have found their separation impossible; and this idea was confirmed by the appearance of the man himself.

At the moment of Pedro's entrance, Abraham Lincoln Leigh was stooping over a frying-pan full of bacon, which was sizzling on the stove; and the instantaneous impression which his visitor received was that the man's name had in some curious fashion influenced his personal appearance. He was very tall, and his leanness was extraordinary. From eye to chin deep lines swept down the forceful jaw, and his overhanging brow and rather prominent nose were rugged in outline. His eyes, deep-set, were misty, but lit up when he spoke as though a veil had suddenly been drawn from before them. It would have been extremely difficult to determine his exact age, though as a matter of fact he was in the neighborhood of thirty-five. He was clean-shaven, and his shock of dark hair was in disorder. He was clad in a linen blouse, and an ancient pair of khaki trousers. Taken all in all, he was a man whose silent and retiring manner led people either to expect much of him or fail to notice him, according to the cast of their own natures; while Leigh himself let both pass by, without comment, if not without thought. All his movements were leisurely, and he took his time about speech. As Pedro entered, he did not even turn his head for a moment, but continued manipulating the bacon deliberately. When it was reversed, he looked up at his visitor, and again the mellow voice rang out like the slow chimes of a church-bell.

"Who are you?"

"I am Pedro," said the owner of that name, flashing his white smile. "I have a letter from Sam Hill."

"Ah!" remarked Leigh, not, however, offering to take the missive, but looking at the bearer, and, as was so commonly the case, liking him. Then, in response to that smile of Pedro's, Leigh smiled, a rare thing in him, and an illuminating.

"Have you had your breakfast?" he asked.

"Why, no! I haven't!" exclaimed the boy, evidently surprised at the recollection of his lack.

Leigh looked him over again, his face grave despite the gathering up of the little lines at the corners of his eyes.

"You're a friend of Sam's?" he asked.

"I am his most devoted one!" exclaimed Pedro fervently.

Again Leigh smiled.

"No, you are not," he said. "However, the forks and spoons are in that bureau, and you'll find a cup on the shelf behind that screen."

Pedro stared at him for a breath, and then, with a laugh he threw his hat and his letter down upon a chair, and went in search of the articles mentioned.

"Gracias!" he said, "I am very hungry. Maybe you know what that feels like, eh?"

"You bet!" said Leigh solemnly.

With alacrity Pedro gathered up the implements wherewith to serve himself, and returned from the corner shelf with one hand grasping a bristly bouquet of cutlery and the other balancing some dishes. Pausing before a sketch in plasterline, he looked at it critically, cocking his head to one side, and half-closing his eyes.

"You ought to push the hind quarters of the tiger

TWO MEETINGS 91

back of the woman, so!" said he, giving an illustrative twist of the hand which nearly sent the cup flying. "It doesn't quite look—look *solid,* you know."

Leigh brought the frying-pan over when he came to inspect. He crouched for a moment before his model. Then he turned to Pedro.

"I believe you are right," he said. "In here is where you mean, of course. Are you a sculptor?"

"Painter," said Pedro, "at least, I am going to be."

A gleam of amusement crept into those strange eyes of Leigh.

"Going to be!" he quoted. "Ah! I see! The novice is always the severest critic."

"But I am right about it," persisted the boy, not in the least abashed at being made fun of.

"I did not say you were wrong," remarked Leigh. "Come and eat. You are in no need of championing your views."

Still on the alert to defend his inexperience, Pedro obeyed, and drew a chair up to a partially cleared table, the opposite end of which was cluttered with a catalogue full of small objects, all of which had to do with the host's work. Leigh followed suit, placing the frying-pan full of bacon atop a heap of anatomical drawings.

There was coffee, and half a bottle of milk; also crisp French rolls from the baker around the corner. While Pedro ate, one eye on the food, the other on the work, finished, half-finished, or just begun, which occupied the main portion of the studio, Leigh perused Hill's letter between gulps of coffee. Its substance was merely that Hill was going away, possibly for a year, and confirmed Pedro's possession of the studio with the fewest possible explanations. When Leigh finished reading it, he attacked the bacon and addressed his guest.

"Tell me," he began. "What's all this about? Did you really never see Hill before last night?"

"Never," said Pedro.

"And what reason did he give for this unexpected desire to leave town?"

"That he wanted to go!" said Pedro with rising inflection, as if surprised that any other reason were necessary.

"Hum!" mused Leigh, thinking instantly of Iris. "I believe I can give a guess, then."

"He took my bear; I took his studio. A very good arrangement, eh?" asked Pedro.

"For you, certainly," said Leigh.

"Ah! but you should see my bear!" responded Pedro earnestly.

The lad was so sincere that Leigh smiled again.

"From something in Sam's letter," said he, "I am pretty sure that I am right about why he has gone. He says I am to look after you. Are you going to need much looking after?"

"Every one does," said the lad, suddenly serious. "Every one needs looking after, because every one is young—always! And every one is alone—always! But," he added with a laugh, "you may depend upon my troubling you only as much as you trouble me; a friendship, is it not? Giving and taking *trouble,* eh?"

Leigh did not answer, but as he drew out his pipe and filled it deliberately, he never took his eyes from his visitor. Something in the boy's personality arrested him, and as he could not quite define the interest which it aroused, he pondered it well. What charm the lad possessed! Like many another, Leigh succumbed to it without further demur.

"And what," he asked at length, "do you wish me to do for you as a starter? Take you up to the art school?"

"*Academy!* No!" exclaimed Pedro.

"What do you intend doing, then?"

"Paint," said Pedro.

"Anything else?"

"Find some one whose criticism I can respect!"

"Ah!" said Leigh, "and who will that be?"

"I have not yet decided," said the boy thoughtfully. "I shall have to see the work of all the best men first."

"And when do you go to work?"

"Now!" replied Pedro. "I must go. There is not a moment to be lost!"

He arose and stood looking as though alarmed at the flight of so many precious moments.

"But later?" asked Leigh.

"When it is dark, I will go with you," said Pedro, responding to the unspoken invitation.

"I shall come around for you at about six-thirty," said Leigh. "We must get to know each other better."

Hat in hand, Pedro turned to flash an assenting smile at Leigh before he went out.

When the door had closed upon him, the sculptor stood in deep thought for several moments. Then absent-mindedly knocking the contents of his unlit pipe out upon the hearth, he put it in his mouth, upside down, and lounged over to the plasterline sketch that Pedro had criticized. For some time he looked at it immovably, and then stretched out a tentative hand toward the hind quarters of the tiger, withdrawing instantly.

"No, by George!" said he aloud, "I think it's all right just the way it stands."

But nevertheless, he went to work upon another group, leaving the diminutive sketch alone.

Half past six (it being then dark) found Leigh on his way to the studio in Muldoon Place, strolling along meditatively through the half-lit mystery of Greenwich.

At the corner of Seventh Avenue he halted, slapped his pockets, unearthed his pipe and pouch, and proceeded to light up. Then, to make up for the few moments lost in this operation, he dived down the little short cut called Paradise Place. It was very dark in the little fragment of a street, and half-way down its narrow span he bumped into two men who were in the act of parting from each other with low-voiced adieux. The taller of these two muttered an apology almost in the same breath with Leigh's, and was hurrying away, when the sculptor, catching sight of the face under the peak of the cheap and shabby hat, called his name.

"Vanderpool!"

The millionaire heard, for he made an irresolute little movement as if to return, but changing his mind, only pulled his hat over his eyes, and walked off rapidly. For a moment Leigh almost doubted the veracity of his recognition. Reginald Vanderpool in what amounted to a disguise! Such a circumstance seemed far from likely! And yet he could not be wrong, for in the folds of the man's coat he had distinctly seen the black ribbon and dangling monocle which were characteristic of Iris' father. Deuce take the man, it was very odd for him to rush off in that manner without speaking! But, for the matter of that, Vanderpool had always been something of a mystery to his acquaintances!

With a shrug, Leigh resumed his walk, only to have it borne in upon him after a few moments, that the second of the two men whom he had interrupted, was preceding him. Even when he turned into Muldoon Place, after having lost sight of the fellow for a moment, there he was again, crossing the little paved court twenty-five feet in advance, and entering at the basement door!

"Well, if that isn't the darnedest thing!" said Leigh as he mounted the stairs, puzzled, but thereafter thinking of it no more.

He found Pedro engaged upon a pencil drawing of a very pretty girl in the act of washing herself with the aid of a cake of soap which she held in a prominent manner. Leigh started slightly as he looked at it, but all he said was:

"Still working?"

"No," responded Pedro, "I stopped when the light gave out."

He waved his hand toward the smaller easel where stood a canvas, upon which a picture—a street scene—had been blocked in. Leigh crossed to look at it, and although the artficial light made any real judgment of what he saw difficult, he bent before it interestedly, though still without comment.

"So you have stopped working," said he. "What do you call the thing you are doing?"

"This is not my *work*," explained Pedro, arising, and laying down the drawing-board. "This is just to live. I have seen many pictures in advertisements like this, often less good, and perhaps I can sell it. Then I need not use the money of Mr. Hill. A good idea, eh?"

"Yes," assented Leigh, still without any change of expression. "You will be able to sell it. Are you going to put 'Pears' or 'Ivory' or what on that cake of soap?"

"Whichever!" said Pedro with a shrug.

"Ah!" said Leigh, "well, come out and play around with me. I never see any one much, except Hill, and as he has deserted the camp you will have to fill his place, since you have undertaken to fill his studio and my time."

"All right," said Pedro.

"Do you know the city? Have you been here before?"

"No."

"Then you haven't much choice as to where we go?"

"No. That will come later."

"I suppose so," said Leigh dryly; "meanwhile, I shall reveal some places from which a choice may be made."

Together they went out. Pedro was good company, and Leigh responded to him readily. Between these two had already sprung up an intimacy that was accepted by both without surprise. It seemed so natural to them to be together, the language that they spoke was identical, and both were so simple in their attitude toward life, and toward each other, that they spoke and acted with the feeling of old comrades from the first.

It was a merry excursion upon which they went, merry and innocent in the way that things are innocent to those who think no evil. Arm in arm they strode into their adventure of the commonplace, the tall ungainly figure and the slight graceful one, keenly observant of their surroundings which were replete with interest for both. With comment, turn and turn about, upon the things they saw, they passed through half a dozen places of amusement, finding themselves at about midnight seated at a little round table in the Café Lafayette; their left hands upon the frosted surfaces of *amer picons,* and their right fists belaboring the little table to emphasize the periods of a cosmic problem then under discussion. Having run the gamut of conversational subjects, they were wallowing in a most complicated and intricate discussion of ethics. A sentence or two can paint the picture of the stage at which their intimacy had arrived within the span of half a dozen hours.

"But why do you not believe in the thing called

sin?" Leigh was protesting, with an earnestness born of the hour of night. "Personally, I am convinced that it is a most potent factor in life. For instance, hypocrisy is a sin (to my mind, at least), and by a sin I do not mean an act, the discovery of which would cover one with mortification and confusion and fear—like murder, say; but a mental process by which one gives one's soul into bondage; which stunts the growth of the spirit, to our own horror in the face of our futile, because tardy, resistance."

"An act whose chief punishment lies in its discovery by ourselves," said Pedro.

"Exactly!" said Leigh.

At which subtle agreement they were each enormously impressed with his own intellectuality.

There was a silence.

"Ah, well!" said Leigh finally, "the night and the city have turned our heads. Let us go home."

Pedro followed him out into the cold night air, with cheeks still flushed from the excitement of his emotion, due to the rare pleasure of being listened to by some one capable of understanding what he said. And Leigh, the while he closed the discussion, watched the earnest young face beside him, with an interest beyond any he had yet experienced. Who was this young man, anyhow?

The question was one that lulled him to sleep that night, and persistently confronted him on his awakening next morning.

Why was the boy so reticent about his origin, his people, his nationality even. Sometimes one would swear Pedro to be a Spaniard; yet he spoke Italian fluently, and French, too. It was Pedro, for example, who had ordered the *amer picons*. His talk was a queer mixture of the elegance of phrase which comes with a literal translation from a Latin language, and the jargon of the gutters. Yet, when he became earnest and wished to press a point, good English seemed to come to him with amazing readiness. And the quality of the boy's work! It was astounding! This latter thought stimulated action.

Slowly Abraham Lincoln Leigh arose from his untidy bed, and in the early light of the wintry morning, strode into his workshop. Half-way across the floor he stopped, adding his ungainly figure to the motionless throng which stood about. For several minutes he stood stock-still, and then, with rapid skilful fingers began to curve back the hind quarters of the tiger in the little plasterline sketch.

CHAPTER VI

THE PEOPLE DOWN-STAIRS

IT has been said that as Leigh entered the front door of the studio building in Muldoon Place, the second, and to him unknown, of the two men whose conference in Paradise Place he had interrupted, entered the same building by the basement way. This latter person was a tall dark man, unmistakably Latin in type, and that the house was familiar to him was evinced by the air with which he manipulated the latch and admitted himself.

The little hall was stuffy and ill lighted by a single gas-burner in a wire cage; and from the rear room came an odor of cooking. But it was not these facts that caused the man to stop short, the crease between his eyes deepening as he stood listening. In the hall above, Leigh's footstep could be plainly heard. The man below approached the staircase with absolute noiselessness, and ascending part way, managed to get a good look at the sculptor without allowing himself to be seen. All unconscious, the latter continued to tramp up toward the attics, and with a muttered oath, quickly suppressed, the watcher returned to the basement as cautiously as he had ascended. At the door of the front room he tapped discreetly, and after a brief interval, during which there was a scurrying sound within and the muffled closing of some interior door, that before which he stood was opened a crack while a smooth voice, with only a slight foreign accent, inquired who was without.

"It is only me. Open up, Ricardo," replied the man in the hall. At which the door was thrown back, revealing a tall bearded man who waved an invitation to enter.

"Ah, Yznaga!" he exclaimed in Spanish. "So it is thou! Enter, my friend, but I beg you will remember that in this house I am Mr. Rowe. Such exclamations, however cordial, must not be made in the public halls!"

"Ever cautious!" exclaimed the visitor. "Now I am not even to speak aloud! Well, you are wise! I obey!"

He seated himself beside the table and mopped his face with a thin silk handkerchief. A fine figure of a man, almost noble in bearing, and exceptionally well dressed beneath his shabby overcoat. Rowe brought out glasses and a decanter, pouring for his guest and for himself.

"The house is at your disposal," he said, after the Spanish manner. Then, this formal courtesy discharged, he leaned anxiously toward the other.

"Did you see him?" he asked.

Yznaga nodded.

"I did."

"And he will buy the necessary armaments?"

"Yes, but he is a hard customer, that Van . . ."

"Hush! Not that name, above all others!" implored the host. "That he will pay is all I need to hear!"

"He will pay for them," responded Yznaga. "Moreover, he is no fool, and intends dealing through me only as an agent. No cash! But we shall arrange the estimate and the bid in such a way as to retain a little for ourselves, eh?"

Rowe growled at this, and the other went on.

"No, our wealthy patron would be very difficult to defraud. He is a man to whose capability I make my bow! And his caution! By the way," he added abruptly, "who lives on the top floor of this building?"

"A painter by the name of Samuel Hill," replied Rowe, "an easy-going young man. He's the landlord."

"Have you any acquaintance with him?"

"No more than is absolutely necessary!"

"Ah! your exclusiveness! Sometimes I think that it is a mistake—that it will attract attention! But of that, later. Tell me, is this landlord of yours a tall homely fellow?"

"No," said Rowe; "why do you ask?"

"Because when He-of-whom-you-know and I were parting just now, such a person interrupted us, whether intentionally or not, I can not tell. But he recognized Vander—recognized him, of that much I am certain. And what is more, he *followed me to this house* and is up-stairs at this moment!"

For a moment Rowe glared at the other with an expression of intent alarm. Then his features relaxed.

"A great tall fellow, did you say?" he mused. Then a light broke upon him. "A giant with a long face and ungainly carriage; that would be Leigh, the sculptor, a great friend of the landlord. And he would know *him,* also! No need to worry about that. As for his following you, that was mere coincidence. He comes here to visit Hill almost daily."

"You relieve my mind, Rowe," replied Yznaga, lighting a cigarette. "And now for our project. He-of-whom-you-know refuses absolutely to commit himself on paper. He will spend, yes! It is for a great purpose, in a noble cause! But he will sign nothing! What have we to hold him by?"

"The money he spends!" replied Rowe grimly.

"Will that suffice? This business is against the law, you know, and—"

"I have something that will hold him," replied Rowe. "I still have the thing by means of which I first interested him!"

"Which is?" said the other suggestively.

Rowe laughed, an unpleasant laugh that was characteristic of him, and reached for the wine.

"That, my simple friend, I am not going to reveal," said he politely. "But its efficacy you need not doubt. Has it not sufficed so far? Why should you doubt that it will work in future, until we have sucked this simple American gentleman dry? Paugh! I hold him in the hollow of my hand!"

"So you possess knowledge of some secret that he fears the exposure of! Ah, I suspected as much."

"I have not said so," replied Rowe, smiling confidently at the end of his cigarette. "Be content, Yznaga, that my knowledge serves its purpose."

"And serves to keep you leader of this enterprise!" snapped the visitor. "Very well. Have it as you will! Thank the blessed saints you have no hold over me! I should dislike to find myself in those nicotine-stained fingers of yours, *amigo mio!*"

"Perhaps you are in them," remarked Rowe, amused.

"I! What nonsense!"

"How about your connection with this affair? Does it not place you somewhat at my mercy? A respectable member of the International Commerce Committee—"

"Hush!" said the other, paling a trifle. "You are right. I admit the precariousness of my position. But granting that you can control him, and myself, what have you to offer the mob? The people, or any body of them, must have an idol, or an ideal for which to fight. Nothing else will really arouse them, nor hold them. It must be politics, or emotion. In this case, as you are well aware, the political side of the question is not sufficiently strong. Can you invent an ideal that will appeal strongly enough to start a revolution? Here we have the cart-before-the-mule. In other words, strong financial backing; a patron whom we (or rather *you*) can absolutely control; a complete knowledge of our country; everything, in fact, except the sentiment of the people. In short, it is a highway to power for us both, blocked by the apathy of half a million ragged half-breeds!"

"Yznaga, my esteemed and admired friend," began Rowe, never losing his amused smile, "you are such a charming, well-bred, representative person that you fit the rôle of pseudo cabinet minister to perfection; and you are such a fool, that you are the ideal minister of state. I don't wonder that our respected patron actually believes you are what you represent yourself to be!"

The man opposite sprang to his feet with an oath.

"A fool!" he cried; "you call me a fool?"

"Sit down, and stop confirming my opinions so nicely," grinned Rowe, "or you may bring the house down about our ears with that yelling."

Yznaga complied, but sat frowning.

"Very well," said he, "say what you like. But calling me a fool will not prove you a wise man."

"Admitted," said Rowe. "But I am wiseacre enough to be forehanded about a matter like this of public sentiment in our beloved country. Let me ask you a question. What would the people rise for? Think well. You know the answer!"

Yznaga was silent for a moment, rubbing the palms of his hands together as he thought hard. At last he spoke, but it was as one who mentions a desirable but unobtainable circumstance.

"There is Signora Daussa and her child," said he slowly. "But of course that is out of the question. No one knows where they are, and in all probability they were killed during the big uprising."

"That was never known as a certainty," said Rowe with meaning.

Yznaga looked up sharply.

"You mean to say—" he began.

Rowe raised a hand, warning him to silence.

"Listen!" he said, "I have for years known the whereabouts of our ex-president's wife, and am in daily—hourly—communication with her. Indeed, she is less than a mile from this very spot! She has practically no English, and therefore it is safe enough to take her about with me a little sometimes. As for explanations; that is easy. She has no money except what she could get for her few jewels, and she has deigned to accept my assistance. She is accepting it for a purely personal service, also, which is confidential, and which consequently I can not tell you. But all this is irrelevant. The main thing that I wish you to understand is the fact that I have in her the one thing which will create a popular feeling. In other words, *her restitution!*"

"If the others—the doubting ones—could but see her once, we would have them with us heart and soul!" said Yznaga.

Rowe thought for a moment.

"Yes," said he, "I had intended that they should, of course, sooner or later. In a few weeks' time they shall see her. In the meantime your work will be to prepare their minds for that event. You must take bogus messages from her to them; give them every confidence that she is in sympathy with the movement. But one thing must be strictly observed. He-of-whom-you-know must be told nothing of her existence until I give the word. Remember that. To be frank with you, I do not believe that she will be in sympathy with us. She cares little for pomp or power. When the time comes for her to see the others, they must be warned to say very little to her, and I shall see to it that she, on her part, does not betray the ignorance in which I think it will be best to keep her."

"As you will!" replied Yznaga. "I am too much dazed by this revelation to dispute with you. I shall go now, and during the next few weeks I shall procure those estimates. And now good night!"

"Via usted con Dios!" said Rowe as to a beggar, closing the door after him.

As long as the sound of Yznaga's footsteps could he heard, Rowe sat staring in the direction of them, nodding his head meditatively.

"He, too, loves her," he said aloud, "and will not move alone, or in the dark, for fear of hurting her."

Then he turned and gathered up the unsigned documents that Yznaga had thrown upon the table, his face clouding again at the sight of them.

"He is right; we are too conspicuous, living so closely," he muttered; "we must go about, and seem like other folk."

CHAPTER VII

A PARTY IN THE ALLEY

FOR the five weeks that led into the heart of the winter, Pedro worked almost incessantly.

From daylight till dark he scarcely left the studio, and only at night (when they were not too tired) would he go forth with Leigh upon what they began to call "perception prowls." At other times they would sit together and read, or talk; sometimes in the wide cushioned ingle-nook at Pedro's; again in tilted chairs, their boots upon the rim of Leigh's stove. Every topic under the sun was brought forth and threshed out; yet the more they talked, the more they found to say, usually ending their arguments by an arrival at similar conclusions. And gradually the magic of companionable silence would creep upon them, while the sculptor lighted pipe after pipe, and the white stumps of Pedro's cigarettes strewed the hearth.

Leigh was a man who made few friends; thus it came about that Pedro met hardly any other people.

But he was well content that such should be the case, delighting as he did in Leigh's society, and utterly satisfied with the gentle adventures upon which the latter led him.

Strange little cafés served them, and sometimes more pretentious places. When Leigh was flush, they dined at Mouquin's, in the mirrored room down-stairs, where Bohemians and friends of Bohemians foregather to sit side by side upon the leather-covered sofas against the wall, hold their ladies' hands beneath the table, drink the excellent and inexpensive wine, and eat that most adorable salad with the garlic in it. Here the air was thick with cigarette smoke and art talk—with talk of work, of salad dressing, and of love—of love, alas! both bought and given. Truly it is a delicious place; but you must go to the café down-stairs.

The symphony concerts began, and from the topmost seats in that vast hall which bears its donor's name, they sat and gazed adown the shelving sea of faces, flecked, foam-like, with fluttering programs, to where, upon the island of the stage, a collection of insects—great crickets, ants, grasshoppers and katydids—brought forth divine music at the waving of a magic wand.

Through the Fall Academy they wandered, too, and smaller exhibitions in the backs of shops, and in the lesser galleries. And from one of these latter visits came about Pedro's choice of the great De Bush as his future adviser. Ah! there was a painter for you!

Once they attended a prize-fight, gaining an entrance with great difficulty, and, with the crowd, being obliged to disperse before the contest was ended, much to the relief of Pedro, who found it not at all to his taste.

Of all the topics they found to dissect, architecture was a favorite, and they would sometimes stand gazing up the front of a tall building, discussing its merits or demerits, with many an emphatic gesture. Soon a little crowd would gather to see what the matter was, and sometimes Leigh would address them, explaining that the building was good, or bad, and why. The crowd generally melted away before he had finished, but the two friends were not in the least discouraged by this, and continued to feel that they were awakening the public taste.

Another evening occupation lay in walking where the crowds were thickest—Broadway at eleven p. m., the Bowery, the teeming avenues at nightfall.

And gradually these began to appear upon the canvases that Pedro started, only to fling away, half-finished. The lady with the cake of soap, he did complete, however, and as Leigh had predicted, he sold it for a very decent price. Thus the smiling soap-lady was providing his food, while the house in which he lived, as developments showed, belonged to his benefactor.

That this rose-colored existence should continue forever was taken for granted by Pedro, whose sole lack was Mr. Jones. But one day Leigh sent word that he had been called out of town by a commission, and might be gone a week or more.

During the span of six days Pedro managed very well alone, simply getting up earlier than ever, and working harder; for Leigh had come to satisfy him so completely that he fancied no one else could take the sculptor's place. On the seventh day, Leigh not having as yet returned, he ate a solitary meal, and feeling lonely, went to the gallery of a theater.

The play was a melodramatic affair, and on either hand sat people who refused to respond to his critical analysis of the dramatist's work; so, after the second act, he left, much bored, and filled with a longing for dancing and companions, for laughter and inconsequential talk: a most natural and wholesome desire for the amusements common to his years.

"I wish," said Pedro aloud, "that I was going to a party."

The night was gray-cold and the sidewalks showed damp, treacherously slippery stains. Around the corners whipped a keen north wind. He turned into deserted Fifth Avenue, and began to walk down-town rapidly. As he went, a splendid mansion, behind whose shaded windows glowed warm lights, attracted his attention. Into its awninged door the guests were pouring, and a faint blast of music came out to him as he paused for a moment beside the yawning canvas tunnel. A miserable cat curled itself about his legs, but when he stopped to pet it, the creature bounded away into the darkness of the area. Pedro walked on, and again he said aloud:

"I really do want to go to a party!"

Then a thought struck him. If a party was what he wanted to go to—why not go to one? There were the cafés—but no! He wanted a real party, with invited guests, and laughter, and refreshments, hospitality offered. From side to side he glanced at the houses as he passed, confident, and hesitating merely that he might choose the better. But no party presented itself, while the trail led farther and farther down-town. Soon an occasional loft building arose between the dwellings and atop the latter, the northern skylights became more numerous. But most of these were dark, or showed only faint glimmers of light, like lamps of timid souls, who feared the subtle night.

Was there really no party at which he might be welcome? The cruel, inhospitable, and self-sufficient attitude of the city now struck him for the first time. Abstractedly he had seen it; concretely, as touching himself, he had not realized it before. Why, why could he find no open door? He was nice; he was perhaps even charming, he thought. Yet he was alone, and he did not want to be. It was so little that he asked—just the right to laugh and talk with his kind—and no place offered save saloons, and dens of . . .

Suddenly he felt like a prisoner, jailed in a prison that is limitless, yet cramped because it is, in fact a prison. To shake off this morbid fancy, he began to run, and sped through the silent frosty streets as though the gruesome sardonic spirit of civilization was speeding after him with handcuffs.

Breathless at last, and indignantly helpless, he came to a standstill beside the open gateway of a little *impasse* that had once or twice attracted his passing attention. From wall to wall it was paved with uneven flagging, and down the center ran an open gutter. The buildings were squat two-story affairs of old brick, and had once been stables, but as he looked more closely, the light of the scattered bracket-lamps revealed the fact that they had been converted into studios. At the windows of most clustered flower-boxes and trellised vines, dead now, and shriveled. An occasional doorway had been beautified by the handicraft of the inhabitant.

Near the entrance, one building, which retained the wide stable-doors, showed a white litter on its sill, as though a stone shop was within, and on the floor above it an immovable silhouette against the drawn curtain proclaimed that a sculptor dwelt there. All the other buildings but one were dark, and like a bit of the old world, the miniature street nestled timidly almost in the shadow of its giant neighbors, the sky-scrapers. At its hospitable aspect Pedro felt better directly. From the lighted building, half-way down its limited stretch, a soft radi-

A PARTY IN THE ALLEY

ance shone out, uncurtained and cheery, and the sounds of revelry came muffled to his ear. Quite shamelessly he walked to where its window met level with his shoulder, and flattening his nose against the pane, looked in.

A dimly lit room full of animated people met his gaze. A youth, with a cigarette dangling from the corner of his mouth, was playing softly on the piano, while just beyond, two people were dancing. Immediately in front of the watcher was a row of heads, their owners being seated upon a bench which ran directly beneath the window. These heads somewhat obstructed Pedro's view of the interior, but they were interesting in themselves. Two were men's, seated at the farther end. One of them was slightly bald, the meager black hair brushed across it in ineffectual whisps. The other's hair was brown, thick and close-curling, with the vigor of youth and health. These two wagged and bobbed in animated discussion. The head next to them was a woman's, gray and ill-dressed. Then came the last two, just in front of Pedro,—those of a man and a girl. Her yellow curls lay aslant his collar in the most naive manner. The youth's head was sleek and dark, and the cords at the back of his neck gave Pedro the notion that he was not comfortable, but did not dare to move for fear of offending the lady.

Suddenly the street door was flung wide to emit a little knot of men who carried between them the limp form of a woman. Pedro drew back into the shadows and watched.

The exact nature of the trouble he could not determine, and neither could he see the woman very distinctly, but the air seemed to revive her, and presently a cab appeared, into which she was put, and driven off with one of the men. The rest then re-entered the house, closing the door with a bang. The little episode affected Pedro strangely. Why should he be so distressed at what was in no way connected with him, he wondered? Could the woman have been hurt, perhaps seriously? But no! The music within had begun again, and some one was singing. Surely nothing very terrible could have happened. At any rate, he would not permit it to depress him. He longed to be gay.

Again he stepped to the inviting window and pressed his face against it, only to be confronted instantly by a mass of red-gold hair! At first he could scarcely believe his eyes; but it was true—

A PARTY IN THE ALLEY

there was no mistaking those gleaming braids—she was there, the Madonna Lady, standing within the warm room, her shoulder turned toward him. Acting on a sudden impulse, Pedro ran to the door, and knocked.

Almost at once, it was opened by a little man with a smooth boyish face and sandy hair. Although far from handsome, the magnetism of his personality struck Pedro immediately, awakening an answering chord in the latter. For a moment the little man looked the boy over, and then his weird expressive face broke into a smile.

"Were you looking for Milligan?" he asked.

"I was looking for a party," said Pedro, smiling in return.

"Well, there's several inside," said the little man, waving a hand toward the dimly lighted room behind him. "Some friend of yours here?"

"I just wanted—" began Pedro, when a girl's voice broke in.

"He is a friend of mine, Don," said the red-haired girl, emerging from the crowded studio. She had noted his entrance and immediately made her way toward him. "Aren't you going to let him in?" she concluded.

One would have sworn that she had been expecting him, thought Pedro. Evidently she had not forgot the roadside encounter.

"Pedro is the humble servant of you both," said he, with that sweeping bow of his.

"And this is Mr. Milligan, our host," said she.

The two shook hands, and even while Milligan muttered something by way of acknowledging the introduction, he was carried off by a phalanx of men who came up, clamoring for more beer. With a swift gesture the girl beckoned to Pedro, and he followed up a narrow winding staircase which brought them out upon the little balcony. The Madonna Lady seated herself upon a divan and motioned Pedro to follow suit. Below them, in the studio, the crowd surged dimly like a wind-blown flower garden in the afterglow of sundown. The corner of the balcony that she had chosen, however, was practically deserted. As he took the proffered seat, she seemed suddenly overcome with shyness. Perhaps the realization of her unusual act had frightened her, and she rather dreaded its consequences. But Pedro was less timid now than when his bear had rescued her, and besides, he was desperately lonely. As he spoke, that musical voice of his, with its soft foreign intonation, was inaudible two feet away.

"Madonna, I saw you through the window, and I could not resist coming in, even though I was a stranger to the house."

She smiled at him.

"You saved me just in time," he continued, "else I might have failed of entrance."

"And you really came because you saw me?"

"For what other reason?" said he. "Madonna, what is your name?"

"Iris," said she, lifting her great eyes that were like those selfsame blossoms. "My father's name is Vanderpool. What other name have you, beside Pedro?"

"I have no other," he replied after an almost imperceptible pause.

She raised her head, as if in disbelief. Ah! that wonderful line from chin to breast! Surely some day he must contrive to paint it.

"I am speaking as I must," he told her. "Will you not believe me when I say that the only name I can give you is that which you have heard?"

This had a perfume of mystery, but while it added

to her already keen interest in him, she maintained her pose of offense.

"If it was only to be unkind, why did you rescue me just now?" he asked.

She laughed a little.

"You once saved me from real danger," she replied; "the least I could do was to spare you, in turn."

The eyes with which she looked at him were kind now. From sheer pleasure of watching one so lovely he fell into her mood. Not to do so in such an atmosphere was impossible. The dimness, the fantastic appearance of the place, the delight of human companionship, all combined to entrap him. Around the piano a group was singing softly in close harmony, while the rest listened, or flirted in whispers, or, better yet, in silence. Swiftly Pedro leaned toward her. In his eyes shone a light that might have meant pure mischief, but this she did not see, for she had turned away her head again. His voice was very sibilant, carrying a subtlety of meaning which was delicate in the extreme.

"Madonna Iris!" he said, "when you turn your head so, it is lovely beyond words! Do you know that the line of your chin and throat is like the silver-white edge of the young moon? Ah! Now you are angry. Forgive me; but I have dreamed of that line since first I saw you!"

There was a tense pause between them. The song below stairs was drawing to a close, its rising cadence swelling tunefully.

"No, I am not angry," she said at last in a low voice, looking intently at the sticks of her fan as she spoke. "You see, I had not forgot you, either."

Again a breathless interlude. The song below was very soft now. Like the echo of a dream it died away. Complete silence reigned for a second. Then a young man, who sat upon the floor in company with half a dozen others, his frowsy head resting against the knees of a temperamental-looking girl behind him, turned his cheek upon the gray-green art stuff of her gown, and gazing soulfully at her, broke the spell with an exaggerated whisper.

"*Je suis si heureux!*" he sighed. And instantly the laughter and applause broke out clamorously. The young man at the piano struck up a waltz. Excitement leaped in Pedro's eyes.

"I shall not give you chance to forget!" he exclaimed to his companion. But before she could reply, a youth who had been watching her, rushed up and claimed her for the dance. With a smile she was gone; and in a few moments he saw her and her partner emerge upon the floor below. She wore a green gown of some silky clinging material, neither defaced with trimming nor detracted from by ornaments, and she danced beautifully.

While he stood watching her, a man joined him, and after a nod and the proffer of a cigarette, which was accepted, stood beside him at the balcony rail.

This new acquaintance was a thick-set young man, blond and rugged of feature. He was not in evening clothes—indeed, only two or three of the men were—and he did not look over-prosperous. But he fairly radiated energy and enthusiasm, and his face was strong and arresting. For several moments they stood looking down into the crowd.

It was an interesting gathering, mainly because of the physiognomy of the people. There seemed to be no repetition of type among them, every face bearing its own special meaning, each having the stamp of a purpose; yet for the moment all were care-free, as is the way of earnest workers when at play. The women were apparently dressed in whatever clothes had best suited their convenience; some in high- and some in low-necked gowns. One even wore a tailored suit, and an uncompromising little hat, as though she had happened in incidentally. She danced, however, with as much enjoyment and abandon as her neighbor in frilled muslin. Some wore the smoothly braided hair, and "artistic" unbecoming style of dress generally affected by the female art student; and others, like Iris, were fashionable in the extreme.

The men were no less heterogeneous, their appearance ranging from the shock-headed to the sleek, with clothing to correspond. Oddly assorted, of widely varying ages, they nevertheless made as real a "party" as heart could desire. Everybody smoked, some even while dancing. Through the overhanging haze, Pedro could see, in a screened-off corner, the man who had admitted him helping a plump and pleasing woman of about thirty to open some bottles. By her busy air, and merry solicitude for all within hailing distance of her, he deduced that she was the hostess, although contrary to the habit of such, she was enjoying herself thoroughly.

"You're new to this crowd?" asked the man at his elbow.

"Yes," said Pedro. Then brazenly—"A friend of Miss Vanderpool's."

"Ah!" said the man. "She's a good dancer!"

"Yes."

"Not like the other, though; eh, what?"

"What other?" asked Pedro.

"Why, Ruth St. Johns, of course! Didn't you see it?"

"I came in late," Pedro explained. "Sorry I did not see it. Tell me who some of these people are," he added. "Who is the little man, the host?"

"Yes, that's Don Milligan," replied the man, seemingly not in the least surprised at finding a guest who was ignorant of the host's name. "He sure is a nice little fellow—a corker, Don is. Not a bad painter, either, though he's never done as good work since he's married. Can't, of course. They have a kid, you see, and they've got to live. His wife's a wonder. Ask any of the boys! That's Bell over there, talking to Gester, the sculptor. He eats with them all the time; just fairly lives here. She's the best little hostess in the world. Why, it's nothing to her to feed a whole bunch at a moment's notice. And witty! And good fun! Say, you ought to get asked here to dinner some time. Talk? Believe me, we have *some* conversations. That's their cousin, Irma

A PARTY IN THE ALLEY

Wise, the suffrage lady, in the pretty blue dress. A regular dandy, too."

"And the tall man with the so sadly drooping necktie?" inquired Pedro.

"Talking to Heskall's wife? That's a bum poet named Nicholls. Hey, you ink-splasher!" he called suddenly. Whereat, the poet looked about him vaguely, as though recognizing his name, and waved an empty beer-bottle in the general direction from whence the sound came. Pedro's informant continued:

"He's dippy about Margot Leeds, with the silver chain around her throat—the lanky girl in the blue window-curtain effect. She makes 'em—I mean the silver chains. Those two fellows eating the sandwiches all up are the Kensalls, who do such a lot of those bully drawings for the cover of Gopher's and the shirt advertisements. They always look glum like that. I think it's indigestion, for they are always eating, and they do it so darned fast."

"Doubtless," said Pedro.

"That fellow with the wonderful figure is a writer. He lived with me in Paris. (We're just back this year.) He's a model, also. You ought to see his arms—Gee! they're *wonderful!* Carrington, who draws half the book-covers in the states—pretty girl heads, you know (rotten stuff, but there's money in it)—he's down there. Looks like a robin. See him, the one with the glasses on?"

And so he rattled on, saying the names so familiar to himself, so suggestive of success, so otherwise meaningless to Pedro, who never looked twice at anything unless it were exceptionally good, and consequently heard most of these names for the first time.

"By the way, what are you?" asked the man, abruptly breaking off his monologue.

"Painter," replied Pedro.

"I'm on the *Sun*," said the man. "Theodore Pell is my name. Not here to do this party, though. All friends of mine here. Wouldn't be such a rotter, you know. What's your name?"

"I am Pedro," said the other with such quiet assurance that the reporter made no comment, and searched his memory frantically, trying to place a well-known artist of that name. The boy spoke as if he said, "I am Sargent." Who the devil could he be?

There was a slight commotion at the lower doorway, and a splendid old man entered.

"Why, there is Rives De Bush!" exclaimed Pell. "Didn't know he came here!"

"Ah! the great one!" cried Pedro. "I must speak to him."

And without further apology he rushed off, leaving the still greatly puzzled reporter staring after him and repeating, "Pedro, Pedro—one of the new Spaniards, I suppose."

While still debating the matter, and frowning over it, he was joined by the friend whom he had referred to as a writer and professional model. This youth was named Blaume, and came nearer to resembling the Greek gods than do the general run of young gentlemen nowadays. He was rather conscious of this, and also prided himself on acquaintance with, or knowledge of, most of the well-known creative people of two continents. At his approach an idea occurred to Pell: he would make a test. Accordingly he sprang his mine almost immediately.

"Do you know that Pedro is here to-night?" he asked, watching Blaume closely as he put the question.

Blaume had never heard the name before, but judging from the other's tone that the person referred to was one with whose accomplishments it was proper to be familiar, he simulated knowledge.

"You don't say so!" he exclaimed interestedly. "Where is he?"

"Down there talking to De Bush," replied Pell, confirmed in the idea that he had hitherto overlooked a celebrity.

"That young fellow?" cried Blaume. "Why, I'd no idea he was such a kid!"

"Nor I," replied Pell.

Whereby Pedro became famous.

At that particular moment he was extracting a promise from the great man to come and see his work, with a view to giving a regular criticism. The sheer audacity of the request was probably what obtained the desired consent. Such a thing, in such a way, had never been asked of De Bush before. But Pedro had smiled, and his earnest starlike eyes had done the rest. When Pell and Blaume approached them, the famous painter and the youthful one were chatting like the old friends which Pell instantly assumed them to be. The boy's lack of timidity, and frank delight in his new master's talk, charmed De

Bush, who was too well accustomed to that loneliness which is the fate often forced upon the mighty by an over-respectful public. The shaggy head was raised in lionine majesty to greet the reporter.

"My young friend here has just been telling me that he is occupying Sam Hill's studio," said De Bush. "Hill is going to be away for a year. We shall miss him at The Players."

"Will you be here all winter?" Pell inquired of Pedro.

"Yes," said he.

"What, in particular, are you going to paint in America?" continued the reporter. Whereat the innocent and unsuspecting Pedro launched into an enthusiastic explanation of some of his pet theories.

In the midst of these he spied Iris (for the moment seated alone) and, excusing himself, he made his way toward her. As soon as his back was turned, Pell pulled out his note-book and began making jottings.

"Said he knew Leigh well. Hum!—friend of De Bush. Great stuff, this! Wonder why I never heard of him before?" he muttered, writing rapidly. Then he slipped into his overcoat, and left hurriedly.

Meanwhile Pedro resumed his little flirtation,

quite unconscious that Iris had been watching him all evening with an increasing disturbance of the heart. How romantic, how charming a figure he appeared to her, he could not guess; nor that the game he played so lightly was already in fair way to become a serious matter in her mind. As she listened to his talk, half jesting, half inspired, always poetic, she could not but compare him with Hill, greatly to the loss of the latter. Of her former lover she made no mention; neither did Pedro have occasion to speak of Hill; so that when they parted, it was without knowledge of their mutual acquaintance. She gave him her address and asked him to lunch with her next day. His first impulse was to refuse. There was his work! Then the thought of how pleasant it would be to go took hold of him, and for once work was relegated to second place. Yes! he would give her one whole precious hour out of the very heart of the day, a rare gift, indeed.

"Madonna Lady, I will be there!" he said, as he helped her into her carriage.

Then he closed its door and allowed her to be whirled away, as she sat very erect, with glowing checks. To herself she was whispering with fast-beating heart, "Have I found my ideal?"

Pedro gazed after the smart brougham, laughed slightly, frowned, snapped his fingers and said, "What's the harm?"

Then, bidding his hosts good night, and promising to return soon, he conceded with alacrity to De Bush's request for an arm, and set off with the rest of the gay throng that poured from the Milligans' hospitable door, laughing, and hasting through the first snow of the year, into which they stepped, surprised.

CHAPTER VIII

OF REVOLUTIONARY SAVOR

MEANWHILE, the cab into which the lady who had fainted had been carried, and which Pedro had seen drive away from Milligan's door before he gained entrance there, was halted after it had gone less than three blocks, and the directions that had been given before the assembled guests, changed to that of a little unknown café opposite Central Park, and some five miles up-town.

Without protest at the distance, or even exacting the promise of a larger fare, the cabby obeyed the order; the cab was wheeled about and headed northward.

Inside, against the cushioned wall Señora Daussa had laid her head, her cheeks pale, but her wide dark eyes showing that she had returned to consciousness. She was a beautiful woman of that rare type, a blond Spaniard (than which there is no fairer), and although she was close to forty years of age, her slender graceful figure and erect carriage made her appear younger. To the man beside her, she seemed the very incarnation of loveliness, as indeed she had always appeared in his eyes. Her dress, distinctly un-American, and by no means of the latest fashion, was yet worn with chic and distinction, and betokened a personal daintiness that was almost extreme. About her head and shoulders fell a large dark cloak, from which her face glimmered like a pearl. Her companion made a little motion, as if to caress her, but instead of responding, she shrank back from him silently.

"Madame, you must not sing in public again! It is very charming, but too conspicuous," he said in Spanish. "You must not sing when we are in public."

She replied in the same language.

"You must not try to touch me again when we are alone."

Impatiently he dropped his hands to his sides.

"Will you deign to be reasonable?" he begged. "Let us keep to the subject. It is essential to our cause that we appear as the best of friends—as brother and sister."

"In public, yes—since you insist," she interrupted, "but when we are alone there is no need to maintain the farce. You have no right whatever to lay hands upon me. It is a breach of trust."

"Forgive me," he answered quite humbly, "I—forget sometimes, because you drive me mad—especially when I waltz with you as to-night. Sometimes I believe you scarcely realize I am your partner, although we are dancing together. You seem to be in a sort of trance. I feel as though it were your soul that was dancing, and I a mere manikin you accept mechanically. But you set me afire none the less! Carmen, it is not without reason that I have served you these many years; you must—you do know that it is because I love you! And this being constantly together, though it has not made my plight less hopeless, has not made it easier to endure."

"I did not mean to seem ungrateful, Ricardo," she answered softly, pathetically even. "Indeed, I know you serve me well, and why,—but let us drop this too painful subject. I can never be anything to you but a friend, and so it is better to keep away from speech of such things as can only cause us both pain. I like you well; that, at least, you know. Did I not dance with you to-night? I danced with no one else but you!"

"Yes!" he said through his teeth. "But it must

not occur again. It is too conspicuous, I tell you! We shall be observed too closely, and then—trouble!"

She was silent for a moment at this; then:

"If you do not wish me to be noticed, why do you make me go about with you at times? It is seldom enough that I go; but I would willingly stay at home altogether, and leave the quest in your hands alone."

"Listen, Carmen," said he; "I shall again explain. We must appear normal people—it is indispensable, believe me! What would seem stranger than that you should never leave your rooms? The minute that any one does the least unusual thing he begins to attract attention and suspicion. Those who appear normal and uninteresting pass unnoticed. Believe me, I am doing all in my power to locate your lover. With your almost total lack of English, it would be an impossible task for you. Truly, I am beginning to think that he may be past finding."

Her voice was chilled by the force of control which she put upon herself as she replied:

"I have but one reason for thinking that."

"Which is?" he queried, peering anxiously at her through the gloom.

"My letters!" she said hoarsely. "Why does he

not answer them? Do they not reach him? And if not, for what reason?"

"I can not imagine," said he. "As you know, I have myself carried them to the post with every care."

"You are kind to me, Ricardo," she said gently, laying her hand upon his in sudden gratitude.

In an instant he had seized her hand and covered it with burning kisses. Moaning, she snatched it away and drew back, shivering, into her corner.

"I—I will leave you!" she cried. "You torment me more than I can endure. It is not fair. I will go, and somehow, I will manage for myself."

Putting her hand on the carriage door, she made a motion as though she actually intended to leap from the moving vehicle.

Suddenly the man grew frightened. On the instant he became quiet, and dissembling his alarm, he spoke gravely.

"You can not go!" he said, forcing her to desist. "There is something else. Do you know where we are bound to-night? Ah! there is a matter on foot of deeper import than you have guessed; and if you leave me now, you will ruin us. Will you do this after my years of service? Do nothing rash, nothing which will bring us before the eyes of the authorities. Don't start so! I have committed no murder, no theft! But listen, and believe me when I tell you that it is of the most vital importance that we remain in oblivion for some weeks yet. Further, I will tell you one thing—the matter to which I refer, and upon which we are abroad to-night, concerns our dear country. More I can not say at present, but I know that this much will be sufficient to your patriotic soul."

"I will stay, Ricardo," she replied, startled by his intenseness. "Indeed, I can do nothing else. As you say, I have no money, no English; how could I go? But promise me, swear once again that no matter what affair may be engrossing you—what politics, what secret—that you will not cease to search for him."

"I swear," said he eagerly.

"For him, and for that other, even more dear," she added, her eyes wide and luminous.

"And the other," he repeated.

As though satisfied she leaned back wearily, and closed her eyes.

The cab was jogging past a row of palaces now, a heterogeneous collection, Venetian rubbing shoulders with Greek, Colonial, Elizabethan, what you will; no type being missing, and many of the structures embodying them all at once. A motley terrace this, yet stately withal and typical of wealth. Opposite, the park loomed dark and silent under its burden of snow. On and on they went, and farther up-town there began to be an occasional gap in the splendid row of houses. Then came blocks where vacant lots made up the streets. They passed the old Lenox Library, mausoleum-like and dark; and later, the incongruous façade of the Art Museum. More and more scarce became the palaces, until finally, when the Park's upper end was almost reached, they approached a tiny wooden building only a single story in height, that stood upon a corner. At its back was a vacant lot, while in front its swinging doors faced those of a gorgeous residence, belonging to one of the greatest money-kings.

The little hovel that imprudently flaunted its vulgar and humble entrance before its palatial neighbor's very eyes, bore the words, SUMMER GARDEN, in a great gilt sign upon its slanting roof edge, and below this, like dependant golden icicles, hung tall letters which, properly grouped and pronounced, informed the passer-by that

RUPERT'S SPECIAL EXTRA BEER could be obtained within. The sidewalk before the hut was wider than elsewhere, owing to the fact of the garden being set far back between the converging ends of the bill-covered fence that enclosed the lot behind it; and on this sidewalk during the summer months, little beer-ringed tables were set out for the greater accommodation of patrons. At this season, however, and more particularly at this hour of night, the little building itself was ample shelter for such customers as were likely to appear. Over the screen of bushes in their little wooden boxes hung a pall of snow, and snow was draped upon the little canvas tent-sign before the door, which displayed the likeness of a foaming mug on one side, and of a plate of ice-cream on the other. Around these misplaced evidences of summer gaiety the wind howled dismally, making the poor little "garden" appear dreary indeed. But that guests still lingered inside was evidenced by the warm light streaming through the opaque glass of the crooked little windows, and by the presence beside the curb of two cabs without drivers, the wretched horses, blanketed but cold, waiting in patient misery.

To these waiting ones, Rowe's cab was added,

and the driver, descending from the box, opened the door and peered within.

"You'd better come quickly, Ricardo," he said. "It's getting late, and Mike won't stay open all night."

The lady gave a little cry of surprise and grasped her companion's arm. Evidently the intrusion of the cabby was unexpected by her.

"Who is it?" she gasped.

"Look close; it is Sancho, can't you see?" said Rowe. "He is here on that matter of which I spoke. There are other friends inside, and I beg that you will enter for a moment, so they may see that you are alive and well. Your welfare means much to them."

"Sancho in America!" the lady repeated as though dazed. "Have you any news?" she then asked eagerly.

"Come inside, gracious one," said the driver.

She arose to obey.

"Keep your cloak well about you," commanded Rowe, as he assisted her to alight. "I have brought you here because it is not safe for them to come to us. There is a reward out for Sancho, even now."

They crossed the pavement and entered the little

hut. Inside were several rooms, for the place was more rambling than appeared from the front; and after a quick greeting of the rosy-cheeked Irishman behind the bar, they crossed the sanded floor to a smaller apartment beyond. In this little lean-to, with its slanting roof and discolored wall-paper, were a table with a red and white damask cloth, half a dozen common deal chairs, and a little round stove, red hot. As soon as the door had closed behind them, the lady, clasping her hands fearfully, glanced from one to the other of the men in manifest anxiety.

"What word have you, Sancho?" she asked of the driver, who had removed his cap and muffler, revealing a small dark face, lined with evil, which contrasted oddly with his bulky frame. Before replying, the man glanced at Rowe, as if for instructions. Almost imperceptibly the latter shook his head without being observed by the white-faced woman.

"None," said Sancho, "except that we are almost certain that he is still alive; our own government, in fact, has communicated with him recently."

"When did you come to America?" she asked, concealing her bitter disappointment.

"Did you not know, gracious one?" he said. "I came early in the fall, before the abominable snow."

"But for what?" she cried, perplexed. "For what are we come here? Are you not going to explain at all?"

"Come!" interrupted Rowe roughly. "You are not to talk, Madame. The walls have ears. Keep silent, I beg. We can not remain here all night, and I have business of importance in the other room. Pardon if we leave you for a moment. You are perfectly safe."

Then, beckoning to Sancho, they left, closing the door with care.

"Is she with us?" asked the latter as soon as they were outside. Rowe avoided meeting his eyes as he spoke.

"Certainly," said he. "Did you get the reports that the government sent *him* last? It is close on two months since we have cornered one. Did you get those that were sent to him in the country?"

"No," replied the other. "I have been trying to see you to tell you, but I met with an accident and have been laid up with a broken leg, and I dared not write. To-night is the first time I have been out, and I only came in response to your urgent note. I failed to get the last ones. The daughter was bringing them from the post-office, and I tried to snatch them from her, when a bear—a wild thing—sprang out of the bushes, and I made off without getting them."

"Leaving the lady to be eaten, I suppose," said Rowe. "Well, it's too bad. We needed them. It must not occur again."

The two crossed the tiny corridor and entered the main room again, going directly to where a group of men, five in all, were seated about a corner table.

These persons all appeared to be artisans of some sort, and by their dress, none too prosperous. All, however, knew Rowe, although they gave him no special greeting. Leaning over in their midst, he spoke quickly in a low voice, again using Spanish.

"The señora is here," he said, "and has pledged herself to our cause, as I promised you she would do. She will receive you all in token of her pledge, but do not talk too much to her, as she is ill, having fainted earlier in the evening, and is also agitated at this adventure. She has come to you, as you see, at great risk to her reputation. Let us spare her as much as possible."

There were murmurs of assent, and Yznaga, who was one of the men, spoke up.

"There are some estimates," he said, "which I

brought this evening. We can secure a fat bit of graft from the Maxman Arms Company, as well as getting the inventory as soon as *he* pays for it."

"Have you them here?" said Rowe. "Let me see."

"Yes," replied the man, fumbling about in his breast pocket. "Here they are. Sit down a minute and look at them. We shall all have to go directly we have seen her. Mike will be closing up."

"Yes, I suppose Mikey must sleep some time," agreed Rowe, slipping into a chair. "And, Yznaga, I wouldn't wear that tuxedo on this kind of an excursion again. When you opened your coat just then, it was a sight to provoke curiosity."

All this was said in a low tone of voice, but the men about the table laughed at it. Rowe, who was himself very inconspicuously, even shabbily dressed, stretched out his hand for the little packet of papers that the man he had just reproved offered him. Evidently, the pseudo-friend of Señora Daussa was the leader among these men. With quick interest he spread the documents, a martial list of rifles and ammunition, upon the table, and at once all seven heads were bent over them, the talk sinking to a humming, scarcely audible three feet away.

It was a curious room in which they sat, and save for themselves it was almost empty. Across one side ran the bar, a machine-carved mahogany atrocity with shining foot-rail and glass-covered counter, behind which ran a large mirror topped by an obscene picture. Other mirrors with gilt fly-specked frames were let into the three remaining walls, and at least six almanacs with colored embossed decorations hung about. Several chromos of ladies in fleshings and spangles further adorned the walls, and the cigar stand was decorated by an immense photograph of a well-known burlesque actress, clad chiefly in a brilliant smile, with a quotation from her most noted song printed below. "I don't care!" it read, and in truth one could readily believe she didn't. Advertisements depended from a little showcase in which some souvenirs were displayed and near this hung a wooden rack filled with postal cards on which were pictured every imaginable subject from the likeness of the Metropolitan Tower to an obviously sham love incident in harsh colors. But these were relics of the past summer, and would not come into use again until several months had passed, when a small freckle-faced boy, a son of the establishment, would peddle them to the passengers who rode atop the electric busses that ply up and down the avenue.

Meanwhile, where in summer an arch (trimmed even now with artificial flowers) led to the scrawny "garden" in the rear lot, a stove had been erected, a hideous affair with brass trimmings, in which the fire was now dying down to a glowing mass of embers. About the floor stood a dozen tables with common cane-bottom chairs grouped around them. Altogether the place was far from festive in appearance, and the observer would have been tempted into doubting whether even the gladness of summer could shed a glamour upon it.

Behind the bar sat Mike, adding up his accounts. He was both owner and barkeeper, and by the grace of the landlord on whose property he squatted and who found Mikey a useful man, he prospered very fairly. A burly young Irishman was Mike, with an innocent open expression that concealed an ocean of guile. He was in politics of more than one kind, and his bar often saw a gathering of those whose names represented an alarming per cent. of the country's wealth, and would have set a socially ambitious hostess to longing. But Mikey was not ambitious socially. He had no cause to be, seeing as he did, a very intimate side of these men, and even being on terms of pet names with them, notwithstanding that they did not bow to him on the street.

But to-night, however satisfactory his reckonings, the hour was becoming unconscionably late. From his ledger he glanced at the wide pasty face of the clock opposite, and then at the group at the largest table. Would they never go home? Their glasses were empty. Then suddenly, as one man, they arose and following Rowe (who was friend to Mikey by virtue of a fifty-dollar bill), went to the inner room. They did not enter, but stood at the door. Mikey strained his ears to hear the lady speak, but whatever greeting she uttered was said in so low a voice as not to be articulate from where he sat. Then the man who had produced the paper spoke.

"We shall not disturb you, Señora," he said, "for you are fatigued. We merely wish to pay you our homage and assure you of our fidelity."

Again that low murmur, and then, one by one, all bowed and left save Rowe and the cab driver, who entered the little room, closing the door after them.

"Aw, some funny things happens," said Mikey,

not however, with any special reference to humor. He stretched himself and yawned. "They'll be going in a minute," he added presently. "Glory be, they are the last."

Suddenly he stopped, remembering a couple who were seated in the semi-obscurity by the stove. Earlier in the evening these two and their bear had entertained the then crowded saloon, and though the throng had grown steadily less, and the coins fewer, they had lingered, loath to be turned out into the storm. Also they had bought, so Mikey let them remain, and now the woman, an ancient soul, picturesque and haggard, had fallen asleep where she sat, overcome perhaps by her last glass of rum. As she lay back, her head resting on the hard rim of the chair, her mouth partly open, she looked like a veritable incarnation of the tragic and terrible essence of life. Yet there was something pitiable, even likable in that curious old face with its lace-like network of wrinkles; and her deep breathing was regular and peaceful as a child's. On closer examination, Mikey decided that her sleep was that of exhaustion, not a drunken stupor as he had at first supposed.

Her companion was a man of perhaps thirty-five, unshaven, shabby in a suit of clothing that had originally been of faultless cut and style. Under his soft hat, his eyes, keen as gimlets, tolerant, interested, impersonal, watched, now the old woman, now the door of the little inner room. He had a debonair carriage, as though he had touched life's realities without fear, and handled its sorrows as a strong man does.

It was Sam Hill, but Hill so stripped of smugness, so shorn of vanity, and so sensitive to the true context of his environment, that his friends would have been hard put to recognize him. At his feet lay Mr. Jones, the bear, asleep, and between his teeth he clutched a short blackened pipe of clay. On the table at his hand a liqueur-glass of brandy stood untouched. To himself he was saying, apropos of Rowe: "Now who the deuce is that man? Where have I seen his rascally face before?" Then Mikey advanced.

"You'll have to get out of this, you two," he said sharply; "come on now, rouse up and be off with you!"

Without otherwise moving, Hill took up his glass and drained it.

"You've a snug berth here," said he. "Why not let us sleep the night by your stove? It's snowing now, and we are honest folk. You'll find nothing missing in the morning."

"That's a good one," laughed Mikey. "Let you sleep here, indeed! I guess not! Come on now, old lady, wake up and shuffle."

He was about to lay his hand upon her shoulder when Sam gripped his forearm and gently pushed him aside. Astonished at his guest's strength, the husky Irishman stepped back, and watched while Hill gently awoke the old woman.

"Awake, Nita," said Hill. "Come, little blossom of the bramble-vine, our host is giving us Godspeed."

Quickly she was awake, regaining consciousness with that speed which is a faculty of those who are old. With a grotesque gesture she straightened the handkerchief upon her head, and gathering her shawl about her with one hand, she stretched the other across the table to her glass.

"Oh, my immortal soul!" she muttered, "just another little drop to keep out the cold, my handsome boy."

"Nix," said the barkeeper, "out you go. This place is going to bed."

"May you burn in eternal fires, even as I shall,"

she quavered angrily, struggling to her feet. "And God have mercy on you if you do, for I am a great sinner."

This, being uttered in Spanish, was lost upon Mikey, who understood, however, from the tone in which the pleasing sentiment was uttered, that it was far from complimentary. Pulling the table to one side, he gave the still somnolent Mr. Jones a kick that awoke him to no gentle mood, and pocketing the money that Hill laid in his hand, he again bade them begone. With much grumbling Old Nita started for the door, which was at the opposite end of the apartment, and beyond that leading into the small room into which Rowe had led his friends. Still puzzling about the appearance of the former, Hill buttoned his coat about him, and gathered up the bear-pole and chain, preparatory to following her. Who the deuce was that man—ah!—no, it could not be—yes, by Jove, it was, though! One of his tenants with whom he had scarcely spoken. A fellow who lived below the studio. He put a supporting hand beneath Old Nita's elbow. One by one the lights were being extinguished by Mikey, till only a single lantern burned near the exit.

"Hurry up, now!" admonished the proprietor.

"Going, Ireland; good night," responded Hill smoothly.

Just then the door to the little inner room was opened and three figures, one of them the woman's, hooded and veiled, appeared directly in their path.

"How much, Mike?" said Rowe, stepping forward. Then he caught sight of the old woman, and stood for an instant as though transfixed with alarm. At the same moment she saw his face, and her own became livid. Rage, fear, and hate were lurking there, and shaking herself free of Hill, she sprang for Rowe, her old hands curled like the claws of some vicious bird of prey.

"Devil!" she screamed, "have I found thee at last?"

With an oath Rowe fended her off, his forearm striking her a stunning blow, and then, quick as a cat, he overturned the last remaining lamp, and, seizing the veiled lady, pushed to the outer door, Sancho, who also seemed to recognize the old woman, preceding and opening it hastily. Old Nita, stunned by the blow, fell to the floor, while Hill sprang at Rowe—but too late. For a fleeting instant the Spaniard's face could be seen, sardonic, unearthly, in the white light from the street, before he slammed the heavy door to, catching Hill on the jaw with the edge of it. Then he was gone with his companions, while over the dark turmoil and confusion in the bar lingered the echo of a laugh, mirthless beyond description.

CHAPTER IX

THE LADY OF MYSTERY

WRAPPED in a brilliant yellow bath-robe, Pedro was finishing breakfast. Having perched himself upon a high stool, he broke the rind of an orange with the tip of a palette knife, while staring contemplatively at a half-finished canvas—one of the many with which the room was littered. Then he ate pensively, and when he had finished, lighted a cigarette and opened the morning paper. From the front page sprang a piece of news that fairly made him jump. The head-line bore his own name.

NOTED SPANISH PAINTER HERE
SIG. PEDRO HAS TAKEN S. J. HILL'S STUDIO FOR THE WINTER. TO PAINT CITY AS IT IS.

This was the caption, after which followed an interview with himself, based upon what he had said to Pell, the young reporter, the night before, but considerably embellished by that gentleman's own imagination. For several moments the reader was quite overcome with amusement. He, Pedro, the impertinent, the unknown, the mere student, thus advertised, thus hauled to fame! In writing the article, Pell had assumed the same sort of knowledge on the part of his readers that he had himself assumed. Thus, upon nothing, he had built the foundations of a reputation.

The lad laughed, and spreading the paper open before him on the table, lighted another cigarette and admired his name in print. He was in excellent company, the column to his left being occupied by a famous millionaire and the young lady to whom the latter was pledged, and the column to his right being filled with the wool-bill, surrounded by clamoring senators and department heads. Below him, at the foot of the column, appeared a very short notice in small type to the effect that nine coal-miners had been killed in an explosion in Nebraska— a mere detail of news, distant, and of no importance in comparison with the really significant events that appeared in capitals at the page's top. With a quick breath, Pedro turned the sheet hastily. Beau-Jean had once been a miner, and his tales of the inferno in which he had labored came too vividly to mind.

He glanced carelessly at that portion of the newspaper wherein there appear the society notes, accounts of expensive entertainments, theatrical criticisms, and death notices, side by side. He saw that a great writer had died intestate, and that a new opera singer liked America; that a hyphenated society lady had fed her kind so fully that she had been forced to make them dance afterward, in order that they might digest what her cook had spent hours in making indigestible. He informed himself, also, as to the movements of several peoples on several streets, neither of which he (nor any one else) had ever heard of before; and learned that a pet dog had won a prize. Moreover, it appeared that some folk had been married—eight in fact, and one had actually been born!

Strange erratic world!

Then an item of personal interest caught his critical eye. Samuel J. Hill, the eminent portrait-painter, whose engagement to Miss Iris Vanderpool, the Asphalt King's daughter, had been persistently rumored, had gone south for the winter; and it would appear that the engagement, if any such existed, had been broken, for reasons unknown. The lady was to remain in town for the season. The paper thought that this news would be of wide interest, both to society and artistic circles, as an announcement had been fully expected.

Again appeared Signor Pedro (C. E. Pedro, this time, for reason unguessable), who had taken his confrère's studio for an indefinite term.

Pedro put the paper down and gave his yellow robe an extra fold about him before sinking into a reverie.

Ah! this explained much—Hill's sudden anxiety to leave town, his unhappiness, his reckless generosity to the first needy stranger whom he met. These two had some silly quarrel, perhaps. It could not have really been so serious as they apparently made it. Why, never were two people more ideally suited to each other, or he, Pedro, was no judge! The dismissal was given by her, of course, and Hill was saddened to the point of desperation. And in the meanwhile what had he, himself, done! Heavens! Last night, what had he said to her? What would she think? How would his sentimentalism appear? It had none too pleasant an aspect in the light of his present discovery. The beloved of his friend —the friend who had done everything for him— who had benefited him beyond any! What a traitor he would appear! Of course, his love-making was the merest joke—nothing but a pretty game, played in an idle moment; and when he started it he had not known it was she who lay at the root and source of his adventure! *His* love-making! He almost laughed aloud at the thought of it. Why, it was only in fun. And undoubtedly the Madonna Lady had understood it so. For surely she was a practised coquette. He had deduced this from her slightest gesture, her lightest movement, which he foresaw and could have predicted to the instant of its happening. Oh, come now! It was impossible that she was serious! It was quite useless for her to be so, at any rate. Pedro was no lover for her.

At the thought he laughed merrily.

But Hill could not know that. Suppose the painter were to hear of his, Pedro's, attentions to Miss Vanderpool! And hear he might, for he had not gone south as yet. Old Nita had written Pedro a letter in badly spelled Spanish, explaining that though none of them would come near him while he was making his career, for fear of injuring his prestige, they would not be far away and would be watching over him so as to be on hand in time of need. How they would know if he were in trouble

THE LADY OF MYSTERY

she did not say, but Pedro entirely believed in her power to succor him if necessary. Hill was with her, and by the freemasonry of the underworld, or even by the newspapers, Hill might learn of his protégé's actions.

Well, now that the little society item had revealed the true state of affairs, there would be no more flirting, that was assured. But a friendship was surely another matter. He liked her so much! Next to Leigh, she appealed to him more than any of his new acquaintances. He really must get to know her better. Then there was that exquisite line of her throat; he simply *must* paint it—a real Madonna, with blue draperies about her head—a leaf out of the book of the old masters, yet quick with life. A Madonna of flesh and blood, far from ascetic! Ah! yes, they would be friends, and he would ask her to pose. But no more of that silly game of love. *Caramba!* It was nothing but a joke, the veriest farce in the world. She, too, must be laughing at it by now; that was a comfort. And poor Hill! How wretched he had been—was still, in all probability. For the conviction that Sam loved the beautiful lady truly was not to be dislodged. Well, the waif, the stray one, would prove a valiant friend to both of them. The saints be praised! he might serve them.

Just as he reached this amiable conclusion the studio door was flung open to admit the vivacious figure of a young woman, all gold and pink and white, from her fluffy head to the hem of her frilled apron of lawn. A Dresden vision, not quite pretty, but very charming, young and debonair. She wore no hat, and in her hand she carried a couple of checked towels, such as are used for the drying of dishes.

This young person was Miss Cassie Goodell, from the floor below—the young lady of the violets.

"Mornin', Pedro," she greeted him. "I've come to do your rooms."

"Impertinent!" he gasped, closing the door behind her. "How many times have I told you to knock before entering, eh?"

"As often as I come up!" she admitted, making a raid upon the cigarettes.

"Some day you may be sorry!" he warned her. "Suppose I were not clothed?"

"Lord bless you, Pedro dear," she replied amusedly, "I shouldn't die of the shock, having posed in a pleasant smile myself for over five years."

"Well, you knock next time!" he said excitedly. "*I* care, if you don't."

She paused in her occupation of gathering up the table silver.

"I used to," she said in a queer voice, "but I don't any more. And I don't even mind not being able to care, worse luck!"

But Pedro did not hear her, even though the sudden silence in which she stood should have attracted his attention. He was examining the unfinished canvas on the easel, wholly absorbed by it. The girl threw back her head, as though shaking off something, and began her work anew, whistling softly the while.

Her task was plainly a familiar one and her execution of it surprisingly deft. There was a tiny kitchenette between the bathroom and studio, and this was scrupulously clean, owing to her care. Each article had its ordained spot, and she put it there with swift hands, almost unconsciously accomplishing the labor while her mind was on other matters.

One day, now almost two months since, she had come up-stairs to make the acquaintance of the new artist in Hill's quarters—the acquaintance of the charming young man to whom she had thrown her violets on the day of his arrival. She had found him immersed in work, while a few late flies, brought to life by the odor of food, buzzed about a neglected table. Her host had not noticed her entrance. Surprised, she had stood watching him, his serious young face wrapt in an ecstasy of striving, and then, perceiving that to speak would be a sacrilege, and to leave the table as it was, a crying shame upon her femininity, she had silently set about cleaning it, still unnoticed by Pedro. Later, on the occasion of that first visit, they had talked, and he had engaged her to pose, but although nothing was said about her voluntary labors, from that time on, she, instinctively knowing that he needed her care, had come each morning and put his place to rights, though as a rule he forgot she was there.

She finished with the dishes and set herself to making the bed, after, as usual, vainly searching for toilet articles to put away. As ever, she marveled anew at the nicety with which his personal belongings were kept in contrast to his shabby housekeeping. Everything was already in order in the bedroom; the bureau was immaculate, and for the greater part filled with Hill's garments, none of which Pedro had ever used. She soon finished what there was to do and returned to the studio, just pausing to prink a bit before the mirror. As she entered, Pedro beckoned to her.

"Hold out your arm a minute, Cassie," he bade her, speaking without coming out of his absorption. "No! So: the shoulder a little higher. That's it!"

Then he worked violently for a few moments.

"Pedro," she remarked presently, "do you like my arm very much?"

No answer.

"Gil Foster says it's the best looking forearm in the city," she volunteered.

No answer. He was too much absorbed to listen. Indeed, he might have been deaf. The picture was coming out right, and nothing else mattered. A lock of hair fell across his eyes, and in brushing it back he left a brown smudge upon his nose.

"You're a funny one," she commented. "Nary a compliment do you hand out; yet you ain't a bad sport by any means. Think maybe I'll learn a psalm to sing while I sit for you; that might make a hit. More in your line, I guess."

Then she, too, fell silent for a little while, looking about her at the familiar objects almost with an air of proprietorship. Had she not dusted them until her care would seem to give her some claim upon them, if not upon the tenant in their midst? Cassie was in a talkative mood this morning.

"Gil is awful fresh," she began naively. "We went to Beer Peter's last night to eat. Say, he bought the best! I've been posing for him three times lately and now I guess I'll have to cut it out. He's married, and I won't stand no nonsense."

Still unmoved, Pedro worked on, his silence making the girl's words fall the louder in the great barren room; and to her own ears they sounded strangely coarse. What had she said that for? Didn't it sound fierce, though?

"Say, I often think of that first day, when I threw the violets," she said rather softly; "do you remember?"

Pedro heard this, because he had just finished what he was working at.

"Rest," he said, then: "That's all. I'm not going to work this morning. I've got an engagement for the noon meal. What were you saying?"

"I—I was talking about the day you looked up at

THE LADY OF MYSTERY

my window and said—and said—'I love you.' "
Her eyes twinkled as she spoke.

Pedro responded instantly.

"Ha! ha!" he laughed; "yes, I remember. Do you know, I was talking to the house; I didn't see you till you laughed! Ha! ha!"

"Then you didn't mean it for me?" she teased, pouting a little.

"Of course not!" he responded cheerfully. "Here, stand still again for a minute, while I sketch in that corner of your shoulder. This composition just needs it to balance. . . . There! That's all!"

She turned to go, gathering up her gaily checked dish-cloths. At the door she paused.

"Is she a good-looker, the lady you're going to lunch with?" she asked mischievously.

He wheeled toward her in surprise.

"Ah! I did not say I was going to lunch with a lady!" he exclaimed.

"So she *is* pretty," said Cassie, with a pseudo-melancholy sigh. "Ah, me!"

Then she was gone, closing the door softly behind her.

"Hum!" said Pedro, staring at the floor. "I invited that! I must be becoming as awkward as a—"

Here he stopped abruptly; put a hand upon his lips, warning himself to silence; took away the hand; found it streaked with brown paint, and straightway fell to washing his besmirched countenance with soap powder of a peculiarly cleansing sort.

.   .   .   .   .

An hour later he was sitting down to "the noon meal" with Iris.

"For," she said, "father is never punctual; if we waited for him we might wait until night."

In the cold light of day, and in the more formal setting of her own house, Iris was finding it somewhat difficult to continue the romantic impetuous atmosphere which had come so naturally in the semi-darkness of the Milligans' balcony. Then, too, Pedro was somewhat less responsive. He was very courteous, but a little reserved. Furthermore, it was proving almost impossible to question him about himself as she had wished. The morning paper had given her the same news that had so much amused the boy, and, remembering her first encounter with him, she was greatly at a loss as to who and what he might be. Was he an impostor, an adventurer, or an eccentric? He might easily be either, but whatever he was, he fascinated her beyond any of her acquaintances. Indeed, she had begun to consider him even more tenderly. Then there was that miniature in her father's desk! Where had it come from? Was it of Pedro? So many mysteries were enough even to overcome that edict of etiquette which bade one conquer curiosity. She really must know about him, even at cost of seeming curious.

"Were you born in Spain?" she asked.

"No," said he. "Have you seen De Bush's exhibition at Knoedler's gallery yet?"

"Not yet," she replied; "I suppose you know all the galleries well. Or haven't you been here before?"

"This is my first visit to New York," he replied, and then, as she was about-to speak again, he held up his hand, frankly stopping her and looking straight into her eyes.

"Madonna, I beg that we talk of something else than myself," he continued. "These pictures of De Bush's *par example*. You must go to them. He is wonderful as an interpreter either of character or personality."

"Very well," said she, not looking at him, for she was piqued at the purely friendly unsentimental glance with which he had returned her somewhat languishing one, "we shall talk of what you suggest. Which do you consider the more important? Which is the more vital—character or personality?"

"Can you have one without the other, Madonna?"

"Undoubtedly. The veriest bore, who gives one no clue to his individual soul, may have a splendid character or the reverse; embodying all the virtues, or all the vices, without your being aware of it."

"Would not the vices stick out a little so that you'd know they were there?" suggested Pedro. "The virtues, I grant you; they would be overlooked and probably leave no mark upon the face."

She laughed at this.

"Yes," she admitted, "that is true, but personality makes itself felt, whether or no."

"And does not have dependence upon any virtue," said he, "nor need its possessor speak, *tv savis!*"

"Exactly," she asserted. "Which do you consider more important?"

"In our servants, the character," said he; "in our friends, the personality. Me, I sicken of a bore."

"Then you relegate all the virtues to the lower classes?" she inquired.

"There are no lower classes, Senorita," he replied, "and, perhaps, too, we would differ on our—er—what you call—our *definition* of virtue. For example, I consider it a sin to be a bore."

"What a difficult creed!" she cried. "At that rate think of the thousands who would suffer damnation!"

"And why not?" he demanded. "A thief who steals your purse, steals trash, as the English Shakespeare has written. Very true, but he who holds an active brain in thraldom, while droning forth matter of little sense and of no moment, steals your immortal soul, than which there surely can be no greater crime."

"I agree with you!" she cried. "Oh! I do, indeed."

Suddenly she smiled a little.

"Is it sufficiently abstract?" she asked, her eyes full of meaning.

With a quick motion, he handed her an olive.

"Try one of these," he suggested.

How he avoided the personal! It seemed as though he feared it above everything, and detecting the approach of an intimate note, changed the theme at once.

"I have a curious sketch of Leigh's with me," he said, changing the subject determinedly; "would you care to see it?"

"Oh! yes, I like that man—Leigh, although he never pays the slightest attention to me—nor indeed to any woman, for that matter. He looks as if he could be intensely interesting if he would only talk. But though I have known him, en passant, for years, I never seem to get at him at all."

"You are certainly right in supposing him to be interesting!" exclaimed Pedro, his eyes lighting up at this appreciation of his friend. "He is a man among men! A great mind; a sincere artist. I have not words enough to praise him. I—I—well, here, I run away from the subject. Ha! ha! you see it is not safe to start me about Leigh. But to the point. One night not long ago we were talking about form in music, and he told me that he had caught Nature herself demonstrating their intimate kinship. Listen—he saw the Pocantico hills against the sunset, and suddenly it occurred to him that if five parallel lines were drawn behind them in a given space (as the foundations of a music score are drawn) the outlines of the hills against them would form a melody where the extreme height and depths of outline occurred. He made a drawing of the hills, cut it out, laid it upon the five black lines, and behold!—a melody resulted, which he showed me upon the piano. He afterward gave me the drawing; it is in this pocket, I think."

He fumbled in the depths of the old green coat, while Iris waited with baited breath. Never could strategy have worked in more successful allurement of a maiden than did Pedro's honest withdrawal from all flirtatious intent. The more frequently his little hostess looked upon him, and the more he withdrew from love, the more certain she grew that she was to love him—perhaps, already loved him.

How good he was to look at; a trifle slight, possibly; but what wonderful hair he had, that curled a little.—"Like the young tendril of the grape."—Where had she read that? And what a fine clean-cut mouth, with its firmly modeled corners! Such a face meant character—power! As to personality, there was no need to ask about his possession of that! Ah! he had found the paper!

Together they were leaning over it as he spread it upon the table-cloth, when a sharp exclamation from across the room caused them to look up hastily. In the doorway stood Reginald Vanderpool, his aristocratic clean-shaven face for the instant blanched, his eyes fixed upon Pedro as though in fascinated unbelief. Iris covered the odd situation quickly.

"Signor Pedro," she said, "this is my father."

On the moment the man's face became impassive, and with courteous grace he advanced to greet the guest at his table. The two shook hands and the host seated himself, giving a low-voiced order to the servant, who brought rice and milk and a little fruit. Either the millionaire's tastes were simple, or his slim figure was maintained at a considerable cost.

"Are you the painter of whom the morning paper speaks?" he inquired of Pedro. "Pardon my not knowing."

"I suppose I am," replied Pedro composedly.

"Ah! I shall be interested in seeing your work," said Vanderpool. But his tone was perfunctory, except for a note of what might have been disappointment. After this he spoke very little, but whenever the conversation between his daughter and Pedro became most animated he would steal a covert look at the youth—a look full of interest and something else, too, which would have been difficult for an observer to define.

Before the meal was ended, a servant, entering with a note, caused a diversion, and as he put the envelope into his pocket, Vanderpool arose, although he had scarcely eaten anything.

"Sorry, but I must run along," he said. Then, with a slight bow to Pedro, he turned to leave. At the action Iris sprang up, and going to her father, she put a detaining hand upon his sleeve.

"Don't go, dearest," she said; "why, you will starve yourself to death!"

The man's face softened wonderfully as he looked down into her anxious eyes.

"There, there, I'm not hungry," he said, with a little crooked smile. "Really, I must hurry off."

With which he went out as abruptly as he had come.

Iris suggested the gray room, and they climbed the stair to it and sat themselves upon the sofa where Hill and she had quarreled. But no ghost of a former love haunted her now. Instead, her infatuation for Pedro burned higher every moment, and with bright eager eyes she watched him as he examined and admired the treasures of the curious apartment. The atmosphere was becoming tense again as she spread her languorous net for him, quite delicately, almost insensibly, and—quite vainly. The more she felt this, the harder she strived, searching about in her mind for some method by which to chain him to her. Suppose, her charm failing, she had too little to offer him in common friendship, and her intellect was not sufficient to attract him to a second visit? What could she do to secure his interest, to cement the more intimate relations which had been theirs upon that magical evening just passed? She might invite him to her house, and he might come or he might not. This usual course left him too free an agent. She must find some method of attaching him and of assuring their meeting frequently, so that she might have opportunity gradually to bind him by more tender ties. Then, too, that miniature in the desk seemed to haunt her—that and her father's start when he entered the dining-room. But among her numerous questionings, one thing she could and would discover: what did Pedro know about Hill?

"Have you known Mr. Hill long?" she asked. "I see that it is his studio that you have taken."

THE LADY OF MYSTERY 179

"No," said he; "I have seen him only once. But I feel a great friendship for him," he added in a significant tone.

She changed the subject hastily. How could this stranger have learned of her former attachment? And yet his tone implied that he had. The little society item that Pedro had read, for some reason had escaped her own notice. If he had heard gossip, she thought, she could deny it. For it was evident that the circumstance, if he had knowledge of it, would make a difference in his attitude toward her. All at once the idea for which she was searching flashed into her mind.

"I hope you will not think what I am about to say, too strange," she began, "or consider me very presumptuous in assuming that you are already sufficiently my friend to permit my making such a request of you; but remember that I owe you a rescue and that we have come together instantly on the same plane without any of the usual preamble. Perhaps indebtedness already incurred is scarcely a ground for claiming further help; but you will understand—ah! you must, for I am in great distress and trouble, and there is no one to whom I can go with my difficulty."

Pedro, who had been examining a vase, turned to her with surprise. Ever ready with sympathy, he put out his hand with a single expressive gesture.

"Madonna!" he exclaimed, "you know I would willingly serve you. If it is in my power to help, surely you must know that I would not hesitate."

"Very well, then," she said gravely. "It is this: My father is a strong man, a brave man, I am sure, and one who is not easily daunted or disturbed. You noticed how he acted to-day? Why, he was scarcely civil to you. Such rudeness, believe me, is far from his customary habit, and there is only one explanation for it. He must be deeply troubled about something, and for it to disturb him so, that thing is a very serious matter; otherwise he would throw it off, or, at worst, conceal it."

"Have you no idea of what this trouble is?" He asked.

"I have tried to get him to tell me," she replied, "but it has been a useless effort. My father and I are close friends, but he persists in saying there is nothing wrong, which simply means that something is very wrong indeed; so much so that he is unwilling to tell me."

"I am sorry," said Pedro, "but how can I help?"

"The case is just this!" she cried, rising in her excitement: "I have good reason to believe that he is being either defrauded by a pack of scoundrels who have managed to deceive him into some questionable undertaking, or that he is being blackmailed. There is one period of my father's life of which I know nothing, and I am sure that the present trouble dates back to that time. Further than this I can guess very little. My father would go to any length to keep scandal from his name on my account, no less than his own, or to keep harm from reaching me. He is capable of the most quixotic actions. In some matters he is curiously sensitive and susceptible to distress, and that is what makes me so sure that this present trouble is purely an ethical one from which we could rescue him. Could you—oh! do you think that you could in any way find out if he is being deceived, imposed upon, and help him, or at least set my disturbed mind at rest?"

"It is a curious request," said Pedro slowly. "I to help your father! Why, he is a great man—a wonderfully successful person. Surely you can not really believe I could serve him!"

"You do not yet understand," she urged. "He is strong and capable, but he is almost ridiculously sensitive on lines which touch his honor, and is quite susceptible to being worked and tormented by unscrupulous people. And I have some real proof that this is happening, although I can not actually show it to you at this moment. Do you remember my saying that I carried papers of value the day you rescued me with your bear? Well, the sight of them excited my father greatly, and ever since, he has been receiving letters which have nothing to do with his regular business or his social correspondence. I know it for a fact, because I stumbled upon them accidentally, in a secret drawer of his desk. They are in a foreign language—Spanish, I think—and he keeps them all with great secrecy. Oh! I am sure he is being harried by some mysterious people. Why, that note he received at luncheon was directed in that same fine foreign handwriting in which the others are written. Now won't you help me? Don't you see that it is an exquisitely delicate matter with which I can not go to every one?"

"Have you no relations whom this would concern?" he asked.

"No," said she, "we have only some distant cousins whom we seldom see and who would not do at all."

"Then," said Pedro, "I will help you. It is a position of questionable honor, almost, which you require for this spying and I can not go about it deliberately. Yet, if you sometime can give me a definite task in the matter, I will make sure to perform it; or should chance throw me any information, I shall not fail to use it and follow it up, and I shall be on the watchout for any such. Still, it is not likely that such a thing will cross my path."

"Thank you!" she exclaimed in real gratitude. "It is a relief to know that I may call upon you if necessary. Then the matter can rest between us two. There is nothing at present that I can ask you to do, but if a clue should arise I shall let you know."

"And I will respond immediately," said he, arising to take his departure. "I have friends—ay, good friends—who are more likely to hear rumors of plotting than I. They probably know most of the sub rosa doings of the town by now, or else they have failed in their habit of other cities! But even so, I am afraid that there's not a very great chance of their stumbling upon the particular information we need. And now, Madonna, I must leave. Will you pose for me? I want to paint the beautiful line which runs from your chin downward, like the edge of the young moon."

"Pose!" she gasped, astonished at this new turn of affairs. Then delight at the prospect flooded her heart and suffused her cheeks with a delicate color. "Pose for you! Indeed, yes. When?"

"To-morrow."

"At what time?"

"At nine, if that is not too early."

"I shall be there," she breathed.

When he had gone she descended cautiously to the library, and finding it vacant, made the door fast. Then, springing the secret catch in the desk, she took out the miniature which lay within the hiding-place. For a long time she gazed at it earnestly. Then a curious discovery startled her. The portrait was Pedro, feature for feature, expression and all; but one item which had somehow escaped her now added greatly to her already deep perplexity. The hair of the picture, instead of being dark, like Pedro's, was of a ripe corn gold!

CHAPTER X

CONCERNING BOHEMIA

ON the following morning, at nine o'clock promptly, Iris reached the top landing of the Muldoon Place house and paused, flushed and rather breathless, before the studio door. On it, below the heavy brass knocker and the plate engraved with Hill's name, was a modest ticket bearing simply the word "Pedro." Tucked under a corner of this last was a folded bit of paper addressed to "Madonna Iris." At sight of it her heart almost stopped beating. Could he have gone away? Did he not wish to see her? With trembling fingers she unfastened it, opening it to her anxious gaze.

At the top of the page was a sketch of Pedro himself, empty handed, and running frantically to the open door of a shop which bore the sign: Artists' Supplies. Then came the words: "The door is unlocked. Wait, I beseech you. I haste; I fly!" Below this was a second sketch of himself running madly, package in hand, toward a door marked Studio.

From sheer relief she laughed aloud, and at the sound a door upon the landing below creaked as though some one had opened it to listen. However, Miss Vanderpool did not notice this, but, turning the handle, let herself into the studio, where she had often been before, to be sure, but never until now unchaperoned.

Closing the door behind her, she stood motionless, leaning against it, Pedro's funny little note crushed tightly in one hand, while she let a flood of mixed emotions sweep over her. Pedro, the adorable! This was his habitation, his workshop! Already his vivid personality had permeated it, blotting out that of his predecessor as effectively here among these inanimate objects, as he was unintentionally supplanting Hill in the heart of his lady. The very furnishings looked different under the slight change Pedro had put upon them—a chair replaced, the sofa shifted to a different angle, thus leaving clear a greater floor space. The somewhat careless arrangement, instinctively changed for comfort rather than deliberately thought out, all bespoke the present inhabitant. Nothing, indeed, that Pedro touched could fail to retain his mark, and here he had lived, was living!

As for Sam Hill! Why could she not think of *him?* Why not feel him here in this place, which was built to his order, ordered by his careful thought? She tried to, but vainly. His spirit seemed gone out of it. Ungrateful was she? Fickle? Ah, well, she could not help it. This new thing was mounting to her head like wine. The charm of this newcomer, the beauty of him, the manner—Hill slipped out of her mind, out of association with the room, as completely as though he had never possessed a place in either, leaving her swamped by her new infatuation.

Slowly she advanced to the center of the floor and smoothed out the crumpled note. How clever he was! With a tender little sigh she folded it carefully and slipped it into the bosom of her gown. Then flushing a little, she removed her long outer wrap and laid it, with her hat and furs, upon the couch. She was wearing a trailing gown of blue, almost medieval in its simplicity, which clung softly to the long lines of her graceful figure. A trifle self-consciously she went to one of the swinging mirrors and smoothed her close-braided hair before it, turning away only when its arrangement had been completed to her entire satisfaction.

When this was accomplished she set herself down upon the sofa to wait, but a sudden nervousness came upon her, and springing up again she began to pace back and forth. What had possessed her to come here alone? What would her father say if he knew of her doing so? Poor man! He seemed worried enough nowadays without her adding the burden of an action of which he would not approve! Oh, that trouble of his! If only she knew what it was! Would Pedro be able to help her? Pedro! What would *he* think of her for coming here alone? On the occasions of her former visits to this place there had been company—many people talking all at once and eating silly food while pretending to look at the pictures.

But surely Pedro could not think less of her for coming unchaperoned. No Bohemian would. And, anyway, was she not a Bohemian herself? Had she not learned to laugh at the ridiculous conventions of life as more hypocrisy? Still—

There was a footstep upon the landing, and the door opened suddenly. Expecting to see Pedro, she whirled about with a word of greeting, but to her amazement, in his stead the doorway was occupied by a woman!

It was Cassie.

For a long moment neither woman spoke, but stood staring intently, one as much amazed as the other.

"Good morning," said Iris interrogatively, the question following swift on the heels of the first pang of jealousy she had ever experienced.

What woman was this who entered his apartment as though by right?

Cassie's smile was disarming.

"Pretty, and a lady—a rich lady," she said. "Why, you must be *her!* Well, I'm glad to see you!"

"Who are you, please?" repeated Iris, smiling a little in response, despite herself.

"Of course you'd have to ask," replied Cassie. "He wouldn't be likely to have mentioned me to *you*. No more has he told *me* anything about you; not knowingly, that is. But just the same, I've no need to return your question."

"You are correct in supposing he has not spoken of you," said Iris, puzzled, but with a cold fear creeping over her. "Why should he have done so? I—I have not known him very long, and we have only talked about— What is your name?"

"My name is Miss Goodell," replied the girl, still smiling, her eyes full of curiosity.

"And who—how do you know me?" asked Iris.

"Men are funny things," said Cassie. "They don't say much when they are really in love with some one. Oh, I knew you must be on the job somewhere the minute he said he had a luncheon engagement yesterday. The *way* he said it put me wise."

"And you were annoyed because you are—" began Iris.

Cassie stared at her in amazement, open-mouthed, as though scarcely able to believe her ears. Then she sprang down from the table with a commanding gesture.

"Hold on a minute!" she cried. "I see what you mean, only I couldn't believe my hearing for a second. You think because I walked in here like that! . . . Lord! Trust a good woman to think the worst! I guess you don't know much about studio life. Come back here, kid; I want to talk to you like a grandmother."

Iris had reached the door, her coat upon her arm, but the swift torrent of words, with the reproof they bore, made her pause there. Pictured upon the model's face was disgust, mingled with amusement, back of which was a wide sympathetic understanding that made the slangy little person, who was scarcely her senior, seem ages old. Disgust! This little feminine God-knows-what felt disgust of her, Iris Vanderpool, the immaculate! That such a condition of affairs could arise was in itself arresting. At recollecton of her hasty words, the younger woman blushed again, turning to the other, half irresolutely.

"Then I was mis—oh! I *am* sorry!" she cried, on a sudden impulse stretching out her hand. "Will you forgive me?"

"Of course I will. Cut the comedy!" said Cassie. "Now, come sit down and have a little chat. You really oughtn't to go off the handle like that. I've been awful anxious to see you!"

"But really, how did you know about me?" began Iris.

Again the girl laughed.

"I pose for him," she said, "and I ain't generally considered to be lacking in charm. Well, the charm failed, and when it does, there's usually a better reason than any lack of looks on my part. You are that reason. I guessed it right off. Are you going to marry him?"

"Oh!" cried Iris, startled by the suddenness of the question; "why do you—how do I—"

"So he ain't asked you yet," observed Cassie shrewdly.

"How do you know that?" Iris flared at her.

"Because you'd have said yes to my question if he had," Cassie replied.

Iris arose in indignation, but reseated herself, biting her lip.

"By the way, what have you come here for?" asked Cassie, watching her closely. "If you ain't engaged to him, a visit by your lonesome is a little— "

"I came to pose," said Iris breathlessly. "Signor Pedro is going to paint my portrait."

"Even so, your kind don't generally come alone, do they?" said the elder girl gently.

"You are quite mistaken!" cried Iris. "It is sufficiently customary. You said just now that I knew nothing of the life of the studios. Well, again you are mistaken. I do. I am in them constantly. That I am not an artist does not prove that I am not a Bohemian, and utterly accustomed to freedom of thought and action!"

In a manner filled with smoldering defiance, although intended to convey an impression of absolutely unconscious habit, she helped herself to a cigarette, lighting it clumsily.

"If you think I am not a woman of the world you are utterly wrong," she added, and then suddenly fell to coughing.

"Don't try to smoke that; it'll choke you!" said Cassie, shouting with laughter. "Put it down! That's right. Now listen to me, and don't cry. There's nothing to weep over. What I'm going to tell you is the straight goods, see? I'm not exactly a lady myself, but I know the real thing when I see it, and this time it's you, with no mistake!"

They seated themselves before the fire now, side by side, Iris submitting meekly to being placed as Cassie indicated. The latter fingered the cheap bracelets upon her wrist as she spoke, rapidly, and Iris listened, her blue eyes wide.

"Now, I'm not a swell," began Cassie; "and probably you'll say I ain't fit to advise you. And so I ain't, but I do know something more about this world than you do. That's pretty clear, and I want to slip you a tip. It's this: You carefully brought up girls think it's a great lark to come into 'Bohemia,' as you call it, and do crazy things, as though you was in a foreign country where you didn't expect to be seen. It's that queer notion, that what people are told not to do, is fun to do, that's brought you here. You came alone because it made you feel like a 'real devil' to do so; lighting the cigarette, the same. But you ain't a Bohemian and never can be, because it's not in you—because all this informal life *is a game to you*. You have to live it unconsciously before you *belong*. You only *play* it. But the trouble is, you can't step back safe behind your locked doors of respectability when you quit feeling it's a game, see? And your kind would always be pounding on them doors, trying to get back once you was really locked out, see? And you'd be unhappy. Now, your set would lock you out P. D. Q. if they caught you coming to studios by your lonesome. Why, *you* know that if you think a minute! You don't really mind my saying that, do you? I mean it the right way."

"I see," said Iris in a low voice.

"And there's another thing," said Cassie. "They are all alike in one thing, the men are. The harder a thing is to get, the worse they want it. Oh, don't mistake! There's no sense in being offish. But there's no use running after them, believe *me!* You'll only scare 'em to death!"

"But I'm not—" began Iris, painfully conscious of having come alone for the express purpose of giving Pedro the greater opportunity for sentiment.

"Then mind you don't!" said Cassie, rising as the door flew back to admit Pedro.

"Madonna!" he cried, throwing the parcel that he carried upon the table and going to Iris with outstretched hands. "I entreat your forgiveness, but there was no paint with which to make the divine blue—see, like this!" He swooped down upon a length of silk which lay near by and flung it upon her shoulder. "I have it now, and you will not be angry because I was absent, eh?"

"Oh, no," she answered, beaming at the sound of his voice.

He next turned to Cassie, the sight of whom did not disconcert him in the least, a fact which Iris noted with relief.

"The cakes were wonderful!" he exclaimed to the model. "Not until a moment ago did I realize that you must have made them yourself. I thank you!" He kissed her hand. "You know this lady, Miss

Vanderpool?" he asked, taking her to Iris. "This is a friend who has been *so* good to me!"

"She has been kind to me, also," said Iris.

"Ah! she is your friend, Madonna? That is good! I did not know. However, we will get to work now if you are willing. Step upon the platform, so!"

Cassie, having gathered up the remains of the little cakes, to which Pedro had evidently referred, was about to take a reluctant departure, when Iris, turning around under Pedro's guidance, stopped her with a gesture.

"Don't go away," she said shyly, moved by an impulse she could not have defined. "If you are not too busy, won't you sit in here? You will give me confidence."

The girl looked at her suspiciously. What did this move portend? Was it really the hand of friendship? At any rate if she consented it would do no harm.

"All right, I'd just as soon," she remarked nonchalantly.

"How delightful that you are friends!" hummed Pedro, busy with the wondrous blue drapery. "Friends, friends; oh, world of friendship!"

"Thank you," said Iris, without spoiling the pose; and thereafter spoke no more during the interval.

The elder girl went silently to the bookcase and stood covertly watching the painter, who already seemed to have forgotten the women. Cassie had simply ceased to exist for him at all, and the personality of Iris had merged into the wider ego of art itself. The line was there; the color was there; the soul he would bring to the very surface of her exquisitely textured skin; but Iris, the *woman,* had ceased to be, as far as he was concerned.

Before many minutes had passed Iris herself became aware of Pedro's detachment, and knew that she needed no guardian to protect her from this abstracted spirit, who, with earnest brow, labored so devoutly at the rudiments of his work; knew, also, that the smaller conventions of life had no existence in his mind, and that he had noted her request to Cassie as little as he had noted the fact of her originally having come alone. He wanted to *paint her,* and he was doing so. That was the main point of her presence, and evidently to him a sufficient one. So far as conversation went, she might as well not have been there.

The morning wore on very quietly, and in the

rests little was said, Pedro simply releasing Iris with a signal, and at once falling to touching and rubbing of the canvas. Then she would resume the pose, and he would begin anew.

One o'clock came and went, and still they heeded not, and it was well on toward two when the first interruption occurred. A timid knock sounded at the door, as though some tiny child were seeking admission, and then, before Cassie could respond to it, the gigantic figure of Leigh slipped in through an incredibly small crack, and looked about him. Iris smiled a greeting, but did not move, and Pedro did not notice the intrusion. Leigh dropped into a chair beside Cassie, with whom he seemed to be on terms of long acquaintance.

"I thought you were going to pose for Elloch this morning!" he whispered.

She looked at him in comical dismay.

"Why, so I was!" she whispered back. "But I clean forgot! How did you know? Ain't you been somewhere?"

"Yes," he responded, "for two weeks. But, I just passed Elloch, who was cursing you out. What are you doing, loafing around here?"

"I am chaperoning Miss Vanderpool."

"*You* are!" ejaculated Leigh.

"I am—honest," she said, with serious eyes.

"There!" exclaimed Pedro, throwing down his tools. "Enough for to-day."

"I should think so!" cried Leigh. "You look exhausted. And you, too, Miss Vanderpool. I didn't know you had met Pedro," he continued, helping her to descend from the model throne. "You see, I have been away, and am behind the times."

"Oh! yes, we are friends," said Pedro, his face lighting up wonderfully at sight of Leigh. "Welcome home! Did you get the commission? Are they delighted with the sketch? But, of course! *Dios!* you are a sight to gladden the heart!"

Pedro's cheeks were aflame, and his eyes shone with excitement. Iris noted this with wonder, and thought that truly his friendship for Leigh must be great, since the mere sight of the sculptor aroused in him an enthusiasm so far beyond any which he displayed for others. And, indeed, at this moment Pedro appeared to see no one but the tall gaunt man, whose hands he held. To break the little tableau, Iris looked at her watch, and noted the hour with an exclamation of surprise. Then she began slipping into her outdoor garments.

"I must fly!" she cried. "When shall I come again?"

"I—er—suppose I call you up and you can let me know?" said Pedro, looking, however, at Leigh. "We must have it soon. Ah! it is good to have you back, *amigo mio!*" he added to the sculptor.

"To-morrow?" said Iris. It almost seemed as if she were persisting. "I could come in the morning."

"Will you be working to-morrow?" Pedro asked of Leigh.

Abraham Lincoln Leigh nodded his long head.

"This day I loaf with you," he said. "To-morrow I shall begin to set up the big group."

Pedro turned to Iris.

"To-morrow morning will be splendid then!" he said. "You will come early, eh?"

"Yes," she replied, "but now I must go."

"And I, also," said Leigh. "I must leave an order at Penelli's for plasterline. I'll be back in an hour, Pedro. Cassie, you'd better hustle around to Elloch's and make your peace! May I show you to your motor, Miss Vanderpool? It's waiting out on the avenue."

"Thank you," said Iris, "I shall be glad." Then

she turned to Cassie, all her original antagonism coming back full force. What right had this girl to dictate to her, Iris? How could this little model know what was wisest and best for a woman so infinitely above her that the very tone of a man's voice changed in speaking to them?

"Good-by," said Iris stiffly, ignoring the girl's outstretched hand. Then she went out with Leigh, her head very much in the air.

Cassie said nothing, but stood gazing dumbly after her. Then she let her hand drop, and gave her shoulders a little shrug. What was the use? Their worlds were too far apart.

"Pedro," she said wistfully. It is not good to be ignored.

But Pedro did not answer. He was in the adjoining room, busily engaged in washing the stains from his hands, prior to adventuring forth with Leigh. As he splashed, he whistled gaily, a waltz that was strange and arresting. Where had she heard it before? Ah! yes! the people on the ground floor played it sometimes. It had a sad little refrain.

"Good-by, Pedro," she said again. But still he did not hear, and with a little gesture as though she let something fall from her hands, she went out, closing the door so softly that the lilt of the tune covered the sound of her going.

．　　．　　．　　．　　．

When Pedro and Leigh went down the stairs, arm in arm, the door of the ground-floor apartment was slammed with violence, just as they passed it.

"Do you know the chap who lives here?" asked Leigh.

"Never saw him," said Pedro. "These tenants are all very quiet. I never meet any of them, except Cassie."

"I've seen this down-stairs fellow," said Leigh. "Disagreeable fellow. Name's Rowe, I believe."

"I have never seen him," Pedro replied. "Where shall we go, eh?"

"Paleri's," said Leigh; "we can talk there. I have made a discovery that I must impart to you. And later, there is a party at the League. They want me to speak. I'm instructor there, you know. Mind going?"

"Never you fear!" laughed Pedro assentingly.

And so they went to eat pink spaghetti at Paleri's on Washington Square (lord! how often we eat), and they talked fluently over the acrid wine. Yes, Leigh had secured the western commission.

Yes, they liked the models rather, but the important thing was the discovery. The discovery dealt with architecture and was, briefly, that the trouble with sky-scraping buildings was that their perpendicular lines were not sufficiently accentuated. A most important fact, this; and he, Leigh, had hit upon a way of improvement. It was thus and so. He drew some diagrams upon the cloth, and "Oh!" and "Ah!" said Pedro, illuminated.

Other vital subjects of the same order came to their minds, and Leigh, completely under the spell of Pedro's charm once more, entirely forgot to inquire further into the friendship with the Asphalt King's daughter, which had sprung up during his absence. They had a wonderful time; for anything seemed interesting, personal, intimate, so be it they were together again. Only now, indeed, did they realize how sorely they had missed each other.

When it was time to leave for the Art League, they swung up Fifth Avenue, arm in arm, and pausing at Forty-second Street, gave one of their "art instructions" to a small and mocking group. The subject was the deficiencies of the new Public Library, and Leigh informed them that its proportions were wrong; the columns were too fat for their height, the doors too small, etc. It was an excellent talk, brief and to the point. Two girls, with painted cheeks, stopped their prowling along the dark wall of the public garden and stood listening to the rich tone of this ultra-masculine person's voice. A college youth, rather "elevated" by a course at the Manhattan bar, and a brace of roistering companions, were there also. Two newsboys stared up into the face of the speaker, and on the outer edge of the circle, half-ashamed, a theater-bound suburban couple lingered. A supercilious policeman and a nondescript loafer or two were in the crowd, and a ruddy-faced old gentleman in evening clothes. Behind him stood three sailors from a battleship, and a professional dog-fighter, with his strong white animal in leash. Nowhere, thought Pedro, could a more cosmopolitan audience be found. This, indeed, was getting instruction to the people. And such a lecture! They could not fail to understand it!

Leigh finished with a short peroration concerning the duty of all citizens to make their city a place of beauty, and of the reaction of beauty upon the public mind. Then he thanked them for their attention. The painted women giggled, and nudging each other, called out some vulgar colloquialism. "Can the comedy," yelled one newsboy, rushing off after dodging the policeman's stick. The loafers shuffled away wordlessly, and an ancient match-woman begged for charity. The suburban couple had not waited for the end, and had soon made off to their dollar-fifty seats. If the meaning of what Leigh said had penetrated to the minds of any of these, they gave no sign of it, but slid away on their own affairs. All, that is, but the ruddy old gentleman in evening clothes. He came forward and shook Leigh by the hand.

"I entirely agree with you in your criticism, sir," said he. "My own plans, which I submitted in the competition for that building, were refused, sir, and they had no such faults as you very justly find here, sir!"

With which he went his complacent way, leaving Pedro and his friend to discuss amusedly the little adventure, and brood upon the tremendous lot they knew about art, the while they reached Fifty-seventh Street and the National Academy Building.

Here, in the well-lighted assembly-room, Leigh, his rough tweed clothing very shabby under the fierce light, made another speech, not nearly so good this time, and delivered rather self-consciously. The wide floor was well covered by a cosmopolitan crowd, seated upon camp-chairs,—students, both men and women, instructors and their wives, and parents of some of the pupils. The students were of varied ages, some very young, not more than sixteen, and some old enough to be the parents of these. Here good artists had sat and graduated; here sat many who would become noted. All were vivacious, some were clean, and the program for their entertainment was furnished from the home talent of the League, both past and present. Edwards, the illustrator, sang to his guitar; surely no one could do it so well as he, so tuneful and so debonair. And Collings, the man who draws the dogs, talked a song which he accompanied upon the piano. An improvised grand opera followed, and then the portrait-painter, whose class it is so easy to enter and so difficult to graduate from, spoke, a trifle pompously. Milligan was there also, jolly little Milligan; and he recited a French-Canadian poem (very badly, by the way).

On the walls of the room in which all this took place hung many paintings, mostly out of frames, and all of them good, though many were too "advanced" to show to the conservative public. It was the "best" room of the League, and later the throng trooped up three flights of stairs to where the class-rooms had been thrown together for dancing. Some one played the piano. How the dancers spun and whirled! Such odd-looking couples! There was one particularly wild-looking girl, with earrings of red sealing-wax. Some said she might be great some day. And the red-headed boy with whom she danced had just won the *Prix de Rome*. Ah, well! there were too many of them, good, bad and indifferent, to take time for the picturing of them all; too many types, ugly and beautiful, successful or failing! Imagine them for yourself; they are in every atelier in the world.

Pedro and Leigh watched them for a while, and even did a "grizzly bear" themselves, greatly to the joy of their audience. Then they clattered down the carpetless stairs and went around to the "Alps" for a little brown drink they make there. Prunes go into the concocting of it, and you drink only one glass—if you are wise. And over this they tackled cosmic problems to their heart's content, until it was close on to one o'clock, when, in a very enthusiastic mood, Pedro saw Leigh to the latter's door. They stood for several moments in the shelter of the vestibule, comparing the English of Oscar Wilde to that of the St. James Bible. Then Leigh found his latch-key and Pedro turned homeward.

But he was not destined to reach the studio immediately.

Before he had gone to the end of the block, he turned, and stood quite motionless, looking up at Leigh's window, where a dim light soon appeared behind the cracked and yellow blinds. Until this light had been extinguished, he waited, looking up with a strange expression in his eyes. Then, when the window went dark, he buried his face in his hands and seemed to purge his soul of some trouble. After a moment or two, however, he abruptly squared his shoulders and resumed his homeward way; only to be halted by the sight of two men, who issued from the swinging door of a little subterranean café and paused together under a street lamp.

At his first glimpse of the taller of the two men, Pedro's heart gave a great thump of surprise. It was Mr. Vanderpool, Iris' father! And who was the disreputable-looking fellow to whom he was talking? Why had the chap such a familiar look? Where had he seen the fellow before? Impossible to remember. But whatever their former encounter, it paled in interest beside the fact that the mystery he had undertaken to unravel was probably being enacted, in part, under his very nose.

Clearly some mischief was afoot. By his tone and gestures, the smaller man appeared to be dictating to the millionaire, who followed his words anxiously. Assuming a careless saunter, Pedro pulled his cap far down over his eyes and walked past the two.

"A week is impossible; too long, by far," the villainous-looking person was saying as Pedro passed. "I warn you, it must be ready by three days from now at the latest."

Vanderpool's low-voiced reply did not reach the straining ears of Pedro, who had stepped into an area-way just beyond, where he could watch through the railing without being seen himself. But he could hear nothing further, owing to the direction of the wind. What was to be done? How strange that chance should have let him stumble upon the action of a mystery which he had scarcely believed in the existence of! And mystery there was, beyond a doubt, else why this meeting in a little unnamed wine-cellar—why this hour of the night? But how should he, Pedro, act? Follow Vanderpool? Perhaps! In all probability the millionaire would go directly home. Follow the other? That might prove more fruitful. While he waited in perplexity his problem was decided for him by the appearance of a cab, which Vanderpool hailed, and getting into, drove off.

After waiting a moment to make certain of the direction taken by the cab, the man with whom Vanderpool had been talking started off rapidly in the opposite way, which led toward Sixth Avenue. On the instant Pedro was shadowing him, dodging in and out of the darker spots and keeping at a discreet distance.

After a few moments he realized that they were bound in the direction of his own studio! He quickened his pace, lessening the distance between his quarry and himself, for they were now on the lighted avenue, where boldness was less conspicuous than stealth. The man ahead was evidently in a hurry and did not pause, nor once look around. And all the time Pedro puzzled his head as to where he had seen the fellow's back before. He had an excellent memory, but in this case it was scarcely heeded, for one of the man's shoulders was slightly higher than the other and he had a peculiarly sneaking gait. Pedro became so much absorbed in trying to place this person that he could scarcely believe his eyes when the man vanished from before them. A swift glance about showed that he was on his home block. There was only one place into which the man could have gone—Muldoon Place! Before him loomed the dark and narrow gate, with its dim lantern, showing the name flickeringly. Breaking into a run, Pedro gained the entrance just in time to see the man he was pursuing gain admittance to the interior house by the basement door. For a moment he stood stock-still with surprise. The basement of the house in which he, himself, lived! Why, that was a part of those people's apartment—what was their name? Ah, yes, Rowe!

Alive with curiosity, he crossed the court with cautious steps, and tiptoeing to the barred window, which was further reinforced by shutters on the inside, knelt down upon the stones and applied his eye to the crack of a lame slat.

At first he could see nothing but a patch of red carpet, so he shifted slightly, bringing into full view the man whom he had followed. At this he suddenly remembered. It was the tramp who had tried to rob Iris! What a mystery was here! First a man tries to rob the daughter and then is seen in secret conference with the father! *Papers!* Yes, she had papers in that little silk purse, and this rascal knew their value, no doubt. But what could they concern? The man had moved aside now, disclosing another, at sight of whom Pedro's heart liked to have stopped. "Ricardo!" he gasped, amazed. But his gaze and his painful wonderment were instantly deflected from "Rowe" to a woman who sat beyond him. Feature for feature, the face she lifted in the light was his, Pedro's, very own. She was his counterpart, all but the color of the hair!

Like a wounded animal, Pedro gave a little moan, and clutching at his heart, dropped his head upon the stone sill and sobbed gaspingly, terribly. Then a noise inside the room startled him. They were coming to the door. Evidently the woman was leaving. Arising, he flung out his arms toward the warmly-lit interior with a single gesture of passionate longing, and turning fled terror-stricken to the sanctuary of his room above stairs.

CHAPTER XI

SUNDRY ADVENTURES

ON that night when Rowe had struck Old Nita, and she had fallen senseless into the arms of Samuel Hill, peace and order were long in coming to the little summer garden.

When a light had been lit to disclose the disorder of the bar, Hill's first thought was to get Nita and himself away before the matter went any further. A swift examination sufficed to show that she had not regained consciousness by the time that Mikey had begun telephoning for the police. Once let the bluecoats arrive and it would be no easy matter to escape publicity. Whatever Nita's grievance against the man, Rowe, it must forego immediate settlement! No good could come of a court-room scene just at present. Besides, Hill was now certain that the foreigner was in reality his tenant, and he could, consequently, assist in finding and bringing him to justice later. But what was to be done for Old Nita? Would she never come to? Seizing a bottle of brandy, he poured out a little and succeeded in forcing a drop or two between her lips, whereat, choking slightly, she came to life. Apparently, she had received no injury more severe than the shock of the blow. Thank heaven she was no worse!

"Old Mother, can you walk?" he queried anxiously.

But she seemed not to hear him. In an instant more Mikey would leave the telephone, and it would certainly be a mistake to wait for that to happen! With an effort he gathered the old woman into his arms, and after a moment or two, found himself in the street. He extracted the old-fashioned key from the lock, and, closing the storm-door, fastened it on the outside. But what to do next? Anxiously he gazed up and down the deserted snow-bound avenue. At a glance it was plain that he could not carry Nita to the car line, and he began, too late, to curse the lack of sense that had led them so far a-field at such an hour. It seemed as though the Irishman must be upon them at any instant now!

At the moment of his despair there emerged from the basement of one of the houses a little down the line the cabby to whom the solitary remaining vehicle before the saloon belonged. Whether he was warmed by a successful amatory adventure, by the wines of an unconscious host in the person of the cook's employer, or by some other agency, must go unrecorded here, but the fact remained that his good humor was such that without solicitation he hailed the little group in the snow with a proposition which seemed like a beneficence direct from heaven.

"Ole lady hurted?" beamed this cherubic personage.

"No, only tired out," lied Hill glibly.

"I'll histe yer to a car," suggested the man. "Never di-serted a lidy in distress. Nope!"

"I'm afraid they wouldn't let us on a car," exclaimed Hill. "Are you going down-town, by chance?"

"No, I'm a-goin' a-purpose!" grinned the man. "Get in; I'll take yer fur es I'm goin'!"

Hill did not wait to be urged further, but carried Nita to the carriage door, which the heavily muffled coachman held open.

"Easy there, with yer ma!" the latter warned him. "Now jump in yerself. This heat is too fierce to lay about in."

The horse, which had stood passively under its meager blanket for hours, scarcely shifting a foot, now scented the bear, and sidled off a little, its city-trained senses scarcely revolting, yet finding in that unfamiliar odor some warning of danger, and the two men noted the action.

"What about the bear?" gasped Hill.

From within the saloon came sounds which indicated that Mikey had discovered the trick played upon him.

"Whoa, my baby!" roared the happy cabby. "Push the damn bear inside!"

In a moment it was done, not without protest from Mr. Jones. And as the bony horse, tossing his old head about with many a suspicious sniff, set off at a tremendous pace, the window of the saloon flew open to disgorge the rotund figure of Mikey, who shouted an unintelligible threat, or command, upon the snow-filled air.

Rocking and swaying, the cab sped down-town, the old horse giving as good an imitation of a runaway as lay within his depleted prowess, the occupants of the vehicle tossing helplessly about in a confused mass of gipsy, man and bear, together with a great rattling of the chain and pole. Outside, upon the box, the joyous cabby sang about a girl, who, if the song was to be believed, was waiting for him by the Suwanee River (or some river). We take it he really referred to the cook in ninety-odd street. The horse, unable to understand why it could not out-distance that bear smell, continued to hurry, much to its owner's delight. Half-way to Fourteenth Street, he dropped the little front window and stuck his head in.

"C. Murphy thinks the bear's a-follerin' of him," he informed Hill. "I'd like to git that there animal as a permanent institution. We ain't gone so fast in years!"

Whereat, owing to lack of guidance, "C. Murphy" nearly collided with a street lamp, thereby demanding the cabby's head, which was promptly withdrawn, and its jovial attention fixed upon its proper affairs.

Meanwhile, Old Nita had not fully recovered, but lay against Hill's shoulder, moaning so pitifully that he began to fear that she was more severely hurt than he had at first supposed, and to regret that he had not let her be sent to a hospital, no matter what consequences might result.

"By jove! Flower Hospital is not far from here," he muttered, peering through the frosted window. "I believe we had better go there."

At sound of his voice the old woman, who seemed to have understood what he said, roused herself with a fearful effort and protested.

"No, *no!*" she gasped. "Back to Beau-Jean! *Not* hospital! *Promise!*"

"Very well, I promise!" he said.

An expression of the most intense relief relaxed the muscles of her face, and she seemed, soon after, to faint. At Twelfth Street the cab came to a sudden halt beside the curb, and the driver, dismounting from the box, opened the door and looked in.

"This is where my stable is at," he announced. "Right down the block. Guess you'll have ter git out. How's yer ma?" he added solicitously, as though to repair his rudeness in ejecting them.

"Pretty bad," said Hill. "Gone off again, I'm afraid."

The cabby wrinkled up his face with a perplexed stare, and removing his hat, scratched his head with one heavily mittened hand.

"I really hadn't oughter," said he, "considerin' the hour and all, but I guess it's gotter be done. Whereabouts do you live?"

"Little Jones Street," said Hill, and gave the number. "I've a bit of money. Could you get us around there, do you think?"

"Well," said the cabby, "I might as well make a night of it, I suppose. Take good care of yer ma, now, and I'll have yer home in a jiffy!"

Then he remounted the box, and soon they were wending a tortuous way through the silent squalor of lower Greenwich village. They stopped at last before a tall tenement, a building of uncompromising ugliness, whose intricate network of fire-escapes was hung now with a fairy drapery of white.

Whining with disgust at being again disturbed, Mr. Jones jumped out clumsily, followed by Hill, who, with the cabby's help, carried the unconscious Nita into the unlighted hallway, which gaped, sinister and forbidding, under the nethermost of the crowded fire-escape balconies. Here Hill, one arm about his charge, fumbled in his breast for his wallet. But the cabby put up a restraining hand.

"Never mind the coin!" he laughed. "Youse need it more'n me, I guess. Better let the doctor take it; you're a-goin' ter need ter call him in! Yer seem all to the good, even if yer *be* dagoes!"

"You're a gentleman!" exclaimed Hill, holding

out his hand. "Many thanks for your kindness. You seem very happy. May I ask why? I should like to congratulate you."

"Oh! it ain't nothin' much," said the cabby sheepishly. "I ain't goin' to be married, thet's all!"

Wherewith he was gone, and Hill, without stopping to ponder upon the content of this odd reply, set himself to carrying Nita up the stairway. At the first landing he stopped and knocked. The door was presently opened by Beau-Jean, a scantily-clad colossus, silhouetted in the aperture against the light of a single candle. With an exclamation of dismay, the man stepped back to admit Hill and his burden, and the painter, staggering across the tiny room, deposited Nita upon a ragged bed that stood beside the cook stove.

"Holy mother!" breathed Beau-Jean. "Is she dead?"

"No! Where are the women?" asked Hill.

In response to the question Guneviere raised herself from her pallet of quilts in the opposite corner, a sturdy unmodern figure, with head swathed for sleeping. With entire unconcern for her negligee, she arose and came to the assistance of the older woman.

"God save us! she is too ancient to survive such injury!" she exclaimed, examining a swelling which was now quite obvious on the crone's forehead. "Hermania! Anna! come!"

From a tiny inner closet came Hermania, clad as for the day, save for the absence of shoes, and her forehead-band of coins, which was at this moment reposing in her bosom for greater comfort with no less safety. After her came Carlos, sleep-stupid and annoyed. In a moment both women were busy over the prostrated form of the injured one; and to the men Hill was giving an account of the adventure that had brought them to such a pass. They listened without being able to throw the smallest light upon the subject, nor identify the enemy who had assaulted the old lady in so cowardly a fashion. By the time all was done that could be done for Nita, and she lay more easily, Anna appeared from the windowless bedroom at the rear, where she had stopped to put a ribbon in her hair before emerging into the light, which would reveal her to Rico's eyes. Her lover followed on her heels and joined the men, while his mistress took her now useless offers of help to the bedside.

"Which of you has ever heard of her enemy?"

Hill was asking. "None, really? And has she no kin whom we should call upon for help?"

"Nay," said Beau-Jean, the ponderous, "she is from the America-of-the-South. If she hath kin, they are too far away to levy claim upon."

"America-of-the-South! What do you mean?"

"Venezuela, I think," said Rico.

"But how is it possible that no one knows anything further about her?" cried Hill. "You have all been with her for years. Surely you must know —or the women will, perhaps."

"No one but Pedro knows," said Rico positively. "They came together; we all know that much. But beyond that—!"

He waved his hand with a gesture expressive of infinite vagueness.

"Then, if anything threatens her, it may also affect Pedro," said Hill.

"Perhaps the Old One will speak soon," suggested Beau-Jean, "and then we can find out."

It was a hope to which they all agreed, but which was not to be fulfilled during the watches of that night. As it became evident that rest was the most important thing for her, and that little or nothing could be done until the morrow, the watchers, one by one, betook themselves to bed.

Where but a moment since the ribbon-girded head of Anna had shone like some rich finely-carved gem against the soiled and tawdry paper on the wall, the flickering fitful light danced upon the silly pattern, for she had gone—useless, beautiful, as though she had indeed been a jeweled ornament, snatched away by the hand of her lover. Carlos, taking the money that the day just past had brought to the late comers, tucked it into the leather bag he carried in his breast, and squabbling with his wife, was ejected in company with Beau-Jean, while the remaining women prepared to share the watches at the sick-bed.

The little room was close with odors of garlic, of clothing, of bears, of living, and the tallow light flung the shadows in wavering masses over the scanty objects with which the place was furnished. There were the cot, the mass of quilts upon the floor, a corner sink, a stove still cluttered with the implements that had served to prepare the evening meal, a battered chair or two and a large deal table. At the single tightly-closed window that gave upon the snow-filled fire-escape, hung a cheap lace curtain, against which leaned the three bear-staves; while from the cornice hung Rico's flute. But of all its contents, the spirit that pervaded the place was its most striking feature; it was a chamber where reality of thought and action was the rule of the day, instead of being the alarming dreaded exception. And this spirit pushed back the narrow walls until they encompassed the earth.

Hill stood in the doorway looking at the upper half of the old woman's unconscious face, where the light fell upon her hooked nose and wrinkled eyelids. As he looked he heaved a sigh of admiration, closed the door, muttered something about having "Rembrandt skinned a mile", and went off to the attic where he and Mr. Jones dwelt in brotherly love and in greater order than prevailed below

. . . . .

The next day a doctor came and pronounced that there was nothing alarming in Nita's injuries, but that she must rest for a few days and have great care. Then he took most of their money, and having drugged Nita, after the custom of certain beasts who prey upon the not infrequent victim to be found among the tenements, proceeded to make a case for himself whereby he could come daily until his patient's finances were exhausted. And for several days his little plan succeeded, for Guneviere was faithful to the nursing, and administered the drug with great regularity. On the days when Hermania remained at home to care for the old woman, she, too, was painstaking and vigilant. But there came a time when it was Anna's turn to watch, and Anna forgot to give the "medicine". For poor little Anna wept at being separated from Rico, and weeping, fell asleep. When she awoke, the day was gone, and what was more, Nita was gone also. The bed was made, the old woman's clothing had disappeared, and on the table the empty coffee-cup and plate, showed that Nita had not gone hungry!

. . . . .

Now the doctor had been a severe drain upon the resources of these people, and just at present Hill was bringing in the most money, for he added to his exhibition, sketching portraits at twenty-five cents apiece. He was usually the first to set out, and last to return, and this was more regularly the case since Nita's illness, for the two older women were much occupied, and Anna's condition was delicate as she was expecting the advent of an addition to the troop.

It so happened, then, that on the day just recorded above, he had gone forth even before it was decided that Anna should remain with Nita.

High-banked on either hand lay the now sullied snow. Up-town, where the carriages go, and glittering automobiles slip smoothly along in shining array, carrying gorgeous ladies and indifferent gentlemen, the streets were cleaned by now; but down here, where the neighborhood must go a-foot, it matters little what they walk upon because they are already so soiled and bedraggled when they sally forth! So the snow had been let lie until it was black and hideous.

Between this dirty rampart and the teeming houses on his other hand, walked Sam Hill, speculative, absorbed in thoughts of Iris, dejectedly thankful that the need for money was driving him to work, for he was firmly resolved not to draw upon that bank-account, which would inevitably bring him in touch with his former life. It was terrible, but not even work could wholly drive her from his mind. Iris, the golden! How cruel, how cold! What had he not suffered at her hands! That period of his life was done with forever. No one could even take her place. How he loved her! How sweet she was! No! he didn't care a rap for her, the silly child! Yes, confound it, he did!

And so on, past tenements, past gloomy little shops, past meager wares set forth at cellar doors, on and on he went, absorbed in thought; and behind him shuffled Mr. Jones, at whom the children stared and pointed; the little dirty children for whom there was not room in the great schools. Women with wrinkled faces and coarse brown wigs stared from beneath their shawls, or from under the massive bundles that they were carrying homeward from the jobber, that the family might be employed thereby in the "home"; on and on past steep and tottering door-step on the little winding streets. Down a back alley they plunged then, man and bear, and emerging upon a wide slatternly avenue, pushed back a slatted swinging door, and entered a saloon.

There were shining mirrors within, and polished woods, with a fine bar, all arrayed with glasses and bottles in decorative and tempting array. Here was a group of men in a post-midnight mood, hilarious and ready to part with small change. Sam made Mr. Jones dance for them, turn somersaults, sit in an armchair and hold a pipe between his teeth, kiss him, be dead, and perform many other intellectual feats beyond the common acquirement of bears. The fruit of this effort was only sixty-one cents, and so, to leave nothing untried on the immediate ground of operation, Hill drew the barkeeper's portrait; an effort which pleased the watchers more than the patron, for Hill, being somewhat absent-minded on Iris' account forgot to be flattering, and drew a coarse fat Irishman in lieu of a sleek handsome one. However, he was paid a quarter for it (a quarter of a dollar for an original Hill, and a portrait order, at that! Modern society has paid a hundred dollars apiece for just such sketches from the identical pencil, as all the world knows), and the resources of this particular saloon being exhausted, they left.

The day, from being overcast, was growing into one of glistening blues and whites, and the thought of a wide sapphire horizon-line, unhampered by the irregularities of building-tops, drove him toward the water-front, while in the depths of his consciousness lurked a determination to steal out to an open meadow before the day was done. Meanwhile the little streets encompassed him like a maze; and he thought and thought of Iris. A hand-organ reeled off an insinuating rag-time tune, and of his own accord, Mr. Jones began to dance. Sam permitted him to do so for the laughter of the children, the sole reward to be obtained from such an audience. Then he strolled away, ever toward the river, in a northerly direction that would ultimately lead toward the open country. And all the while Iris filled his heart and mind, as, indeed, she had done almost every moment since his angry parting from her.

It came to pass, that, being occupied with the thought of a red-haired girl, such as bore locks of a similar color arrested his eye more frequently and with a more personal interest than did any other type: and so it followed in natural sequence, that when he caught sight of a Titian head (elaborately puffed, and curled, to be sure, and quite unlike Iris' gleaming braids) behind the confusion of feminine articles of apparel in the window of a tiny notion-shop, he fancied a resemblance, and stopped to stare. And equally inevitable was it that she should feel that stare through the window glass and over the mass of articles therein displayed, as people have a way of feeling a stare; and looking up, she smiled upon the handsome gentleman whose gaze was riveted upon her. She was no more like unto Iris than the cinnamon-pink to the Ascension lily;

nor was she at all pretty. But Sam obeyed a sudden impulse and entered the tiny shop, followed by Mr. Jones.

Together they stood before the little counter upon which were piled coarse stockings, underwear with cheap lace trimming, unsubstantial neckwear, boxes of ruching, gingham aprons, bandannas (printed on one side only) and the headless, armless, stockinet torso of an extraordinary figure, presumably female, upon which was laced a purple satin corset. Overhead, petticoats of bengaline and sateen waists hung like banners at a festival, and neckties, alternating with balls of wool and mending cotton, festooned the edges of the shelves. A case of many-colored spool-silks, like a brilliant treasure-chest, and made up of shallow drawers such as gems are kept in, formed the background against which the shop-girl stood as she greeted him, while before her was the only unoccupied part of the counter—a twelve-inch square of painted wood upon which the tips of her long freckled fingers rested. She stood there, saying nothing, but smiling. What should he ask for? It was awkward, decidedly. Yet here he was, and somehow or other the situation must be managed. Very vaguely he uttered what seemed to him an inanity.

"I—I would like some buttonholes," he stammered, and then blushed furiously at having said such nonsense.

But the young lady seemed in nowise disconcerted by the extraordinary request.

"White or black?" she inquired calmly.

"Eh?" said Hill incredulously.

"I said, did you wish white or black buttonholes?" she smiled.

"But—but, great Scott! you don't mean to say you actually *have* 'em?" gasped Sam.

"Of course. This is a notion-shop; didn't you read the sign?"

"Notion-shop! I should say it was! How the deuce can a hole have a color? Is that one of the notions?" said he.

"I thought you didn't really want them," said the girl, "but we do keep 'em—embroidered on strips, you know, of black or white stuff—and you sew 'em in!"

"Oh!" said the enlightened male, "would you really not mind if I don't have any, though? I don't really need them. You see, you smiled, so I just . . ."

"So I guessed," said the girl, "but it ain't any use. I'm engaged."

"Ah!" said Hill, suddenly relieved of the absurd situation which he had brought upon himself. Then he added gallantly, "You don't expect me to be surprised, do you? He is such a very lucky fellow!"

"He is a rover," she said plaintively.

"A what?" queried Hill politely.

"A wanderer on the face of the earth," she elucidated. "He is in the lunch-wagon business, and not havin' a regular stand, it takes him to distant parts a lot. You seem to be the sort that travels, too," she added, "you an' the bear. Ain't he the cute little feller!"

Hill gave a huge sigh, and looked at her sentimentally.

"I wish you would say as much to me," he told her sweetly, and then felt almost as much of an ass as he looked.

But the lady spurned him with the air of a tragedy queen.

"You shouldn't ought to say such things," said

she loftily. "No matter what chances offer, I am ever true to Mr. Lovejoy."

The plain little lady's charms were so few (beyond the color of her hair) that Hill thought the dangers that awaited her at the hands of adoring swains were probably *non est*. But this conception seemed so at variance with her attitude, that he played up, and leaning over the counter in an attitude of intense admiration, said aloud that her temptations must be many.

"Mr. Lovejoy takes a great risk in being away so much," he added; "some day he will return to find that you have been stolen, kidnaped, Miss, Miss . . ."

"Call me Lola," said she; "my name is Lizzy Hinkle, but I like Lola La Farge better. I read it in a book."

"Miss La Farge, you are a wonder," said Hill sincerely. "When is the doughty lunch-wagoner going to marry you?"

"Soon's he can get the money," she confided to him.

"And shall you join him in his roving life, when that happy day arrives?" asked Hill.

"Yes!" she sighed. "It must be lovely to travel. I got this from him, recent. You see it's posted clear over in Jersey. And this one is from Yonkers. How I shall enjoy seeing the world!"

She gave two picture postal cards into his hand. They were warm and somewhat crumpled from being carried inside her pink shirt-waist, and had evidently been read to shabbiness. He took them, believing her to be joking on the question of journeys, but her earnest face betrayed the truth. Her lover's wanderings were, to her mind, travel. Hill examined the bits of pasteboard carefully in order to gain time in which to compose his expression. One of them bore a view of the Grand Hotel, Newark, in colors never yet seen upon a building made by hands; the other had the legend "I am thinking of you" printed upon it in red ink.

"Have you never traveled at all?" he asked as soon as he dared to raise his eyes.

"Oh! yes!" she answered. "I've been to Coney Island twice. But I've never been up-town. And I've always wanted to see Harlem, too. I've heard such a lot about it."

"Surely you're kidding me?" he asked.

"No, I *ain't!*" she disclaimed. "I was born right

around on Eighth Avenue, and I know more'n one that's been away less than me. And my ma is terrible strict, too. She's never let me go nowhere. Besides, there's the shop. I've been minding that ever since I left school."

"I don't wonder you want to get away!" exclaimed Sam.

"When I can go honest!" she added. "But meanwhile I do love to get picture-postals! It's next best to goin' yourself. I think this hotel must be swell, don't you? Round here there ain't so much color, is there?"

She held up the lithograph horror admiringly.

"No, not so much color," assented Hill; "and I'm afraid that even if one went all the way to Newark, one would find there post-cards depicting yet more distant spots which would seem more colored than the surroundings of this wonderful hotel. But such is life! However, may I send you a postal or two if I happen to wander to some far-off place—say Bronxville, for instance—or would Mr. Lovejoy object?"

"Oh! that would be grand!" said Lola, the freckled. "Thank you awfully, Mr. . . . What was the name?"

"Hill," said Sam, who usually answered so impulsively that he seldom remembered to lie.

"Mr. Hill, you are real kind," she beamed. "Mr. Lovejoy, he won't have no objections, I guess. Anyway, he won't know."

Though not pretty, she was a sweet little thing.

"True," said Hill. "There are many simple innocent occurrences that don't hurt us if we don't know about them. For instance, Mr. Lovejoy couldn't object because he wouldn't know if I . . . hum!"

Here Hill leaned very far over the counter, and Lola leaned very far toward him, doubtless to discover what he was referring to, which she quickly did, for he kissed her lightly upon the lips.

Then he turned, and went out, hurriedly, much astonished at himself and leaving Miss Lola La Farge *alias* Lizzy Hinkle, equally astounded, though not so much at what had happened, as at her own lack of any proper distress and regret. . . . A harmless, unaccountable little incident it was, one of the things that somehow do manage to happen, and leave us surprised, perhaps, but none the worse, and, as a matter of fact, none the less faithful than before.

So Lola tucked her post-cards into the bosom of her pink shirt-waist, straightened her ruffled red hair, and put away the buttonholes. After all, one does not need to have been to Harlem to be educated. . . .

.   .   .   .   .

As for Hill, he wandered off toward the river.

When noon came, he stopped at a dairy, and obtaining milk and doughnuts, sat down (by permission of the proprietor) upon the door-sill of that exit which led into the back yard, and the two men fell into conversation. For a while the talk was desultory, for customers came and went, but at length, this being the slack hour, they talked more consecutively and, falling upon the tariff, became absorbed. Suddenly there came a crash from the shop behind them, and they rushed in, just quickly enough to see Mr. Jones, who had overturned the protecting glass case, waddling off into the street, his paws filled with comb-honey which he had stolen from the counter.

"Stop, thief!" yelled the dairyman.

"Shut up! you'll collect a crowd!" yelled Hill. "Here, Jonesy! Here, Jonesy! come back, you villain, sir!"

"Hi! stop him, stop him!" shouted the dairyman, dancing upon the door-sill, but making no effort to run after and interfere with Mr. Jones. Already the neighborhood was beginning to take notice, and a little band had gathered interestedly about the shop, while half-way down the block a second group was following the sedate progress of the bear; maintaining a respectful distance, the while.

"Keep quiet! Cut it out!" said Hill to the dairyman roughly. "Here's all the money I've got. I'm sorry the case got smashed, but arresting me won't do a bit of good. I'll send you more money later."

With which he rushed out after his animal, leaving the little milk-seller still dancing for rage upon the door-sill, his white apron fluttering in the wind.

At the street corner sat Mr. Jones, busily engaged in consuming his stolen sweets. With great difficulty he was persuaded to part with some of the remainder, which a watchful urchin instantly seized upon and ran off with, followed by most of the little crowd; and the bear, dropping upon all fours, submitted to being chained to his master, and off they went toward the river, leaving a sticky trail upon the pavements as they passed.

Over the housetops the gray clouds of commerce

were flying to the unsullied heavens. Where, oh! where was a wide horizon-line? He turned up-town. All his money was gone again, and more he must have before returning to the tenement where Old Nita lay ill. A gradual progress brought him to Riverside Drive, and he had by then collected over a dollar. That was very little. Perhaps the children of the rich would pay.

Along the steep embankment he paraded his bear, and drew crowd after crowd of laughing youngsters, but the returns were small. A ferry-boat scuttled into dock, and the asphalt walk bringing him, on an abrupt turn, to the landing's very gate, he followed an impulse (and the bear) and stepped aboard.

"I shall go to Jersey City," said he, "and buy a postal card."

It proved a profitable trip, for the passengers gathered about Mr. Jones delightedly, and when the hat was passed (the bear did it) another dollar had been gained. Then the farther shore was reached, and the painter scrambled up the steep roadway to the top of the cliffs.

"Now that I have done my duty," said he to Mr. Jones, "I shall loaf; I *must* loaf. I *must* think of her uninterruptedly for a while. You know whom I mean, Mr. Jones: I'll leave her unnamed, as should be the case between gentlemen, but you will understand. I simply must have breathing space in which to think of her, and look at a wide expanse of sky. We shall walk along these cliffs until we are weary. Then we shall wander down toward the evil metropolis and take a ferry that will bring us out near home."

Mr. Jones grunted in reply, and they set off.

And so it came about that, what with one thing and another, Hill remained in Jersey until night fell, ate his supper from a crowded lunch-wagon near the docks, and afterward gave the wagon itself a minute and critical examination. The result of this last was, that as soon as he had done, he went to the nearest news-stand. Here he bought a postcard upon which was depicted a pea-green likeness of the local soldiers' monument, and wrote in the space for correspondence—"I had supper to-night with Mr. Lovejoy. His wagon is superb, and at the present rate of the business he has, I shall expect a wedding invitation inside a month." Then he signed his own name, appended the Jones Street address, and posted it. Then, much exhilarated by his "long thought" of Iris, and the piquant coincidence that had befallen him, he determined to turn the night to profit, and set to work among the river-front resorts.

. . . .

At midnight the Jersey shipyards are very still, and down toward where the docks are fewer, and farther apart, it is quiet indeed, once darkness has fallen. Here and there one hears the baying of humanity (so called) belching out from the swinging doorway of some low-ceilinged, evil-lighted den, the resort of poverty and brute strength, where the enormous energies engendered by outdoor work, find vent under the name of recreation. Against the outer darkness loom masses yet more dark, and sometimes a crimson light, like a dull jewel, smokes at the crest of these, when the indefinable bulk is a ship. The giant machinery of coal-yards and gas-tanks are but shadows upon the shades of night at this hour, their strength a hypothetical thing that you allow or ignore at will. Long spaces of cobbled irregular paving stretch away dimly, their darkness rendered deeper rather than relieved by the infrequent lamps. Again, at wide intervals, a flaring light illumines a throng of toilers, who, like the distorted creatures of a dream, rush about in methodical disorder, accomplishing the loading of some vessel that must sail at dawn. From the gaping mouth of such a hold, comes a stream of fire and a roar as of a prehistoric monster, where the rumbling trucks rush in and out. Then again the water-side stretches on in mystery, in darkness and silence. But whichever lies before one, the darkness or the inferno of light and noise, it is a wonderful picture; one to arrest the observer with its vast suggestive quality and arouse the desire to linger and watch.

Hill thought of this when he came out from one of the low saloons into the tingling cold of night, and saw the strange panorama that melted away on either hand. Mr. Jones did not agree that the shipping was of any interest whatsoever; *he* infinitely preferred the warmth and gaiety of the close little cabaret they left behind them. But Hill felt otherwise, and, being the more intelligent, had his way, and they walked slowly and scrutinizingly in the general direction of the down-town ferry.

Presently they reached a small covered dock where a greenish light was burning, in the glow of which some score of men were at work, loading great cases into the hold of a small third- or fourth-rate steamer. Although the scene was less flamboyant than several that they had passed, Hill was interested by the color of the light, and the manner in which it fell upon the group whose labor it illuminated: and so, unobserved by the watchman, he walked out to a dim sheltered corner of the pier, and stood quite still, making mental notes of the scene before him.

There seemed to be curiously little disorder or excitement in connection with this embarkment, a fact which soon impressed itself upon Hill's mind. Nor did the men appear to be in any particular hurry. Then a question obtruded itself. If they were not rushed, why did they work so late at night? It was rather odd. The cargo was odd, too. From the size, shape, and weight of the wooden cases of which it principally consisted, the shipment was evidently composed of pianos. Where on earth could so many pianos be going to? With a little effort he remembered the sign at the entrance to the dock—"The Venezuela Fruit Steamship Co." Ah! that accounted for it! Of course, it was only reasonable to suppose that Venezuela turned out very few pianos, if any. How quaint, though! He began to muse upon the melodious consignment, and, therefore, to observe the cases more closely. How odd that they should be put aboard at night! Then another thought flashed through his mind. Had he not read, or seen advertised somewhere, that these steamers sailed only bi-weekly? And this being a Monday, they would not sail before Wednesday. Why choose such an hour for loading them? How beastly uncomfortable, how unnecessary!

A man who had been directing the work, his back toward Hill, now turned about so that the light shone full upon his face, and at the sight of it Sam gave an involuntary cry of recognition, which, however, was lost in the general noise. It was Rowe! His tenant! Confound the man, there was something mysterious about him! What was he doing here, and at such an hour? The memory of their last meeting, and of Old Nita, came to him in a flash, and his hands clenched ominously. Here, perhaps, was a chance for retaliation! But before he could act on the impulse, several things happened all at once.

A piano-case, which was being lowered from a truck, was allowed to drop in such a way that it split open. From the aperture several objects fell out upon the pier. They were rifles! Field-rifles, new and shining!

With a snort of amazement Sam sprang forward, and at that same instant he felt himself seized upon either shoulder. Looking around, he saw that he was captive between two huge longshoremen, who proceeded to propel him toward the ship. As they came up with Rowe, who was cursing roundly, but had already managed to get the rifles out of sight, one of the ruffians called out: "Here's a detective, mister, disguised as a dago. We caught him spying just before the case broke."

With an oath, Rowe whipped around, and for a moment the two men stood glaring at each other.

"Take him aboard," said Rowe, breathing hard. "Captain's room, I'll be there directly."

"What the devil . . ." began Hill furiously. But he was cut short by Rowe, who struck him across the mouth.

Dazed by this needless insult, and wholly unable to retaliate because of his captors, Sam suffered himself to be led aboard, his custodians still holding him fast. No sooner was this done, and the door shut upon them, than it was opened again to admit Rowe, who was followed by a dark little Spaniard, presumably one of the ship's officers.

"Sit down," commanded Rowe, locking the door.

Hill paid no attention, standing speechless with rage. Rowe drew a revolver from his hip pocket, pulled up an armchair to one side of the table, and pointed to a second seat, which was placed opposite. He indicated the chair with the muzzle of his weapon.

"Sit down," he repeated politely.

Hill sat.

"Now, my dear mysterious landlord," began Rowe, "I have at last discovered your real trade. I always thought you were a rotten painter, but I never dreamed that you were a detective—a spy!"

"But I'm not!" exploded Hill, vainly endeavoring to appear calm. "Let me explain. I'm not watching . . ."

"Pardon me!" said Rowe. "Our last meeting, taken in connection with this one, explains the situation far more fully than any words of yours are likely to do. You are a government spy, and I suppose you are chortling at having caught us 'with the goods' as you Americans say."

"I haven't caught you at anything, so far as I know, except striking a tottering old woman!" responded Hill. "And, by God! I'm going to make you smart for that! As for being a secret-service man—you are all wrong, there!"

"Paugh!" exclaimed Rowe, flushing angrily, "what's the use of bluffing? Why don't you make a show of arresting us?"

"Look here!" exclaimed Hill, restrained from assaulting the man only by the sight of the gun that the other was still caressing. "Look here, you can't keep me like this, you know! I'm not a detective, and I don't even know what the devil you are making all this fuss about."

At this all the other men shouted with laughter. Rowe leaned over the table, an evil leer on his cunning face.

"No detective! ha! ha!" said he. "You don't really expect us to swallow that, do you? Why, next thing you'll be telling us that you didn't know it was contraband to take arms out of the country, eh?"

Hill sat back, shocked into momentary silence.

"I did not know it," he said simply.

The quiet that followed these five clear-cut words was charged with electricity. Then, Rowe, his face very white, his eyes fixed upon Hill, rose to his feet.

"By God! I believe you are speaking the truth!" he said at length.

"That's one joke on you, Ricardo," said the little Spanish officer with a short mirthless laugh.

"Well, he knows it now, if he didn't before!" put in one of the longshoremen.

Hill said nothing at all, but sat staring at the group in wonderment. What on earth did it all mean?

"That's true. You needn't inform me of it," said Rowe bitterly, "and detective or not, he'll inform now if we let him go. But he's a service man, all right," he added, his confidence in himself returning. "Wasn't he up at Mikey's? Hell! something must be done with him; and something *will* be done, never fear! I will get the Señor Chief, and he shall help us decide the matter."

The little officer nodded, and Rowe, slipping out of the cabin, closed the door behind him. In silence they waited, while a thousand conjectures whirled through Hill's brain. What had he stumbled upon? In exactly what nefarious business were these men engaged? Could he trick them into letting him go?

What would they do to him? Suddenly he missed the bear. What had become of Mr. Jones? Doubtless the poor beast would be hopelessly lost. . . .

In a moment more, footsteps were heard outside in the passage. The door handle grated, and Hill, bracing himself for whatever was to come, swung about and found himself face to face with Iris' father, the Honorable Reginald Vanderpool—Millionaire Asphalt King.

CHAPTER XII

A COMPROMISE

THE day on which Iris came to Pedro's studio for her second pose was not that which had been appointed, but one nearly a week later. During the intervening period the young painter had remained locked in the studio as long as daylight lasted, emerging only at night, in company with Leigh.

Pedro had given her no explanation for putting her off, simply sending word that he could not have her at present, but would get some work done on the background of the portrait. To Leigh he had made no reference to the sudden depression that had settled upon him like a pall, and Leigh bided the time when Pedro would confide in him. It is to be noted that this great test of congeniality was successful, putting the final link to their bond of friendship; for the trouble, although untold, drew them closer, instead of creating a breach between them.
. . . Incidentally, this was an excellent moment

for such a mood to have come upon the youth, for the two were arranging for a little exhibition, and it gave them ample opportunity to avoid personalities. They were giving the "two-man's-show" partially to please themselves, partially because Theodore Pell's unconscious boost through the Associated Press was bringing about results, and the time seemed ripe.

Iris had telephoned several futile invitations, and at last, catching Pedro on the wire, had arranged for a sitting. At the hour appointed, she mounted the stairs slowly, with fast-beating heart, starting and trembling at every sound within the ancient building. What if Cassie should see her? For, notwithstanding her resolves to the contrary, Iris had again come alone! These last few days, when she had been unable to see Pedro, had but added fuel to the flame she already burned at his shrine, and it had come to such a pass that she felt it almost a necessity to her continued existence to be with him— alone with him in that exciting atmosphere which his personality created, and to which she was not as yet conscious of contributing largely herself. That he always appeared unconscious of this electrical atmosphere, mattered not at all. Whether he wished it or not, she must see him, must be with him, at whatever cost to her pride or vanity.

She reached the door unchallenged, and rapped upon it.

"Lady! Most gracious Madonna!" he cried in greeting. "See, here is the blue robe—quick, quick! I am all impatience to begin. Do you know the good tidings? Of the ridiculously audacious thing I am going to do? Exhibit my pictures! Yes! *me*. Pedro! Ha! ha! I am not unknown, it seems! Read the newspapers. I am Pedro, the great Spanish artist! I do not know how to paint, but it matters not: they will say 'an impressionist—Matisse outdone!' Ah! ha! your portrait will be the chief gem of the display. In two weeks comes the exhibition, so I must finish it soon, soon!"

"Where are all the canvases?" asked Iris, looking about her. "There were simply shoals, and now—"

"Leigh has taken most of them," he laughed, "some to be framed for the show, and some for himself. And De Bush, he has two. I am rather frightened at my sudden fame. I have already orders for two cover designs for magazines. And Leigh made me say two hundred dollars each, no less!

A COMPROMISE

Wait, *wait!* I must tell you the most funny part of all—*they are going to pay it!*"

"You seem surprised," replied Iris, who, it must be remembered, had no reason for doubting the newspaper story which was the gage of Pedro's position that she had decided to accept.

"Surprised?" said he, with a lift of the eyebrows. "Tut, tut! Of course not! Am I not Pedro, the great Spanish artist?"

Whereupon he burst into a gale of laughter, and set about arranging the light.

Iris slipped into her blue robe, slightly puzzled by his wild mood, but finding it charming none the less. How far removed from her he always seemed! Here she had come full of sentiment, of personal interest, and he met her with a gaiety and an impersonal enthusiasm that were only for the model which would enable him to continue work on his picture.

During the first part of the pose, he, contrary to his usual habit, talked rapidly.

"It will be a lovely exhibition!" said he, "there will be Leigh's stuff—beautiful marbles, rich in form, and with such textures and high lights. *You* know! And the virginal white bas-reliefs—the joyous one of the ladies dancing—what a difference it makes which way one says it. 'Ladies dancing,' or 'dancing-ladies'—English, eh? And there will be his group with the lions, and the fountain that he did for H. G. Ball. The General Grant, too—the equestrian—a small cast of it. That is for the center of the gallery. And around the walls, between these things will hang many gorgeous paintings by that great Spanish painter—myself."

Iris could not but laugh with him.

"And of all these fine pictures," he continued, "the most lovely will be a Madonna with hair that is red-gold, like joy! Calmly she will gaze down upon the vacant room. Then the exhibition will open. Oh! the anxious hearts of that great sculptor and that noted painter! Pretty soon, in will come two girl art students and one newspaper reporter. The reporter will not look at the pictures or the sculpture; he will take a catalogue from the little stand by the door, and as he goes out again he will say to the young man in charge, 'Are they any good?' and the young man will reply, 'They must be: they have already paid for the use of the gallery,' by which, perhaps, the reporter will be influenced and write a favorable criticism accordingly. The two art students will run around quickly, saying 'rotten, rotten!'—peck at everything, and go out—still saying—'rotten, rotten!' Then, some one who is tired will wander in, because there is a bench to sit down upon. Then more students, who will say 'rotten', and go out. If it rains, it will be much better. Probably many will go in if it rains—it is a free shelter—and afterward, they will say at dinner parties: 'Have you been to the exhibition at Mason's? I dropped in the other day. Very poor, very poor!' and feel themselves art patrons, even as they say it! I hope it rains. It is thus that one becomes famous."

"Pessimist!" she accused him.

"Merely contemptuous," he assured her. Then there was silence and he worked fiercely, cruelly, for, as usual, he forgot the rests, and it grew late before either spoke.

At last, exhausted by the long pose, by his indifference, by her own emotions, she could bear it no longer, but holding out her arms toward him, she swayed slightly, and said his name in a broken voice.

"Pedro!"

Then he saw how white and drawn her face had become, and with a little cry he dropped his palette and sprang to her side.

"Madonna!" he said, "forgive me! Come down! So! Let me help you. Lie here upon this couch. Oh! I am cruel and thoughtless!"

Whimpering a little, she clung to his arm, burying her face in the crotch of his elbow, fondling his hand.

"Pedro, Pedro, I am so tired!" she said over and over again.

Distressed, he tried to sooth her, stroking her hair, adjusting the sofa pillows with a surprising deftness, and accusing himself bitterly. Then he gently disengaged his arm and made her lie down.

"I know! A little sherry!" he exclaimed. "A bite of luncheon! You will see now what a splendid housewife I can really be, at need. We will have a charming meal directly."

He poured wine into an antique Venetian glass, and brought it to her, clasping both her hands about the fragile thing as one would clasp a child's untrained fingers around a precious toy.

"Drink!" he commanded, "and lie quite still with your lovely head among the caressing pillows. You are an Eastern Queen now, and I your humble serving-slave. See! Like magic the feast shall appear!"

With an encouraging laugh, he twisted a bit of

A COMPROMISE

crimson silk about his head for a turban, and salaamed before her.

All this was not what Iris had wanted when she held out her hands with that piteous little cry; but beggars must take what they can get, and so she lay obediently among the cushions, a faint color coming back to her cheeks, a tremulous smile playing about her lips, and in her eyes, all the love and longing which Pedro would or could not see.

Meanwhile, he drew up a little round table before the hearth, stirred the dying embers with fresh wood, threw an Arabian cloth over the table and proceeded to lay the feast.

"*Foigras*—behold!" he said, with a flourish as he placed it before her. "Knives, one fork. Ah! lovely plates from Dresden, and biscuits from London. Sardines, too. I saw such as these caught in blue water—ah, so blue!—and they flashed and glittered in the nets like captive quicksilver! Here are grapes —your own gift to me. In this magic urn I will make coffee *a la turc*. And do you know this cordial? 'Forbidden fruit'—it is called. And cigarettes of Russia with little paper holders growing on the ends! The nations serve you, oh, queen!"

She sat up and allowed him to feed her. The solitary fork gave them much cause for mirth, for she insisted that they share it, and before the meal was finished they were playing like children.

Pedro's moods were generally irresistible, and he was determined that she forget and forgive his thoughtlessness. As he sat opposite, seeing her cameo-like beauty, he thought for the hundredth time that Hill had chosen well. Small wonder that the latter had been driven to despair by her! And she—did she still care for the absent painter? She seldom spoke of him, and that argued well for Hill's cause. And what had parted these two? Some silly, silly quarrel, he again assured himself. How well matched they were, how admirably suited to each other! But how about the girl's attitude toward himself . . .? A subtle smile crept to the corners of his mouth at the thought, and he hastily took his eyes from her face, looking intently at the glowing cigarette between his fingers instead.

"What is the matter?" she asked. "A second ago you were merry. Now you look quiet, wise—*dangerous!* How you change!"

"Dangerous! Far from it!" he exclaimed, pushing back his chair, "that is, unless you call overwhelming curiosity dangerous. Personally I think it less dangerous than a lack of curiosity; to the individual, at least."

"And what makes you curious?" she asked.

"You would think me impertinent."

"Never!" said she with such vehemence that he looked up in surprise.

"Yes, you would," he said.

"Try me!" she begged.

Then Pedro, who did not know how to lead gently up to any subject, plunged in.

"Were you engaged to Hill?" he asked abruptly.

Without answering, she arose and walked away to the window, where she stood for several moments before replying, her back turned.

"Yes," she said at last.

"And do you still care for him?"

To her own intense surprise she found that she could not reply at once.

"I beg your pardon, Madonna," said Pedro softly.

"Oh! you don't understand!" she cried wildly, throwing out her hands. "I don't care, I *hate*—oh! why did you ask me?"

"I think I *do* understand," he said very distinctly, looking straight at her.

A wave of crimson flooded her cheeks. What did

he mean? Unable to face him longer, she buried her face in her hands. He came toward her and stood where he could have touched her. One hand was in his pocket, the other held his glass of cordial, the "forbidden fruit", and that subtle smile played about his mouth and eyes, as though he were at once sad and amused.

"Sam Hill is a great soul," said he softly. "He is generous and good. He is talented, he is . . ."

"He is nothing to me!" she gasped, looking up.

"He is my friend," finished Pedro firmly.

She flung her arms wide, and turned to him with an appealing gesture, her face revealing an emotion she made no attempt to conceal, nor he to ignore.

"Pedro!" she began passionately, "you will think me mad for saying it, but ah! I can not help it—you *make* me! Pedro, I love . . ."

There was a crash as his liqueur-glass fell to the floor.

"Hush!" said he.

"What is it?" she asked, for the moment startled into normality.

"Nothing!" said he, "only that you are not to finish your sentence. Never mind the glass, it was done intentionally. Let us talk of other things."

A COMPROMISE

"But, Pedro," she said hysterically, "I can not! I am possessed! How can you be so cruel?"

"Please, *please!*" he begged her. "Madonna, I am abject; I am in torture! Have pity!"

"It is akin to pity," she replied.

There was silence. Outside, upon the snow-filled ledges the sparrows squabbled noisily, and from the street came the sound of a barrel-organ playing an aria from a defunct Italian opera.

Pedro walked to the hearth and stooped to mend the fire. Then he straightened up and spoke.

"Impossible!" he said quietly. "Utterly impossible."

And she, watching him intently, knew he had believed her, although he presented this denial. She felt, too, that her cause was nearly hopeless.

"You do not care, then," she said in a low voice.

"Madonna Lady," he said sadly, "I care for you a great deal, but not as Hill does; not as a man should, to be your lover. You charm me beyond words; you are lovely as a dream, and if I could love any woman, it would be you—but, you are not for me."

"Why not?" she asked sharply, between her tortured breaths.

"The reason is beyond my power to alter," said Pedro.

"Then," said she, "I suppose I had better go. Shall you wish to finish the picture?"

"Iris!" he cried in a suddenly changed tone, "come here, listen! Of course, I want to finish the picture; it is going to be good! And what is more, if you will be so gracious, with your permission *we* will finish it, and renew our friendship at the same time."

"Friendship!" said she, with a mirthless little laugh.

He threw back his head proudly.

"We are not of the common herd," said he. "And we can do things which weak persons are unable to accomplish! Surely we are bigger than the circumstances in which we are placed. At least, we can become so if we will."

"Become friends?" she asked.

"Certainly!" said he. "For us that is perfectly possible. For the ordinary man and woman, no! I grant you it would be too hard. But for *us!* Ah! that is quite a different matter, I assure you!"

There was a pause, during which she hesitated, biting her lip.

"Very well," said she in a resigned voice. But inwardly she was resolved far otherwise. He recognized this, but the situation had lasted long enough.

"Come!" he cried, with an attempt at putting the incident behind them, "I must talk to you about something very important. You asked me to help you find out who was troubling your father."

"Yes," she assented, without much interest, however.

"Well," said he slowly, "I am most distressingly placed, Madonna. I am almost certain that he is being either blackmailed or misled in some manner, and yet my hands are absolutely tied. I can do nothing."

"What do you mean?" she demanded, aroused.

"I seem fated to be a man of mystery," he lamented, "but I can not help it! I have ascertained that a man of doubtful character is in communication with your father; that much I learned last week. But at the instant of my discovery of this fact, a circumstance arose that makes it impossible for me to continue as your detective. More than this I can not say. But you will have to find some one else to help you."

Iris was turning the matter over in her mind very rapidly. Did Pedro really not care for her? Hardly! Why he said such things . . . He had followed her from the country! Had he not begged to paint her, and paid her such compliments as no one yet had done? That night at the Milligans came back with a rush of memory. Ah! he had surely cared then! What had since occurred to change him? Samuel Hill! That was it! He had learned of her former attachment, and meant at all costs to be loyal to the man who had befriended him. It is not easy to believe that one's love meets with no return, and this theory fitted her need very nicely. And now, she decided, that he might the more easily maintain his resolution of loyalty, Pedro was determined to cut off that claim to intimacy incident to the investigation of her father's trouble. But he should not do so. No! a thousand times—no! Something must be done to make him see, quite clearly and unmistakably, that his sacrifice to Hill's trust of him was a vain and useless thing. But how was this to be accomplished? Meanwhile, Pedro was still talking.

"I say with regret, that I have every reason to believe that your father is being defrauded in some way. The character of the man with whom I saw him, is sufficient to justify my saying this. Also, alas! this same man now appears to be standing in such a connection with me as makes it impossible for me to inform any ordinary person of the facts. I might injure an innocent—undoubtedly innocent— person by so doing, to say nothing of perhaps letting out a secret which your father's actions prove he wishes kept dark. For a whole week I have been trying to see my way clear, and at last I know that it lies only in refusing to help you."

"And yet," said Iris slowly, rising and putting on her wraps, "I would reward the right person to the best of my ability, if only the work of helping, perhaps saving, my father could be continued."

He gave her the muff for which she stretched out her hand.

"I wish indeed that I could help you," said he. "I know the danger of confiding so delicate a matter to any one. But, perhaps, for a reward—what would it be, this reward?"

For an instant the audacity of what she was about to say rose like an impediment in her throat, holding her silent, while her heart beat violently. Then, at last, she found her voice.

"I would marry him, no matter though he thought there were insurmountable objections," she said with meaning.

He stood astounded, scarcely able to credit his hearing, and could only look and look at her, open-mouthed. Then a gleam of light swept across his face as though he were suddenly possessed of a glorious idea.

"Iris!" he gasped "will you—will you put that down on paper? Make an—what you call it—affidavit?"

"Affidavit?—yes!" she replied.

"Then do so!" he cried, pushing pen and paper toward her.

"Do you really want it?" she asked, looking straight into his eyes.

"You bet!" he shouted joyously.

She laid down her muff, and drawing off her glove, she wrote:

"I hereby promise to marry you on the day you can tell me my father is not being subjected to danger, or has been rescued from that, if any, which now imperils him. And I furthermore agree to overcome any debatable objections you may have to the marriage. IRIS VANDERPOOL."

A COMPROMISE

"There!" she said, laughing a trifle hysterically, when she had finished, "will that do?"

"Splendidly!" said Pedro, and thrusting the folded paper into his breast pocket, seized her hand and kissed it with the grace of a courtier.

Iris blushed, watching him with tender eyes. Then she submitted to being led down-stairs and shut into her coupé. No sooner was this accomplished than Pedro fled across the little court and up to the studio as if all the devils in the demonology were after him, and slamming the door behind him, he proceeded to dance the coquette at a mad pace, upsetting several articles of furniture in the process.

"And now to find Mr. Samuel Hill!" he shouted gleefully, waving the paper above his head.

"Ah! *Meestre Samhill,*" was echoed in a wail from outside the door. "Where, oh! where is he?"

CHAPTER XIII

SOME ADVENTURES WITH VARIATIONS

PEDRO stared at the door as if transfixed, and then, the wail being repeated, he opened his portal. On the landing stood Guneviere.

"Madre de Dios!" he exclaimed, "what ails thee? Come in."

"Oh! 'tis terrible!" moaned Guneviere, "that Anna! that irresponsible one! We left her in charge, and when she awoke Nita had vanished. And every one was away. And now *Samhill,* he, too, is gone! Oh! Merciful Mother!"

"Sit down and be calm!" cried Pedro. "Tell me all. What has happened?"

"Lucky it is that *Samhill* left the address!" exclaimed Guneviere. "And lucky, too, that I could find thee. Now, all will be well!"

"Thanks, oh! smooth tongue, for thy faith in me," replied Pedro. "But what has happened? Tell me, quickly!"

"Yesterday we left her with Anna," began Guneviere, and told of Nita's illness, and strange disappearance.

"How very queer!" he commented, when she had finished. "How unlike Nita! And Hill? What has he done?"

"He has not come home!"

"But there is nothing strange in that!" objected Pedro. "Does he not often stay away all night, eh?"

"But the bear came home!" wailed Guneviere.

"Mr. Jones! *Alone!* Impossible!"

"A policeman-of-the-law brought him," explained Guneviere, "saying that he found the bear near the river. The name was on the collar, and the number, *tv savis!*"

"Saint Joseph! but that does look serious!" Pedro exclaimed. "Quick! is there nothing more?"

"Only that the policeman-of-the-law made much noise when he found that four bears dwelt within the tenement. He says we must move out. Four bears are not permitted. One bear—*perhaps,* if much money be paid. But four! No, that is not allowed!"

"And what have you done?"

"We have arranged to go into the *back* tenement," said Guneviere, evidently convinced that the change would solve the difficulty.

"But, Hill! Something must have happened to him? And the bear left him!" said Pedro, walking up and down excitedly. "He may have been hurt! Near the river, eh? Good heavens! I scarcely dare guess what has occurred!"

"The hospitals?" suggested Guneviere with some faint return of her usual practicality.

"Ah! yes," he exclaimed, "I shall telephone them at once, and then I shall go to Jones Street with you. As for Nita, we shall have to find her without help; she has made me swear never to invoke public aid in her behalf, you know."

"Yes, yes!" said Guneviere, "you will come then?"

"Directly!" he cried. "No time must be lost."

But as it proved, time mattered little, for the hospitals told nothing, and neither did that grim lost and found office, the morgue. For two whole days Pedro alternated between his studio and the rear tenement on Jones Street, his mind in an agony of uncertainty. He could not work for nervousness, and the combined suspense and inaction played havoc with his spirit. Leigh had been called out of town to see his mother, who was ill, and there was no one else whom Pedro dared go to for advice and help.

Hill himself had forbidden that his affairs be made known to any one but the sculptor, or Pedro might have asked Milligan's assistance. As it was, he could only fume impatiently, and eat his heart out with worry. At last, no longer able to endure doing nothing, he called a council of war in the tenement kitchen. To the assembled bear-dancers, with exception only of the still mysteriously absent Nita, he arose and spoke.

"I am going to find Sam Hill, if he is on the face of the earth!" he announced. "I am convinced that some misfortune has befallen him. In half an hour I am going to take Mr. Jones with me, and I am not coming back till we have succeeded in discovering the whereabouts of my friend."

"*Bien!* And I," said Beau-Jean, from his seat on the foot of the bed. "I will go with you to find that *Samhill,* who is my friend, *avssi.*"

"But Rico must not go!" cried Anna, with an anxious glance at her lover.

"No, I will remain with thee, little blossom that shall bear my fruit," said Rico tenderly.

"Since thou hast learned of the coming child, thou art of no earthly use!" grumbled Guneviere. "Go thou, my husband, and be right arm to our Pedro."

"Have I not said it already?" demanded Beau-Jean.

"Carlos and Rico will have to provide while we are gone!" said Pedro, with the air of a general. "Guneviere, pursue your search for Nita, and we also shall be looking for her. Most likely we shall find the partners together, in perfect safety."

"How we have missed thee, little one!" cooed Guneviere. "Now that thou art here amongst us again, all will go well."

"Very good!" said Pedro, "all is arranged. Come, Strong Arm, we will go."

On the instant they began collecting the few traps necessary for a short absence, and while they were in the midst of these preparations, the door was thrown open to admit an old woman.

"*Nita!*" yelled Pedro, springing toward her.

Instantly the room was in an uproar, all talking at once, laughing and weeping, shouting questions, making offers of help, proffering food and drink, crowding around the crone with such clamor and persistence that Pedro could scarcely manage to get her to a chair. Then she sat beaming upon them all, apparently in the best of health and delighted at the welcome afforded her. Her clothes were, if possible, a trifle more worn and soiled than usual, but, otherwise, she seemed to have suffered no harm.

"Where hast thou been? What hast thou done? Where is *Samhill?* Art well? Tell us!" they shouted all at once.

"Aye, I am well, lucky for me!" said Nita, with twinkling eyes, "for I have been a bird in my day, and I am in no haste to meet what awaits me in the hereafter."

"Beloved Nita!" exclaimed Pedro, kneeling beside her, "how I rejoice that thou art safe! But where is Mr. Hill?"

"*Samhill?*" she queried. "I have not seen him, nor thought of him! I have been abroad on other business. What of *Samhill?*"

"Don't you know?" cried Anna. And then the clangor began anew. Not know where *Samhill* was? Where could he be, then? Did she not even know of his disappearance? What had she been doing? etc., etc.

For answer, she took Pedro's face between her old hands that were like withered leaves.

"Dost thou know who is in the city?" she asked. "Thine enemy and mine, Ricardo! He struck me, and I was senseless. But when mine eyes opened, I arose and went in search of him. I took the long slender *machete* with the handle of pearl, but I found him not. There was a woman with him : . . ."

"Yes," said Pedro, "my mother."

"Then thou, too, hast seen him! Where?" she asked eagerly. "And with thy *mother?* Surely you are mad?"

"Not mad, only bewildered, and frightened," he answered. "I know where they are, but not for what purpose! I shall tell thee all that I have seen, but not now. Can't you hear the others saying that my benefactor has vanished? Before anything else we must find and help him, if need be."

"Where is Ricardo and thy mother?" asked Nita, her eyes fixed upon Pedro's, and her hand closed tightly upon some object that was hidden among the bundled shawls and scarfs about her waist. Pedro's eye followed the movement.

"It is very far from here, oh, ancient lady," he lied glibly, "and I shall not tell you where until I return. Then we shall attend to your little matter, and I shall see why and how my mother comes in such company. My mother!" he turned away and sighed. "I had forgotten how I love her!" he said as though to himself. Then he picked up the pole and chain, and signaled to Beau-Jean that he was ready. Nita arose to her feet.

"Where is the murderer, the seducer of my daughter?" she screamed. "Where is Ricardo?"

"At the other end of the city," said Pedro. "Come quickly, Beau-Jean."

And with that they were off, leaving Nita screeching imprecations at them from the stair-head, in the most healthy manner. As they reached the street Beau-Jean asked:

"What is all this murder business of which Nita talks? Couldn't we manage to avenge her, when we have found *Samhill?*"

"Perhaps," said Pedro soberly, "for this man, Ricardo Valdez, is a very wicked man. He used to live near my home. Nita was my nurse, once, and her daughter was my foster-sister. When she was only fifteen, Ricardo stole her away. Then he deserted her, and when she came back to us, she killed herself and her baby. Ever since then Nita has been looking for him, to avenge her child. But she is so old now, that I think we had best not let her do it. I am sure she would really prefer dying with us, to dying in jail!"

"I agree," said Beau-Jean.

"And now, which way shall we turn?" said Pedro.

"As the bear came from the river, let us to the river go," suggested Beau-Jean.

"A good notion," said Pedro, "and as likely to prove fruitful as any."

"More likely up-town, than down, from here," said Beau-Jean, and again Pedro assented.

And so, in accordance with the plan, if plan it could be properly called, they made their way westward, straight toward the docks, and once reaching them, began a pilgrimage up-town, wending an intricate way among trucks, cabs, autos, longshoremen and sailors, Jew-pedlers, market-wagons and ambling horse-cars.

Just what they expected to find, it would be hard to say, but they went along hopefully, stopping now and again to peer into the recesses of some covered dock, or through the dim windows of a water-front shop, sometimes stopping to exchange a word or two with the proprietor, or whomsoever was about. Suddenly a doubt came to Pedro.

"Are you sure this is the right river?" he asked. "There are two—one on the East Side."

"This is the one," said Beau-Jean, and they continued up-town, past old houses, cheap houses, tall clean warehouses, and tall dirty warehouses, until they came to Thirteenth Street, where the railroad runs, unfenced, unprotected, upon the open avenue. Here the tenements were more in evidence, and the little children ran out over the tracks as they played. Between the winding crisscross of rails were dirty scarred remnants of the snow, and on the narrow pavements lay the refuse from the dwellings. Buildings for the storing of foods, and shacks belonging to the railroads, were placed at irregular intervals throughout the yards, and in between these and the street, wound the tracks. The obstructing buildings often made it impossible to see an approaching engine part of the time, and the intricate network in which the rails were laid, made guessing which direction the train would take, a difficult and deceptive problem. Twice, within a few blocks they were nearly run over, and when Mr. Jones pulled Pedro down a side street out of the dangerous thoroughfare, Beau-Jean followed with a sigh of relief.

Mr. Jones now began acting in a most peculiar manner. Something on the sidewalk had attracted his attention, and nothing could divert him until he had made a thorough inspection. To Beau-Jean and to Pedro there appeared to be nothing on the pavement but a good deal of dirt and refuse; but one particular spot seemed to have fascinated Mr. Jones, and there was nothing for it but to stand waiting while he nosed about.

"Shall I chasten him?" asked Beau-Jean, who was accustomed to using this method with Koko.

"No, certainly not," said Pedro, "I believe he's been here before. Perhaps he recognizes something. Let us watch!"

Pedro's surmise was an eminently correct one, for Mr. Jones had recognized—*honey!* Very shortly he raised his head, found the scent, and came upon a second spot of interest. How delightful!—this was the neighborhood in which he had found that nice hive where there were no bees to sting, and where the honey was so plentiful! He really had not taken half of it last time! And here were his own footsteps, his sticky honey-made footprints, which would help him to find the treasure again. St. Bruin be praised! They washed the sidewalks of this neighborhood no more than they did the forest-trails. Again he sniffed and pawed, and the two who followed him began to be of a single mind regarding his familiarity with the place. Meanwhile, the children were crowding about, following the animal's slow progress. Thus it happened that in time they reached the doorway of the little dairy, which Mr. Jones recognized with a joyful bound, and a sort of purr, which brought the dairyman (who had spied him through the window) to the entrance, with a shower of abuse ready at hand.

"Get out of this, youse!" shouted the milk-vender. "Don't you dast ter come in, any of youse! I ain't-a-goin'-ter sell yer nothin'. Get off, you smashin' murderin' bunch of dagoes! I'll set the cop on yer if yer don't skidoo!"

"Why?" asked Pedro, wildly excited. "But why won't you sell to us?"

"Go on now! none o' yer back-talk!" growled the man. "I sold to one dago feller with a bear last week, an' the brute eat up all me comb-honey! So get out; quit talkin'."

"A man with a bear?" cried Pedro, scarcely able to believe his ears. "I'll bet it's the one I want to find. That bear he had belongs to me."

"Well, what do I care for that?" said the milk-vender sourly. "Get out, or will I call the cop?"

"Which way did he go?" persisted Pedro—"same way as we came?"

A malicious smile came upon the weazened features of the dairyman. Here was a chance to mislead and annoy a bear-dancer, and to do so was a wondrous source of satisfaction.

"He went this way, bad luck to him!" he lied, pointing east, "if yer catch up with him, I hope the bear eats both of yer!"

With which Christian sentiment he slammed the door, and the interested crowd set up a laugh. Angrily, Beau-Jean shouted them away.

"Shall I thrash them all?" he asked of Pedro.

"Nay, let them be," responded the lad, adding eagerly, "let us be off! This news may lead to something."

"I think the man was lying," said Beau-Jean. "Let us retrace our steps."

"I don't agree!" replied Pedro. "This way seems to me more likely."

And as usual, he won his point. Once more they joined the busy many-hued shifting panorama of the crowded street. They steered a straight course, for they knew not what else to do. Both kept on the alert, and after them a little straggling crowd of children followed, like the ragged tail of a kite.

When they had been walking for about half an

hour, Pedro laid his hand upon the arm of his companion.

"Look, Beau-Jean!" said he. "Look, there, in the window of the little shop of women's finery! See the girl with the red-gold hair? I am painting a picture of the Holy Mother, and the hair is of just such a color!"

"Indeed!" said Beau-Jean soberly. "It is a terrible color. Do you think that the Holy Mother will be pleased?"

"I had not thought of that!" replied Pedro. Then he added suddenly—"Oh! see, the shop-lady knows Mr. Jones!"

It was true. The red-haired girl had given very animated signs of recognizing the bear, and lifted her gaze to the persons in whose company he appeared, with a smile on her lips, which swiftly gave way to a look of disappointment as she met their eyes.

"Wait!" said Pedro, halting before the door, "that lady has seen this bear before, or I am much mistaken! And what is more, she expected to see some one she knew, when she looked at us! Come in, I want to buy some thread."

Whereupon, he opened the door, and with the bear, entered the crowded little shop, leaving Beau-Jean gasping out on the pavement.

Behind the purple satin corset and the dangling neckties stood the smiling Lola La Farge, *alias* Lizzy Hinkle.

"What can I do for you?" she asked, laying aside the bit of knitting upon which she had been engaged.

"Thread, please!" said Pedro, flashing his smile at her.

"What color?" she inquired, admiring his eyes and teeth.

"Er—ah—green, please!" said Pedro, because her eyes were rather of that color, and consequently it came first to mind: "Green, and a needle, please."

"A needle!" she exclaimed, "you mean a package of needles!"

"I only need one at a time," he told her. Would she speak of the bear? Ah! she was going to!

"Seems as if training bears and sewing didn't go together very good," she giggled. "There was a gent in here not long ago, who didn't know much more'n you! He had a bear, too!"

"Yes?" said Pedro.

"Yes, indeed," she responded, busily getting out the articles he had named. "I do declare to goodness, I thought this was the very identical bear, when I seen you coming!"

"It is the identical bear," remarked Pedro.

"What!" said she, with a little shriek of surprise—"well, I never! How is the other feller? Ain't he got the bear with him then?"

"No, I've got him!" said Pedro dryly.

"You don't say!" exclaimed the girl, peering over the counter, as though seeing the animal for the first time.

"And so you know my pal, eh?" said Pedro. "Now that *is* nice!"

He smiled again, and, as was usually the case, hypnotized her into instant response. Encouraged by his interest, and by the fact of their mutual friend, she drew a postal card—*not* from the bosom of her pink shirt-waist—from her pocketbook.

"Well, I certainly *do* know him!" said she. "I had this postal from him only three days ago!"

Trying not to seem over-eager, he took it and read the postmark and the signature. It was Hill's and came from Jersey City! At last the scent was getting warm. What good fortune! But he must not seem too anxious, or she might grow reticent. Diplomacy, diplomacy!

"You are treated better than I am!" he complained whimsically. "I haven't even had a card! But then, you are a lady, which makes all the difference. Ah! woman, lovely woman! How you fascinate and abuse us!"

She giggled self-consciously.

"So this is the latest news of Hill!" said Pedro. "I suppose you write to each other frequently?"

"Well, no!" said she. "You see, I'm engaged. I told Mr. Sam it was useless, but he's so persistent."

She giggled again.

"Poor Sam!" said Pedro. "You are very cruel!"

"Do you happen to know his Jersey address?" she asked, thereby giving Pedro the information he wanted, to wit: that she was unaware of Hill's present whereabouts.

"Oh! he was only there for a day!" said Pedro, putting the coin which she indicated out of his handful, upon the counter. "He might drop in here any time. If he does, tell him Pedro was asking for him, will you? And now, good-by; I must be off!"

He leaned over the counter to pick up his package, and she leaned over the counter to help him, perhaps. Her face was very near, and her puckered mouth sweet and red, despite the fact that she was so far from pretty. Yet Pedro took no base advantage of the opportunity, and having secured his infinitesimal bundle, lifted his hat and bowed her a graceful farewell. Pouting a little, she flung him a taunt as he reached the door.

"I like Mr. Sam the best," she said.

As Pedro joined his waiting companion outside, he was met with a string of reproaches.

"Never before have I seen you tarry so long with a woman, oh, waster of precious moments!" said Beau-Jean. "How shall it benefit thee?"

"It has already done so!" declared Pedro. "Come, hasten with me. We are going to Jersey City. I shall explain on the way."

So off they went to the ferry, Mr. Jones, the inadvertent detective, shuffling after.

To discover where the picture post-card had been purchased, would have been almost impossible; but to locate the district in which it had been mailed was easy enough, and that, combined with the hour which had been stamped upon it, was sufficient evidence to show that Sam had been near the waterfront at some time between eight and ten o'clock on the evening of the previous Monday. Consequently, the next problem that confronted them was what Hill had done after dropping this exquisite chromo into a district "X" pillar-box? Pedro at once tried to picture his own probable actions were he to find himself in such a district at such an hour, with, presumably, no company but Mr. Jones! Ah! of course! the cabarets—the saloons of the dance! That seemed the obvious answer, but he consulted with Beau-Jean, to be certain. . . . Yes, Beau-Jean would make straight for the cafés, and Hill had probably done the same, if one were to consult him, the Provençal! In these low drinking places were many sailors and longshoremen, who were free with their money and laughed very much to see a bear perform. Doubtless, *Samhill* would go to some of these. And certainly their search should include them, for they were of a character where one would be only too apt to meet with foul play. Fights were frequent and even the officers of police let them alone. But he, Beau-Jean, was mighty of arm! He was not afraid to explore them, if Pedro was so disposed. Pedro was so inclined—determined, in fact, and decided to try them at once.

Thus it came about that the shades of evening

found them loitering from one low-browed ramshackle dive to another, ever inquiring for Hill, of whom they found no further sign. The night fell, cold and black, and still they pursued their weary search, which promised to be fruitless. Not only did they learn nothing of the missing painter, but no one seemed to have the slightest recollection of the bear, a hope on which they had counted strongly. Finally, when nine o'clock had come, and still nothing had been discovered, Beau-Jean suggested that they postpone their effort until the following day, and rest their weary brains and bodies for a while. But Pedro would have none of these suggestions.

"But I am hungry!" protested the giant. "Here it is, of an hour, and we have eaten nothing since noon. Moreover, the bear is famished. Presently he will begin to growl."

"Well," admitted Pedro reluctantly, "I am hungry myself. Let us go and eat and smoke. Afterward, we shall feel more inclined to search. Where shall we go?"

They were standing on a desolate street corner when the consultation took place. To the south stretched the bleak darkness of sealed warehouses before which the faint lamps marched away, block after block into the dim starlikeness which distance lent them. On the other side, a group of buildings in more active use flared about a ferry terminal, some three blocks below. This looked more promising.

"I think there is a lunch-wagon down by the dock," said Beau-Jean, "let us make an examination."

"All right," Pedro assented, and they set off at a brisk pace, in the direction of the lights.

Sure enough, there was a lunch-wagon backed up against the ferry-house, and as they approached, it took on an increasingly familiar air. Pedro's interest was now quickened by more than the thought of food. Where had he seen that gaudy decoration before? . . . Holy Saints! it was his own! At the same instant, Beau-Jean recognized the movable hostelry of Mr. Isaac Lovejoy, with a whoop of glee, and they quickened their pace to a run. The worthy proprietor was occupied in serving a pair of customers—car conductors, or ferrymen, they appeared to be—but when he caught sight of Pedro he dropped the slice of pumpkin pie that he was in the act of transferring from platter to plate, and entirely disregarding this small mishap, he stretched out both hands to the boy, a broad smile of welcome spreading over his now ruddy face.

"Well, well, I'm blessed!" he cried. "The great little feller! and the big husky one, too! Well, well, ain't this grand? Come in, come in and eat. It certainly does my eyes good ter see you."

A very different person from the fat but despondent lunch-wagoner whom Pedro had met in the grimy little suburban square, was the present smiling and prosperous I. Lovejoy, who beamed, who laughed, who pressed his best viands upon them. True, he was still very fat—fatter than ever—but the world had gone well with him, and he seemed to have used his smiling likeness on the wagon's exterior as an example to be lived up to.

"Well, well! What brings you way off here?" he asked, when they had eaten.

For a moment Pedro hesitated and then, looking into the honest red face, decided to give his confidence and related the cause of their sudden appearance in the wilderness of the Jersey docks.

"You *don't* say!" said the fat man, who had listened with great interest and attention. "You *don't* say! Why, I seen the very feller! A likely-lookin' chap he was, too—and a friend of my girl's."

"Really? What good fortune!" cried Pedro. And then Lovejoy went on to describe the meal that Hill had eaten with him, omitting nothing, down to the very number of doughnuts and the strength of the coffee that Sam had imbibed. All this was related with an air of deep significance.

"And what are you a-goin' to do now?" he concluded.

"I don't quite know," admitted Pedro, "but what you have told us makes me sure that we are on the right track. We might keep on going through the saloons near by."

The fat man looked thoughtful for a moment, scratching his head in silence. Then: "Lookey here!" he burst out, "them low-down money-gettin' dives are no ladies' cafés, and it ain't safe to wander round in 'em 'cept in company. Now I like you— you done for me what I can't repay, but I'll have a try. I'm a-goin' to lock up this place and I'm a-goin' with you."

"Good!" exclaimed Pedro, holding out his hand,

"you are—what does one say—a *brick!* Isn't he, Beau-Jean, eh? But it is not necessary, and I beg that you will not disturb yourself."

" 'Twon't disturb me none," said Mr. Lovejoy, "and I liked that young feller. I hate to think he may be a-lyin' dead and cold in some wine-cellar, pierced through the heart with a dagger, or a hatpin, maybe. I'm a-goin' ter help you re-venge him, yes, if I lose money by it, by jingo!"

"I beg that you will do nothing to make yourself a loss!" cried Beau-Jean, who did not relish the prospect of this addition to their party.

"Although every fifty cents lost keeps me just that much further from my Lola," said Lovejoy solemnly, "I'm a-goin' to make the sacrifice this time."

Wherewith, he concealed a long bread-knife in the inner pocket of his overcoat, and extinguishing the light, announced that he was ready for action.

"Where now?" asked the giant, as the three, followed, of course, by Mr. Jones, strode out into the night.

"There's Beer Peter's," suggested the new member, "have you tried there?"

"No," responded Pedro, "where is it?"

"Follow me," directed Lovejoy, "it's a likely place."

They set off at once, and trudged on in silence until a low frame building, abutting on the river and built partially on piles, was reached. Pushing open the felt-covered doors, Lovejoy paid for their entrance, and in another moment they were in the long low-ceilinged room that formed the main portion of the building. A devastating odor rushed out to meet them, like a blast from some evil furnace. The place was blue with tobacco smoke, and at the far end, beyond a sea of little tables, a girl was singing to the accompaniment of a cracked piano. Coarse faces greeted them on every side, and voices were raised in noisy talk, despite the music. At more than fifty beer-ringed tables, little groups gossiped and glowered. There were sailors, loafers, nameless men, and shame-bereft men, and gentlemen, out at elbows, all the chaff of the city's wheat; and burly workingmen, to whom this rough imitation gaiety represented all they knew of amusement. As for the women, they were sad-hearted, brightly dressed "daughters of joy," for the most part victims of a ghastly inheritance of weakness and ignorance.

> "Hurry up, there's something missing,
> We'll have lots of kissing,
> Pa and ma have left me all alone!"

So sang the girl on the little platform, and began to dance very poorly. She was dressed in a light-colored cheap satin tailored gown, which was far from spotless, but lacked nothing in chic and effectiveness. She wore no hat, and her dark hair, cut in a fringe which reached her eyebrows, gave her for all the world the hallmark of Montmartre! Save for her unprofessional dancing and the lack of subtlety in her song, she might have belonged in any den beloved of the *Apache*.

At one end of this charming resort, which was typical enough of its class, stood the glittering bar with a shining array of glasses, mahogany and polished metal, while opposite the entrance, in what appeared to be a single-storied addition, was a room for dancing. Near the wide opening into this section, sat Theodore Pell, the reporter, in company with three companions—Elloch the painter, and two women. They were all very hilarious, but catching sight of Pedro, Pell excused himself, and began a somewhat uncertain progress in the direction of the newcomer. At the same instant a man who seemed to be in authority there, accosted the three and demanded to know if they wanted to have Mr. Jones perform.

"The house takes half of what you get," he added.

"Do you often have dancing bears here?" asked Pedro.

"Nope, never yet," said the man, "but it might go. Try it on after the next dance, if you like."

"Maybe I will," replied the other. Then, as the proprietor moved away, he added, speaking to Lovejoy in a low tone, "Let us get right away. This place is too open. Nothing serious could happen here, and besides I am almost certain that Hill has not been here, from what that fellow said."

"All right," replied Lovejoy, "we might try the back room at Murphy's, or Spikey Joe's place."

"Good!" said Pedro promptly, hustling them out before Pell could reach them. This escape did not, however, prevent the morning papers from bearing an account of how Signor E. C. Pedro, the noted Spanish painter, went slumming in disguise.

It was to the little unnamed wine-cellar known as "Spikey Joe's" that the rescue party went next. Here the very scum of the docks was gathered, and the women were of a kind one never sees by daylight. There were thieves and pickpockets, dancing and amusing themselves just as though they were human; and sickly-faced young men whose profession is unnamable; a terrible group of weary young people, calloused, yet sensation-hungry. The three companions had scarcely entered before it became evident that here at last was a place in which Hill had been, for a girl with flaming cheeks and an unbelievable coiffure turned and pointed to the bear, with a scream.

"There's a Teddy," she called out, "a cute little Teddy-bear, just like the one the other guy had. Oh, the cute little—"

Here followed a joke which made Lovejoy wince, but which elicited a roar of mirth from the habitués. But Pedro cared not at all for the import of the latter portion of her speech. Not for nothing had he lived with Nita the Sinful. With an inviting gesture he beckoned to the girl, and made the motion of one who drinks. With a laugh, she left her partner and came to him, and then, in company with the two others, they sat down at a long bare wooden table and Pedro paid for the poisonous mixture she ordered.

"Dancing a bear must be a hell of a swell business!" she remarked. "You've got the coin, ain't you, sweetheart?" and she stretched out her hand to touch his face. Upon the heels of the rebuff that followed there was a laugh at her expense.

"Can't kidnap that young one, Pearlie!" sang out her ex-partner.

Pedro had her glass refilled.

"Tell us about the other bear-fellow," he suggested. "I'd like to know who my rival is."

"Sure, cutie, I'll tell you," she smiled. But all she had to say was that a nice fresh feller (presumably Hill) had been there three days ago, had made his bear perform, got no money for it, and had gone away peaceably. When it was clear that neither she nor any one else there could give him any further information, Pedro arose and signaled the others to do likewise.

"Don't go! Whatcher hurry—'tain't morning yet," said Pearlie invitingly. But they were not to be persuaded.

Once again they stood in the keen night air, on the brink of the long dark vista of the streets. Here they consulted again, doubtful as to where to turn. Lovejoy opened his watch.

"The night's young yet," he remarked, "only a

quarter past eleven. We've got lots of time to find him before morning."

Pedro and Beau-Jean agreed to this, more for the sake of saying something than from any conviction.

"But where can we look next?" added the former, with a despairing gesture.

"I don't really know," responded Lovejoy. "We might as well walk till we come to some place, though."

At this suggestion they began moving again.

Now it happened that they soon came upon a portion of the one-sided street where the walk had been torn up, and perforce they had to cross to the cobblestones beside the water. Here were some covered piers, and beside one of them Pedro stopped the trio that he might light a cigarette. Beau-Jean followed suit, and Lovejoy, saying that he had promised Lola not to smoke, shook his head, and stood looking up at the semicircular sign above the dock entrance.

"Venezuela Fruit Steamship Company."

He spelled it aloud slowly.

A strange expression crept over Pedro's face as he listened.

"Let us look at the boat that goes to that glorious country!" he said impuisively. And they began moving toward the ill-lit entrance. The gates were open, and in the dim light some men were working about the hold. As they approached, they saw that a small corrugated iron house, a story and a half in height, was jammed up against the dock; the watchman's dwelling, perhaps, or the company's offices. This little building was so situated that there was no other structure except the dock within at least two hundred yards on either hand. All about was quiet and dark, and save where the men labored in the depths of the pier, there was no sign of life.

"What the devil do you want to go nosing around here for?" complained Lovejoy. "The cold is something fierce!"

"Just a moment!" pleaded Pedro. "I love that country so—Venezuela!"

"What's he up to?" Lovejoy whispered to the giant. But before Beau-Jean could reply, a lot of things began to happen.

In the absorption of the moment Pedro had slackened his hold upon Mr. Jones' chain, and the bear, giving a sudden tug, found himself free, and bounded off toward the little corrugated iron house, some twenty feet away, and at once began scratching frantically upon the door that opened upon its porch. Instantly the three men ran after him.

"Come here, you bear!" yelled Lovejoy.

"Don't! Let him alone!" cried Pedro. What on earth could the creature's action mean? Then knowledge came to him in a flash, and running to the door at which Mr. Jones was now sniffing and giving little growls of joy, he put his ear to the panel. Holding up a hand which warned the others to silence, he spoke in a distinct but quiet voice.

"Are you there, Sam Hill?"

After a breathless pause, as if of unbelief on the part of the occupant of the room beyond, came the answer.

"Yes; who are you?"

"Pedro," was the reply. "Are you a prisoner?"

"Yes!" said the voice of Hill. "Good heavens! how did you come to find—"

The rest of the sentence was lost in a shout for help from Lovejoy; there was a sudden sound of scuffling, and Pedro, turning to his aid, was met by a blow on the head from a burly fist.

CHAPTER XIV

TO THE RESCUE

WITH magical swiftness the semi-darkness began to swarm with struggling shapes, which sprang from everywhere and nowhere.

Returning the blow of his assailant with all his puny strength, Pedro managed to scramble into position with his back against the house, where, from within, he could still hear Hill's voice shouting directions which, however, were unintelligible to his distracted attention. Somewhere near by, Beau-Jean's string of rough oaths roared upon the turmoil, and Lovejoy began yelping for the police. At this latter cry there was a slight wavering among their unknown assailants, but it was quickly mended by a new onrush.

The men who had been working at the ship, now left their tasks and joined the fracas on general principles, siding with neither party, but laying about them with vigor and a splendid lack of discrimination. Only the desolate character of the

TO THE RESCUE

neighborhood accounted for the non-appearance of even greater numbers, ready to fight for the fight's own sake. But it was already quite a fierce struggle, and Pedro very soon began to find it difficult to keep his feet. The man with whom he was confronted had an overwhelming advantage in height and weight, while Pedro was slight and soft, and truth to tell, rather badly frightened. He had all he could do to protect his face, fending off the other's blows as best he might. How hot the man's breath was! What a tower of strength he seemed, like some minaret of a citadel come to life and marching upon the enemy. To strike him with such strength as he, Pedro, possessed, would have been about as futile as striking a stone wall. What would the end be? If only he could manage to keep the fellow from knocking him out till Beau-Jean and Lovejoy managed to win, or the police arrived. But what if he should fail?

It seemed as though they had an army against them, though as a matter of fact, there were not more than ten in all. Twice he with difficulty suppressed the temptation to call upon his friends for help, and with sobbing indrawn breath fought on wildly, elusively, striving desperately to prevent his opponent from grappling with him. A solitary policeman (a night roundsman) had come up. Pedro could hear him shouting above the din, but his efforts at establishing order were absolutely ineffectual. Two or three watchmen from the nearest docks now joined the row, and like the stevedores, not knowing the nature of the trouble, only added to the strife and confusion.

By now, Pedro was fast losing strength. It seemed to him that at any instant he must succumb, and sink to the ground. Only a horror of being trampled on sustained him, and his head was growing light. Then his antagonist, who was bent upon his injury or capture, infuriated at being held off so long by this mere slip of a boy, managed to get a leg hold upon Pedro. It was too much, and the boy's courage gave way.

"*Au souceur!*" he screamed. "*A moi, Beau-Jean! Au souceur!*"

Then somehow, he never quite knew in what manner, the giant was beside him, and the black menacing shape of the other man hurtled through space and landed among his fellows, scattering the fighters for an instant. Then Hill's voice arose again,

TO THE RESCUE

and this time, Pedro, leaning breathless and panting against the house, heard and understood.

"*Open the window,*" Hill was yelling, "it's fastened from the outside. *Open the window!*"

With aching arms, Pedro strove to obey, but the heavy iron bar that held the galvanized shutters closed, resisted his effort. With a groan he was obliged to desist, and pause for breath, while his heart seemed to have swollen in some mysterious manner, and to be choking him. Beau-Jean, meanwhile, was a veritable windmill, and one of the stevedores had ranged himself beside the Frenchman, feeling, no doubt, that it was desirable to fight with, rather than against, this powerful person.

"*Open the window!*" yelled Hill ceaselessly. Pedro bent all his strength to another effort, and at the same moment there came to his ears the rapping of the lone policeman's club upon the pavement, a signal that was not wholly without effect upon the entire crowd. Again the heavy iron bar of the shutter lifted an inch or two, and again it slipped back into its socket. Then some one struck him upon the shoulder and turning to defend himself, he looked up into the fat dripping face of Mr. Lovejoy.

"God bless me!" puffed that worthy, "that was a near thing! Thought you was the enemy! Here, you sausage! (This to his next neighbor in the press.) Take that for mustard!"

The fellow reeled back at the blow, and in the hair's breadth interval that followed, Pedro managed to gasp:

"The shutter-bar! Help me!"

In the twinkling of an eye the heavy iron lath had been extracted and was being brandished over the lunch-wagoner's head, a deadly weapon that swept a space clear about the window, which now burst open to emit the disheveled furious figure of Samuel Hill, who was armed with an improvised cudgel, evidently the leg of a table taken from the furnishings of his prison.

"United we stand!" he shouted, springing into the fight with relish. Then came a cry that was echoed on all sides.

"The reserves, the reserves, the police!" and the crowd began to scatter.

Almost as magically as they had been surrounded, they were left alone, but now, to be so left was fraught with almost as many dangers as had beset them a moment sooner; for that the police should not lay hands upon them was the paramount thought in the minds of all. Hill was the first to act.

"This way!" he called, darting off toward an ill-lighted, ill-paved street, flanked only by poster-covered fences. The others followed in the order of their prowess, Beau-Jean close upon Sam's heels, Pedro next, and the panting puffing Lovejoy after him. Last of all came Mr. Jones, loping along on all fours. It was his tardy body that caught the eye of a stout Irishman in the city's uniform, who came waddling along in the van of his fellows. Seeing the vanishing bear, and taking him for one of the reprehensible characters who had necessitated his untimely exodus from the warmth of the station-house, he started in wrathful pursuit, striking the creature with his club as he came up with it. At this insult, Mr. Jones stopped, arose to his full height and emitted a blood-curdling howl.

"Holy Mother of God!" yelled the policeman, and fled, leaving Mr. Jones, considerably accelerated in speed, responding to Pedro's familiar whistle.

By great good luck the rescue party managed to escape pursuit, and in less than half an hour they were seated (somewhat weary, but except for a few bruises none the worse for their experience) in the light and warmth of Lovejoy's wagon, while they discussed their adventure over hot coffee and the inevitable doughnuts. Outside, the beginning of a new snow-storm was filling the air with white petals.

"And why, in the name of the Gracious Madonna, were you locked up?" inquired Pedro. "I can not understand it."

"There is some mysterious illegal business afoot among that crowd," said Hill thoughtfully. "They have got that boat chock full of ammunition and arms, and all under cover of being pianos, and such stuff. It's against the law, you know. They sail the day after to-morrow, at dawn, and as I had accidentally stumbled upon their tricks, they decided to keep me safe until they got away. I've no doubt they would have let me go after that, without any fuss, but it was beastly unpleasant being locked up that way."

"You must give the information to the authorities," said Pedro.

Sam seemed to be in some doubt about this, but at last he decided that an explanation was due to these good friends who had risked so much for him.

"You see," he began, "there is somebody—that

is to say, somebody's near relation—mixed up in this, and I—well, damn it all! I can't very well give him away!"

Instantly a thousand conjectures sprang to Pedro's mind.

"Is it—is it Iris' father?" he said hesitatingly.

Hill stared at him in amazement, a doughnut arrested half-way to his mouth.

"Great Scott! how did you know?" he exclaimed.

"Because—well, I'll tell you later. But the reason is that which made me come and look for you," he answered. "You'll excuse us," he added to Lovejoy, "but it's a private affair, about a lady."

"I will indeed," responded the fat man, "ah! ladies, ladies!"

"We must talk this over at once!" exclaimed Hill, glancing at the clock, which showed that the hour was almost 1 a. m. "Come, let us go!"

The three arose, and with many expressions of gratitude to their host, took their departure, and were soon settled upon the dingy benches of the north-bound ferry. They were almost the only passengers on board, and lulled by the warmth of the cabin, Beau-Jean fell asleep, using Mr. Jones for a pillow, and the bear, also glad of the rest, followed suit. Here, then, was an excellent opportunity for talk, and the other two immediately proceeded to take advantage of it.

Pedro spoke first, and related the story of his acquaintance with Iris and her request for his help in the matter of her father's secret trouble. From this narrative he omitted nothing except her infatuation for himself, and at the end, came to the little paper on which she had written her promise. At this point Pedro began to mix fiction and fact.

"I could not undertake to help her," he said, "because I soon discovered that some one dear to me would be involved, and would in turn involve me: but, more of that later. I then suggested that you be called upon, but she was unwilling—you have had a little quarrel, eh?"

The speaker watched Hill's eager face closely, to note the effect of this remark. The result was confirmatory to his own deductions.

"Yes," said the elder man, "it was a silly quarrel about nothing."

"Aha!" said Pedro, "so I felt sure. But she—ah! she thought you would not come to her aid. I knew differently, and so I told her. Then she wrote this little paper (he spread it out upon his knee) and I set out to find you and give it to you."

Hill took the fluttering bit of white, and read, with glad incredulous eyes:

"I hereby promise to marry you on the day you can tell me my father is not being subjected to danger, or has been rescued from that, if any, which now imperils him. And I furthermore agree to overcome any debatable objections you may have to the marriage.
"(Signed) Iris Vanderpool."

"For me!" said Hill tensely. "She sent it to me!"

There was an instant's pause, and then Pedro lied manfully.

"Yes!" said he.

Hill let out such a whoop at this that Beau-Jean and Mr. Jones woke up long enough to shift their positions.

"Tell her that I shall claim the reward within the week!" Hill exclaimed exultingly; "so she had better prepare to pay up! When will you see her?"

"To-morrow night there will be a masquerade at the Milligans," replied Pedro. "She is to be there."

"Then tell her—" Hill began.

But Pedro stopped him, for every moment was bringing them nearer to the city, and he had not yet finished.

"I will," said he. "But listen now to my own part of the story. You people know nothing about me. Well, I am—but no, I shall not say that until I have to. But this I must tell you. By some strange circumstance, the character of which I have not yet solved, my mother is in New York in company with Rowe, whose real name is Ricardo Valdez, an ex-minister of the Venezuela government. He is as much a villain as my dear mother, my lovely girl-mother, is an angel! Until a few days ago I imagined her safe in her own home, and now I discover her here, and with that man! Some reason that seems good to her must have brought her, but what it is, I can not even guess. But this I know—whatever of evil Valdez is engaged in, she is innocent, and to you I must confide her interests, and beg that you allow no harm to touch her."

"But why don't you look after her yourself?" gasped Hill in amazement.

"I can not!" cried Pedro, his eyes full of distress. "You see, I ran away—oh, long, long ago, because she would have forced me to—oh! I can not explain! But if she once saw me, she might betray me to that Valdez gang—for my own good, as she thinks—and then I would have to go off to a far country, and take up a job I loathe—that would kill me, *that would stop my being a painter!* And even for my mother, I could not submit to that!"

"But how the devil can she make you go against your will?" demanded Sam. "And why did you leave her in the first place? It's all very mysterious!"

"Yes, I know it sounds strange," replied Pedro, "but I can only explain a little. You might take her side. Indeed, almost every one does, except Old Nita. They seem to think that to be rich and powerful . . . Oh, they do not understand. They have given me too much freedom for their purpose, and now they can not tie me down. . . . As for having left her, it was really she who left me. I had a little escapade—very harmless mischief it really was—but afterward Valdez told me that my mother would not receive me any longer. I gave him a letter to her in which I begged her to relent, but she never answered it, nor my others. Were it not for my love of her, it would be a relief to have severed my connection with my past, because of the different life I would lead should I go back, and now that I have begun to paint, to lead my own life. . . . But, please, I beg of you, as I have served you, promise to protect her, and ask me no more. Some day I may be able to tell you everything, but not now."

"Very well," assented Hill reluctantly. "But I may call upon you to get her out of a difficulty if it should prove absolutely necessary to do so?"

"Yes," returned Pedro. "But remember that for me to take any active part in the matter would have terribly serious results for me. Now tell me about Mr. Vanderpool."

"I don't know much to tell," replied Hill. "He recognized me, allowed himself to be persuaded that I should be locked up till this damned boat had reached its port, whatever it was, and gave orders that I was not to be hurt. Then he went off before I could get a word in edgewise, and I haven't seen him since."

The ferry-boat had reached its slip, and they aroused their sleeping companions.

"Will you go to the studio?" Pedro asked when they had landed.

Hill considered for a moment.

"No," he said, "I shall go back to Jones Street

with Beau-Jean and the bear. I'm going to get at the bottom of this business before to-morrow—that is, to-day—is over. I have not yet decided on a plan of action, but in all probability, I shall be better able to work from the stratum of the tenements than as myself. In the meantime, thanks, and good night, and God bless you for this!" He tapped the breast pocket wherein lay the promissory note signed by Iris.

"Good night!" said Pedro, bestowing a violent embrace upon Mr. Jones. "Good night, Beau-Jean, tell Nita I shall be with her soon!"

Then they shook hands all around, and Pedro watched half-wistfully until the swinging doors closed upon them, and then, turning up his coat collar, prepared for the cold journey homeward.

CHAPTER XV

SNOW AND DOGS AND THINGS

AS Pedro emerged into the street, that snowy white carpet which appears so magically lay soft and muffling over the pavements, deadening the sound of such little stir of life as was still abroad at this most silent hour.

A distant chime struck the quarter, and proclaimed that two o'clock of a new morning was at hand. The wind was biting and Pedro, ploughing along ankle-deep in the shifting mass, shivered beneath the insufficient covering afforded by the old green coat. How silent the world was! Even the "link" of the elevated trains seemed deadened and unreal, while the whole city looked fantastically theatrical in its new mantle, like a stage scene wrapped in cotton-batting for the performance of a pantomime. From window-ledge and cornice hung great rolls of snow; the street lamps all had on white bonnets like peaked night-caps, and even the narrowest wires and branches bore ridges of snow, piled higher than ever human hand could have built them.

Oh! the silence, and the rows upon rows of blind houses, standing shoulder to shoulder! Round about him swirled the soft flakes, blinding him, whirling about his feet in eddies as though to betray his steps. Never had he seen the town so quiet. Only one pedestrian passed him in a dozen blocks, and not another living creature seemed to be abroad; only the night-capped arc-lights, standing frozenly in their wan circles of light, and the dancing mocking snowflakes. At every step walking became increasingly difficult; twice he stumbled and once he fell; fell face downward in the white shifting mass that felt soft upon his cheek like the cold hand of a treacherous mistress.

Down the narrow chasms of the streets sang the wind—a dreadful symphony, too cosmic for the cold traveler to listen to, and tuneful only to the ears of those who lay snug and warm at home.

Painfully fighting the blast, Pedro turned up lower Fifth Avenue, hugging the buildings in vain search for shelter, and regretting that he had not tried to get a street-car on the other side of town. Still, all the public conveyances must have practically stopped running in such a storm, and in a few blocks more he would be home! From the distance ahead emerged a black object that presently resolved itself into a cab whose motive power, an old white horse, advanced it slowly, slipping and sliding with stiff knees. Half a block above Pedro, it stopped at the curb, and he watched a young man spring out, almost knee-deep into a drift, hand the driver his fare, and make the best of his way up the broad steps of a splendid old mansion. For a moment his white shirt-front gleamed between the sables of his coat, as, swaying slightly, he stood fumbling with his latch-key before stumbling into the dimly-lit hall beyond. The cabby, like an ancient turtle, drew his head into the massive shell of his thick overcoat and muffler, gathered the reins into his clumsy mittened hands, and off went the old horse again, slip-slide, slip-slide, into the dim white distance. Then again only silence, and snow.

With head bent and shoulders hunched, Pedro had gone past his corner by mistake, and suddenly realizing this, he glanced up to find himself confronting a building that had often attracted his passing attention. It was before the old First Presbyterian Church, with its snow-laden trees, and

SNOW AND DOGS AND THINGS

white-mounded garden, that he paused and turned his back to the lashing gale. From under his hat brim, which was pulled well down over his ears, his eyes shone with excitement, as though he pitted his puny strength against the elements for the pure joy of a combat into which he entered for the sake of the tossing about it would give him. Now that the wind was behind him, the storm became sport, and tired as he was, he no longer felt in such a hurry to reach shelter. Just as he began to retrace his steps, allowing the wind to push him, he heard a low moan, as of some one in pain.

For a second he hesitated to trust his hearing, and walked on for a pace or two. Then it came again, faintly, against the wind, and this time he stopped to listen. The sound seemed to come from the portico of the church. Going up to the iron gate, he found it open, and peered inside. Apparently no one was there, and he was about to leave, when within the dark central doorway something moved, and a gleam of white flashed out of the gloom.

In an instant Pedro had bounded across the snow-filled space between gate and door, and was kneeling on the flagging of the vestibule, groping about. Then something warm and moist touched his hand,

and he discovered the sufferer to be a large black dog with a white star on his face, who lay as though one of his hind legs had been crushed—perhaps by some passing automobile, earlier in the previous day. The animal was a nondescript creature who might have been of any variety of lineage one could well imagine, and in size he was somewhere between a setter and a Newfoundland. His coat was coarse and short, and his tail, in direct contradiction, long and bushy, with white fringes. Like half-moons his eyes rolled at Pedro, and without hesitation the long muzzle was laid into his hand. At the touch Pedro's heart leaped.

"Good dog!" he said huskily. "What shall we do about it, old fellow, eh?"

The dog whined a little, and snuggled closer. Pedro put an arm about him. Beyond the gothic arch of the vestibule fell the mottled white curtain of the snow, now steadily, now waveringly, furled by the wind. Pedro arose.

"Come on, boy!" he said.

The dog made a pitiful effort to rise and follow him, but failing, sank back upon the steps with a whimper. Pedro looked about him despairingly, but no help was in sight. Never once did it occur to him to abandon the animal to its fate; the only thing that troubled him was a method of taking the beast home. The dog was plainly too much hurt to walk. Then it must be carried. With a sigh he stooped and lifted it into his arms, a by no means easy accomplishment, for the dog was at least half his own size, and heavy at that. After a yelp or two it submitted quietly to this operation, seeming to understand that the move was for the best, and with this new impediment Pedro staggered out into the street and again began his homeward journey.

It was a heavy task he had undertaken, and several times he was obliged to pause and seat himself in some doorway for a moment or two, and before he had arrived half-way to his destination it began to seem to him that he could get no farther. Then, as he arose for a final effort, he raised his eyes to the building before which he had last rested, and recognized it as Leigh's dwelling-place. Furthermore, there was a light in the sculptor's window. With a breathless exclamation he clambered up the steps and pounded on the door.

It was several minutes before the janitor responded, and when he found that he had been summoned from his comfortable basement chamber for the sole purpose of admitting "that dago boy an' a fierce old cur" he flatly refused to help in the animal's removal to the upper regions. So Pedro did it alone, and reached Leigh's door breathless and exhausted. At his knock, the door flew wide, revealing Leigh, clad in an old brown dressing-gown and slippers, his pipe, as usual, hanging reversed from the corner of his mouth.

"What the devil—" began the sculptor.

"The dog—he's badly hurt!" exclaimed Pedro excitedly. "I couldn't carry him any farther, so I brought him in. Let us make him a bed by the stove, quickly!"

"All right, Doc!" replied Leigh, gathering up sofa cushions indiscriminately, "we'll fix him up."

For twenty minutes they fussed over the animal, and when they had done their best for it, and it had gone to sleep with its head upon Leigh's rolled-up overcoat, the two shook hands.

"When did you get back?" asked Pedro.

"Only to-night. I went around to your place at dinner-time, but it was locked. Where have you been?"

And then Pedro, keeping back nothing but Iris'

SNOW AND DOGS AND THINGS

attitude toward himself, gave Leigh a full account of the week's adventures. When he had done, there was a long silence, during which Leigh sat staring into the fire, as though obsessed by some idea that he was unable to shake off. When at length he spoke, Pedro thought that the deep voice had never been so resonant and sympathetic.

"Sorry I wasn't here," said he, "and as for this about your mother—I don't have to tell you to call on me, do I?"

Not a question did he put, not a word of praise; but there was a look in the strange eyes, and a note in the rich voice that meant more to Pedro than the greatest eloquence.

"When I decide what course I am going to take, I shall let you know," said Pedro in a low tone. "I am glad you understand that I am not deserting her, or shirking. Why, I would die for her, if she would gain anything by it. I am not afraid to die."

"That is no boast!" replied Leigh, with a tender laugh at the youthfulness of this speech. "Every one is competent to die; who, though, is competent to live? The simplest problems of life are so difficult if one is honest in considering them."

"Yes," said Pedro, "the problem of the universe is in every minor point of difference."

"True enough; it is appalling!"

"Not if one dismisses the problems with ridicule!" said Pedro.

"Paugh! ridicule is the last resort of the unreasoning!" retorted Abraham Lincoln Leigh.

"You are too epigrammatic for me to-night," said Pedro, rising, "and I am very tired—too tired to floor you with a brilliant retort."

Leigh laughed.

"Hold on a minute, though," said he, "there's one thing I must get off my chest before I turn in to-night. I've been meaning to say it and, indeed, have started to several times, but always forgot, somehow."

"Well, what is it?" asked Pedro, smiling. "I'm old enough to hear it, I guess, eh?"

Leigh smiled up at him through a cloud of tobacco smoke. "It is the dream of the very young to be old and steeped in sin," said he, "even as it is the dream of the old to be young and innocent."

"A truism, not an epigram," commented Pedro. "But what is the solemn communication?"

"It's about Miss Vanderpool," replied Leigh, his

smile fading. "You see her too often, and it won't do! Are you not aware that she is engaged, or as good as engaged, to the very man who has made it possible for you to know her. Don't do it, boy, it's not fair!"

"How would you have me act? I am painting her."

"Don't see her at other times, then."

"Eh? Not go near her? Polite, wouldn't that be!" exclaimed Pedro, just for the wickedness of leading Leigh on.

"You know what I mean," said Leigh, and he was watching Pedro very closely as he spoke. "When, for instance, do you expect to see her next?"

"To-morrow night at the Milligans' masquerade," replied Pedro. "She will be there."

"Then don't go!" exclaimed Leigh. "I hate to flatter you, Pedro, but you are not without attractions."

Pedro lighted a cigarette.

"I think I shall go," he said, eying the smoke meditatively, his handsome head cocked to one side; his eyes half-closed, and a queer little smile playing about his lips.

Leigh swore an oath.

"Don't be a cad!" he said shortly, arising.

Pedro grew solemn at his tone, and yet a wicked spark lingered in the depths of his eyes. Going up to Leigh, the boy placed a hand on the giant's shoulder and stood looking up at him.

"I don't know quite what that cad you say is," he said; "but from the way you speak of it, I am sure it is not good to be one. Yet, I am going to that party, and simply in order to see the Madonna Lady. And in telling you this, after what you have said about Hill, I must beg you to believe that no matter how often I should see her, there would be no disloyalty in it to my benefactor. Such treachery as you suggest would, in my case, be absolutely impossible, for more reasons than I can explain, or you could possibly guess. An affair with her is totally impossible for me. Will you not believe this, *amigo mio?*"

As he spoke his face had grown more and more grave, and at the end he seemed struggling to hide some deep emotion. Very seriously and intently Leigh watched his face until he had ceased to speak.

"Very well, I'll believe you," he said finally, "but it's a tricky dangerous matter, and mark my words, you'll be sorry if you run your head into her trap; she's a charming young woman!"

"Yes!" said Pedro. "And now I must go."

"Go!" cried Leigh in amazement. "In this storm? What nonsense, man! Sleep here on the couch."

For reply Pedro seized his hat, a panicky expression blanching his face.

"No, no!" he said. "I must go!"

"But it's nearly morning!" objected Leigh. "Why the devil shouldn't you stay?"

Pedro's fingers were on the latch. Hat in hand, he flung back his answer.

"*Because!*" he replied and rushed out, banging the door behind him.

For a long time Leigh sat looking at the closed door, thinking hard, all the lines in his face springing into prominence as he bent upon his subject with special concentration.

"Because!" he repeated aloud. "What a strange answer. *Because!* Why? Why? Why?" Taking a single impulsive step toward the door he flung his arms out before him.

Then, like a blind man who had been suddenly given sight, he staggered across the studio and flung himself upon the couch.

CHAPTER XVI

A BYZANTINE PRINCESS

TIRED and disturbed in heart and mind, Pedro crept wearily up the long flights of stairs to his apartment, and, as he paused upon the landing next to the top, the little clock on Cassie's mantel-shelf rang four clear silvery notes into the dark silence of the musty stairway. With a sigh he commanded his stiffened muscles for a final effort, and mounted the last remaining flight of creaking steps between him and bed. Ah! grateful thought! It made him hurry, and caused him to glance eagerly toward his goal before the top step was fairly reached. There he paused in surprise.

A light was shining out from beneath the door! Could there be a burglar in the room? It would scarcely be a visitor, at such an hour, and in any event, how could a guest have obtained admission? It was very puzzling! Cautiously he crept over to the door without making any noise, and putting his ear to the panel, listened intently. No sound! Whoever they were, they were quiet enough! But who could it possibly be? Of his friends, there was none save Leigh who would possibly visit him at such a time, and Leigh was at home, and doubtless asleep by now. As this seemed to eliminate all other possibilities, it must be an intruder who was burning his oil. Once convinced of this, Pedro, being tired of fighting, and having had his fill of battle for a long time to come, was loath to bring a new row down upon his head. Again he listened at the door, and at first heard nothing but the distant roar of the elevated cars, and the tense 'audible' silence of the sleeping tenement. Then a faint stirring and—was it a sigh?—came to him from within the room. This was a sound not to be withstood, and, very gently, he turned the door-knob, at the same time fitting in his latch-key. Then, with a swift stealthy movement that was like a panther's maneuver, he opened the door a crack, slid through, and quickly closing it after him, stood motionless with his back against it. A curious scene met his gaze.

Two old Spanish lamps that hung from the ceiling had been lighted, and on the hearth glowed the embers of a dying fire. By the soft red light of these the room took shape, and gigantic shadows stirred in the corners. A heavy scent of fresh flowers and of flowers that were dead hung in the air, and he could see that some of the many blossoms about had been there for days. Others were fresh, as though newly arrived. On the card receptacle lay a small package and a note, and on top of these lay a single glove—a long white suede, crumpled and soiled. On the model throne stood a basket of rare fruits, undisturbed from their original packing, but showing some sign of wilting. Evidently the gifts that Iris had grown into the habit of sending had not ceased to arrive during his absence, and had been carefully bestowed by the janitor. But who had lighted the lamps and kindled the fire?

At first the apartment seemed unoccupied, but a second glance showed this impression to be a mistaken one, for even as he turned toward the couch, there was a gentle stirring among the cushions and one of them, jarring a stand full of long-stemmed roses near by, sent a shower of crimson petals fluttering over the sleeping form of Iris herself.

"*Dios!*" whispered Pedro.

For a breath or two he stood staring down at her, and then, being careful not to awaken her, he drew up a large armchair to the opposite side of the hearth, and dropping into it, sat regarding her intently, his hands clasped about his knees, his head bowed. How strange and lovely this woman was, who lay among the loaming shadows, the rose-petals dropping upon her! All desire for sleep had fled now, leaving him keyed up to a highly nervous pitch, his brain abnormally active from over-tire.

That Iris had been at a ball or festivity of some sort was plain from the gown she wore; a thin gauzy stuff made heavy and clinging with silver spangles, and low-cut, so that it showed her gleaming white shoulders and the swell of her bosom. In her red-gold hair was a jeweled fillet. Over this gorgeousness she had thrown on the blue robe in which she was wont to pose for him, and its classic folds, concealing yet revealing the jeweled gauze beneath, gave her an appearance that was far from saintly. Rather, she seemed to be some princess of ancient Babylon, resting on the rose-strewn couch of a court feast, while the torches flickered and flared in the darkness before dawn.

It was a thought that pleased him, and, feverishly his tired brain completed the metamorphosis.

Her hair seemed washed with melted gold, after the manner of the ancients, and her carmine lips, half parted over the little, even white teeth, might have been stained with henna, so red they were—so very red—like a wounded poppy—and her skin was so very, very white, yet creamy, too. Had she stolen that wonderful color from the carved ivories on the palace walls? And when the black slaves waited upon her, and knelt before her with basins of perfume and jars of scented oil for her rose-tipped fingers—was she not most wondrously white, then? Had not their bodies been created black only that their swarthiness might prove how fair she was? The curve of her delicate nostril was cruel . . . and her mouth was tremulous with unconscious passion. Upon what captive creature would she lavish the force of her maiden affections? A tamed chetah, perhaps, fringed of ear and treacherous, whose wicked green eyes would feast upon the pulsing column of her throat the while he licked her hand . . . a royal chetah, such as the mighty princes take forth in golden cages, and turn loose upon the terrified slim-ankled antelopes, the antelopes with little flecks upon their bodies . . . white flecks that were soft and clear like the down on the slender neck of Iris.

"Princess of the past ages," he murmured softly, "your soul shines through the flesh of to-day!"

Around her slender little feet the blue drapery had caught. Those little feet! To look at her one must believe that they had danced on marble floors; strange floors, wherein each piece was of a different color, and none was larger than the coin that bore the head of Cæsar. . . . Had not the torches flared from the porphyry columns, and the hot wind from the desert tossed their flames in harmony with her floating veils of gauze? . . . The long thin horns of the black musicians blared their brazen notes, and the women smote their lyres. Between the vast columns, whose tops were lost in the darkness of the high ceiling, the courtiers and slaves stood to watch her, fearfully, and as they watched, were slaves in very truth, Roman and Nubian alike, and even the temple-servers, with their oiled and curling beards. . . . Like light thrown from a prism glass she danced before the straining love-smitten eyes of the tetrarch; her electric body wrapped in an ever-changing veil of filmy cloud, star-spangled, and oh, the tender twinkling feet, the fluttering little feet, so white, so pearly white, and tipped with pink. . . . The elusive dancing feet that sped among the rose-petals, among the poppy petals, across the curious marble floor. . . .

He sighed and closed his eyes.

Outside was surely a strange moon-filled scene —some terraced landscape steeped in night! In the door that led out to it would be hung a great curtain, heavy with tapestried designs of crude, keenly articulated men, of strange implements of war, and lions that had human heads and wings. Beyond, a garden,—a garden rich in spices and rare fruits, and in its midst a pool, motionless as the sleeping pelicans upon its margin, wherein the lotus grew tall and firm, and lifted wide-mouthed chalices to the moon. . . . Below, flat roofs in terraces, lower and lower, tier upon tier, to where the lions roared faintly from the desert; to where the silver streak of the river showed gleaming far below the balustrade of the hanging garden. And over all the benediction of the moon; the subtle, discreet, voluptuous moon . . . and silence, silence. . . . Within the palace, gutting torches, the strewn remainder of the feast, trampled flowers and bruised fruit, the heavy scent of spilled wine, and perfumed tresses unloosed, the canopying shadows of the stone roof, the waiting

A BYZANTINE PRINCESS 333

couch, silk draped and soft, the weary dancer, crimson-mouthed . . . the drawn curtain, heavy with strange embroideries, that would hang straight and guarding until the winds of dawn. . . .

Pedro arose, and bending over her, brushed a new-fallen petal from her lips. And Iris awoke, looking at him with love in her eyes.

"I knew you would come to-night," she said smiling. "Something told me so!"

She held out her hands, and he assisted her to a sitting posture.

"How did you get here?" he asked.

"I was at a ball, my own carriage was not to call for me, and I directed the cabby to bring me here. You are not angry?"

"Not angry," he repeated. "Who let you in?"

"It was the caretaker, he has a key."

"Ah! Yes! And the flowers—you did not know I was away?"

"I have telephoned every day, but to-night—to-night I felt somehow that I must see the room, at least, and the things you handle, or I should . . . I must have fallen asleep. . . . But are you not going to greet me?"

"What made you think I would be here to-night?"

he asked, his voice still low and level. "I did not know it myself."

"I was not sure, of course!" she protested. "It was only that I felt you might be, and I—oh! I was mad to come, I suppose, and you will think me . . . yet, I could not stay away. Something seemed calling and calling me! Are you not glad to see me? I—oh!—say you are glad, for I am so ashamed!" She had arisen and stood before him with downcast head.

"Why?" said Pedro.

"Ah! If you need to ask that, then I am not ashamed!" she cried. "You always understand! I knew you would . . . that is, if you were here at all!"

"This time I do not quite understand, Madonna," said Pedro, "but you are very gracious. Will you not be seated?"

He pulled the large chair forward, but she seemed not to see it, and sank back upon the divan.

"Sit beside me," she commanded. And he obeyed, choosing a spot some length from her.

"I was frightened when I came in here," she confessed. "The studio is so vast at night, and so full of shadows, and then, coming up the stairs . . .

that is, the unusualness of it all, you know! And I have been so worried about you!"

"But why?" he asked again.

"The paper that I signed!" she laughed nervously, her fingers straying to the truant locks of his hair. "The paper, and the mad way in which you seized upon it. Then this mysterious absence without warning. And yet I knew you would return; my presence here proves my faith in your ability to win out. Have you any news?"

"Not yet," he said, thinking it best to let Hill tell his own story in his own time. "But tell me, Madonna Lady, is it conventional in America for young ladies in society to go about alone at such an hour as this?"

He was watching her intently as he spoke, and she, wondering how innocent the speech was, felt the hot blood mounting to her forehead.

"No—no!" she stammered, "but *we* . . . surely you understand! No one keeps account of my coming or going, and as far as my household is concerned, I might easily be at the dance until even later than this! Then we are such—we have been such good friends, surely we are different. The ordinary conventions do not concern us."

"Don't they?" he asked softly. "Not me, poor waif, perhaps—but you! The world is small and full of gossiping tongues."

"The world is idiotic!" she declared tremulously. "It never believes in friendship between men and women!"

There was a tense pause. He was leaning toward her now, and her breath was coming fast. The very air pulsed with the situation, and he could feel how fear and passion fought within her for the mastery; how tradition and the world-force were striving together. Then he spoke, and the words fell sharp as knives upon the thick emotion that she had conjured up.

"*Are* we friends?"

The question held much more than the spoken query. It was a denial, and a challenge. At once it dismissed the possibility, the pretense of a friendship between them, and declared her his supplicant, demanded her confession. It was a tightening of the already taut string upon which they had been harping, and which, at another twist, must surely snap.

Oh, the terrible, the sweetly fearsome portent which, to Iris, the little sentence seemed to bear!

Her heart beat to suffocation, and it seemed as if she must swoon for very ecstacy at what would surely follow. Intensely sensitive to his nearness, to the dramatic setting, to the strangeness of the hour—an hour when all waking humanity is keyed to the highest emotional pitch, she waited in painful yet delightful expectancy. The dear expectancy of the moment hovered like perfume before her distended nostrils, like color before her half-closed eyes.

"*Are* we friends?"

Her voice was low and vibrant as she made her reply, her words, like his, carrying a double meaning that was equally apparent to them both, under its pretense of being matter-of-fact.

"I don't feel very much like a 'friend' of yours," she said.

"How do you feel, then?" he asked gently.

"How do I feel?" she cried. "I feel like—like *this!*"

And slipping from the sofa before he could prevent her, she fell upon her knees in front of him, and clasping her hands as if in worship, gazed up at him adoringly, almost touching him as she knelt.

"That is how I feel," said Iris.

"Don't, don't!" said Pedro in a broken voice.

"I love you!" said Iris. "Why, you surely know it—you must have seen it!"

She spoke with the glad note of one who confesses what they believe to be the most desired of facts.

"Don't!" Pedro pleaded again.

"But why should I not?" she asked radiantly. "I love you! Do you not like to hear me say it? Does not my having come here in this manner prove it?"

"No!" he cried in agony, springing to his feet as though to defend himself from something. "No, it proves nothing of the kind. You do not, can not love *me!* It is impossible, *impossible*. I have already told you so. Ah! I can not endure to have you act so! And this is Hill's own room!"

"But I *do* love you!" she cried, following him. "Pedro! touch me—tell me that you care! Kiss me, Pedro!"

"Never!" he said fiercely. "You do not love *me* —you love *Hill!* Yes, yes, you do, although you do not realize it. I am really nothing to you but a reaction—a pastime!"

"That is not true!" she sobbed.

"It is!" he shrilled. "You have loved Hill all

"I am past pride."

along! *Me!* Why, it is out of the question that you should care for *me*. It is against Nature! The atmosphere of the studio is what you love here, the informality, the careless freedom; but, me—ah! no. You love Love itself primarily, and to-night it has mastered you. But the *man* whom you love is Hill."

"Ah! so you care nothing for me, after all!" she moaned. "But I am past pride; kiss me, Pedro!"

"I will not!" he cried, retreating from her. "I love you in my own way—as much as I can love any woman—but I will not kiss you! You are mad to-night. It is the environment, the situation, not me, that has so aroused you. You must go home!"

"Kiss me, Pedro," said Iris with outstretched arms.

Roughly he flung her away.

"Listen!" he commanded, "you don't know what you are doing. You are nothing but an infatuated little animal to-night. You no more love me than you love that lamp—than the hovering moth loves it! There is a splendid man who does love you, and you return his affection, although you do not appear to be conscious of it; but take warning—and open your eyes to the fact. Do so before you succeed in singeing your wings at some such earth-fire as you have tried to light to-night! Love is a sacred, a wonderful thing, and it comes to us but once; Heaven forgive us if we fail to recognize it then, and desecrate or lose it. And heaven have mercy on the torments we shall endure in such a pass. Guard your love as a pure flame upon the highest altar of your individuality; keep it in that secret inner chamber wherein is hid the force which links you to your fellow-beings, and which is called the soul. . . . Listen to me!—With every kiss you give lightly, you rob, not only your true lover, but your true self. Each small affair will make the great one less great. Believe me, to make comparisons is unavoidable. How, then, will it be, when the dear one kisses you, to say to yourself the while, 'Harry did it differently, Tony did it such a way, and Pedro, too, he had a style—but this is better!' Will it not belittle that so sacred kiss, eh? And do you think you could avoid making such a comparison, eh? Ah! Madonna! take no lesser loves; wait for the great one, though you die a maiden; it is better so!"

But she had not been listening.

"Kiss me!" said she.

"No!" cried Pedro.

"Touch me, then!" she cried wildly. "Take my hand—anything! I am mad for the touch of your hand!"

"Will you not listen to reason?" he implored. "I can not endure that you should belittle yourself so! I can not love you as you wish, and again I repeat, you do not love me: I have been nothing but a reaction—a spite, perhaps,—a vent for your emotions. You are led on only by passion. There! I have spoken it. Say what you will, it is the truth. I am sorry, but I know not how to drape such matters with prudery."

She gasped a little, and then came to him swayingly, and placed her hands upon his shoulders, the blue cloak sweeping about her seductively. The scarlet mouth was raised toward him.

"I do not care!" she breathed. "You may not love me—but I love you! Take me if you will, on any terms. I am ready."

Silence. Then—

"It is impossible!" he ejaculated.

Another short pause.

"Why did you lead me on to speak?" she demanded, a note of anger creeping into her voice.

"Because I knew it had to come. The sooner the matter was explained the better," he answered.

"But you are making no explanation," she complained tenderly. "Come! I shall not let you go until you do!"

And she slid her hands down to his, gripping them tightly.

"I can not!"

"But you *shall!*" she insisted. "What is this mysterious reason why you can not love me—why it is impossible?. Tell it to me! I will prove to you that it is a mere phantom! For despite what you say I know that I mean a great deal to you. I see it in your eyes! Only tell me what it is and I will prove that this monstrous difficulty can be overcome!"

"I can not tell you," said Pedro wearily, "and even if I did, you would be helpless to alter it."

A sudden alarm blanched her face.

"You love another woman?" she whispered.

"I love no other woman," he told her.

She drew a deep sigh of relief.

"Ah! then it *can* be overcome!" she said. "Tell me, what is it?"

"I can not tell."

"You must!"

"I will not. It is my secret!"

"I will keep it!"

"You would intend to, I know, but I dare trust no one."

"This is unfair to me!" cried Iris. "You torture me, and yet you give me no reason for doing so."

Pedro drew a long breath. If it was unfair to her, why then . . .

"I will tell you," he said unhappily.

The world was very still. One by one the lamps had guttered and burned out till only a single taper was left, and the embers on the hearth were dead. The room was very cold, and strangely silent, as she waited, with bated breath. Through the great skylight the first faint blue of dawn was creeping in, making the vast apartment weird, unfamiliar; and a chill odor of snow was in the air. Would he never speak? The silence seemed interminable. But at last he raised his head and looked at her with great unhappy eyes that reproached her for the tribute she exacted. Then his lips formed words that refused to make themselves heard. He ran his red tongue out to moisten them. Then he tried again.

"It is because I am not a man!" he articulated.

"Not a man!" she gasped. "God in heaven, what do you mean?"

"That I am a girl," said Pedro miserably.

CHAPTER XVII

PLOTS

NOW on the evening of that day upon which Pedro first learned of Hill's disappearance, and shutting the studio door behind him, sallied forth in the wake of the anxious Guneviere, the ground floor of the Muldoon Place house served to stage a curious scene.

It was past eight o'clock when the first actor appeared, and entering the large old-fashioned parlor, proceeded to light the lamp upon the center table. It was Rowe, or Ricardo Valdez himself, and the anxious manner in which he glanced at the clock betrayed the fact that he was expecting the arrival of some one. After he had settled the light to his satisfaction, he went to a small safe that occupied one corner of the room, and taking a key from his watch-chain, worked the combination, and presently swung open the heavy door.

He knelt before the open safe, and extracting a little packet of official-looking documents, proceeded to compare one of them with another which he took from his breast pocket. The comparison seemed to satisfy him, for presently he put all back in their pigeonhole, including that which he had been carrying, and then looked at the clock again. It still wanted a moment or two to the hour of his appointment, and he utilized these to place in security a considerable sum of money in bank notes. Then the door-bell tinkled, and hastily locking the safe, he arose to answer the summons.

The man who stood, hat in hand, at the entrance was none other than he, who, in disguise of a wayfarer, had attempted to rob Iris on the lonely road that autumn day, long past. Now he was shaved, garbed in the inconspicuous clothing of respectability, and it would have taken a second glance to tell the chance observer that the face was untrustworthy. Rowe made a welcoming gesture, and the man stepped in, laying aside his outer garments.

"I am the first, I see," said he in the same language. "Why do we meet here? Is it safe?"

"Hill may be missed," explained Rowe, "and we are certainly being watched. Consequently, this place is safer than any other. To all appearances it will merely be an evening party. Any news?"

"Yes," said the other, "I have something for you."

"Give it to me before the others come," said Rowe nervously. "It is from Venezuela, of course."

"Certainly!" said the other, "and fortunate it is for you, my friend, that I am in the employ of the post-office of the United States. Otherwise it is scarcely likely that the millionaire asphalt contractor's greetings from the Venezuelan government would come into your hands."

"You are well paid," retorted Rowe, "and in the future you shall be paid even better, but of that later. Let me see what they say. Of late it has been very difficult to alter the communications in such a way as to render them sufficiently antipathetic. They are growing rather friendly toward him, and on several occasions I have been obliged to suppress letters entirely. That one which you allowed to reach him was nearly fatal to our plans."

"But you repaired the damage!"

"With infinite risk and pains!" retorted Rowe. "Although I have opened and altered so many epistles both of his and theirs and have become pretty expert. You must remember that the man we are dealing with at this end, at least, is no fool."

"Yes, Vanderpool is no fool!" agreed the man.

"Hush! No names, I beg!" warned Rowe, "and lower your voice, my friend." Then he continued in a more composed tone. "It is essential that he should go on believing that we are necessary to his success. Once he discovered that the Venezuelan secretary of commerce would be willing to treat with him direct, we should lose our hold upon him, and with him, our chances of improving our fortunes! But come, let us see your latest find!"

The man fished for a moment in the inside pocket of his coat, and then brought out a letter similar in appearance to those that Rowe had concealed in the safe. The latter took it eagerly, and examined the seal. Then, going to the alcove where a number of dishes and arrangements for light housekeeping were stowed, he lighted an alcohol burner of great power. After heating a small instrument in the almost invisible flame, he skilfully removed the seal and in another moment the letter lay open before him. As he read, the crease between his eyes deepened. Then his face cleared.

"This will give little trouble!" he exclaimed. "'Can' must be changed to 'can not', and there is plenty of space in which to do so. Then it will appear to our patron that the Honorable Don Juan del

Costa *can not* agree to do as he is asked in the little matter of bringing the asphalt question before the government! Well, to-morrow will do for that! The envelope has not been stamped at this end, I see."

"Of course not!" said the other. "Who is that?"

A second time the bell tinkled, and Rowe put the letter in his breast, carefully preserving its fastenings.

"It must be Casablanca and the captain," he replied. "Do you admit them!"

The postal employee did as he was bid, and in another moment there entered two men, both Latin in type, one of them being the little officer whom Hill had seen aboard the ship, and the other, a larger man, who was the vessel's captain. At sight of Rowe they bowed politely, a courtesy that was returned with all possible formality, and then, the four having drawn chairs up about the center table, the captain turned a swarthy face upon his host and put a question.

"Signor Valdez," he began, "I presume that something of vital import has moved you to summon us here to-night?"

"You are correct in your surmise," replied Rowe, "and we shall come to the point without delay."

The captain looked about him in surprise.

"But Vanderpool, he is not here!" he commented.

"No, for a reason that is of the best," declared Rowe, "and Signor Captain, I beg that we do not use the name—it is more discreet."

"Ah!" replied the man addressed. "Then it is some matter of which Mr. ——, the gentleman is to have no knowledge?"

"You anticipate my meaning exactly," said Rowe.

"Well then, what is it?" asked the man who had arrived first.

"My friends—my very good friends," began Rowe slowly, tracing the table-cloth designs with a stiletto, which, in its capacity of paper-cutter, lay at hand, "I shall tell you all; but first let us review the situation as it stands. To begin with, then, there is to be a revolution in Venezuela, in which we are engaged—a fact that we are absorbed in to the exclusion of all else at this time, being good patriots all, and having the best interests of our splendid country most sincerely at heart. Secondly, our patron, who shall be nameless, is backing this patriotic and righteous enterprise with his good American dollars. Now, to those interested and active in this most glorious undertaking, he has represented frankly that he is not so much interested in the overthrow of the present rotten and corrupt government because it *is* such an iniquitous administration, as because of his immense asphalt interests there, and the disproportionate export-tax which is at present being put upon it, and which a clean new government would promise in advance to diminish. All this he has told you and it is true as far as it goes. But there is another and a deeper interest which is the real motive behind his assistance, and which is known to me alone; more, without my holding out this interest as bait to him, there would be no money forthcoming, and consequently, no revolution at all!"

There was a moment of stupefied surprise. Then the captain brought his fist down upon the table resonantly.

"What do you say! No revolution! Are you trying to make fools of us, or do you really hold such a secret? Come, no playing, we are busy men!"

"I have made no exaggeration of the truth, señors," replied Rowe. "And it will take but little time to prove as much. Let us speak of Señora Daussa!"

"Ah! the brave and noble señora!" exclaimed the little officer fervently. "It is she, whose presence among us and whose interest in our cause, gives us the so much needed courage! Whose immense popularity will be of such value to us!"

"Wait!" said Rowe. "Let me inform you, first of all, that the honored signora knows no more of this revolution than this table does!"

"Knows nothing of the plans! Why, Valdez, is it not her interest which has banded us together, which—," began the captain.

"Her interest! You have only my word for that," said Rowe. "You have never—not one of you—spoken a single syllable with her on the subject!"

It was too true. Save for that one interview, when little or nothing had been said, Signora Daussa's sympathy and support had been taken entirely upon hearsay, furnished only by Rowe and Sancho.

"This is most extraordinary!" exclaimed the captain in bewilderment. "Will you please to explain this action of yours in so deceiving us—and furthermore, what bearing it has upon Vanderpool?"

"The last is the easiest to reply to," replied Rowe, "and, therefore, to take it first. What bearing has it upon Vanderpool? Good captain, *she is the bait!*"

"*Dios!*" exclaimed the first man. There was a pause, then:

"Is it permitted to ask how?" said the captain with exaggerated politeness.

"But certainly," replied Rowe cheerfully. "Vanderpool has been in love with her for years; he believes her to be a prisoner in Venezuela. *I alone of his acquaintances know exactly where she is!* Ha! ha! behold your revolution! It is very simple."

"And she! How do you hold her, and where?" demanded the captain, his face purpling ominously. "How comes she to be with you?"

"That is soon told—at least, part of it," said Rowe, who, for hidden reasons of his own seemed bent on making a considerable confession. "She also has been in love with him for many years, and I am supposed to be assisting her to find him. Find him, while all the time I am in constant touch with him! Meanwhile, I tell her that the search is hopeless— that I can not find this lover of hers! Ah! ah!"

"And where is she?" growled the captain, never taking his eyes from Rowe.

"That is another question," snapped Rowe. "That is something that I do not intend to answer, save that you are not likely to learn."

"Then in the devil's name, what is your scheme— what do you want to do?" roared the captain. "First you mislead us into joining the revolution on the strength of Signora Daussa's influence, proposing to make her son president, even as his idolized father was; and now that we are in too deep to withdraw, you tell us that she knows nothing of the plot, and by that, of course, intimate that she would not approve it! You defraud Vanderpool, playing him and the señora off against each other, and then, at the eleventh hour you summon us and disclose this astounding matter. What does it mean? Explain, for by the Holy Mother, you shall not leave this room until you have done so!"

A subtle inscrutable smile played around the corners of Rowe's mouth, and he lighted a fresh cigar with much deliberation before replying. Then he looked the captain squarely in the eyes and his jaw took on a determined set that made it seem squarer than ever.

"I intend to be dictator of Venezuela," he said very distinctly.

Again silence. On the old-fashioned marble mantle-shelf, an ornate little clock ticked loudly, and from somewhere near at hand came a low moan, so low and faint that none of the men heard it, preposessed as they were with the stupendous statement that had just been made.

"And how do you intend going about attaining this mild ambition?" asked the second officer with mock courtesy. A look from Rowe cut him short, and wiped the smile from his face.

"I have already gone about it," Rowe said in his precise way. "It only remains for you gentlemen to make a decision between the situations. On one hand, you support me, lend me the power which you control—a no mean force as I am quite aware— and I will present you each with the official appointment which you most desire in the Venezuelan government—you shall be ministers, admirals, premiers —even treasurers—any thing you will, when once I am seated in the presidential chair. On the other hand, refuse, and I will simply bring my two turtledoves together, and there will be *no revolution.* Mark my words—the tariff on asphalt is only a minor issue with our friend. Once he has the lady, he'll risk neither life nor money in our enterprise!"

"I do not believe you!" cried the second officer hotly. "I think you are lying!"

Rowe looked straight at him, meeting him eye to eye.

"You know I am not lying," he responded slowly. "Try it, if you doubt me!"

"You would be ruined if we did so and it proved true," murmured the captain.

"I'd rather see us all ruined than fail of my pet plan," rejoined Rowe.

A long silence followed, which was broken at last by the captain, who arose with a sigh.

"Well, Valdez," said he, "you have got us at your —shall we say—mercy? I think the other gentlemen will agree that there is nothing for us to do but consent to help you, and incidentally, ourselves, if you are to be trusted to fulfil your promises to us, which I doubt. Any other course we may take seems even more likely to land us in prison than this does."

One by one they agreed and then, with a regal gesture, Rowe dismissed them.

"To-morrow we shall talk," he said. "I shall meet you all here at ten o'clock in the evening. Meanwhile, sweet dreams of our future power."

Then, one by one, they left, stringing out down the steps, and clanking across the little paved court, leaving him alone.

"*Gracias a Dios,* that is over!" said he, stretching luxuriously.

"It is not over!" said a voice behind him.

He wheeled about, and there stood the señora, her golden hair in disorder, her face white as death.

"I have been outside for ten minutes," she said, "and I have heard everything!"

"Heard—you—you listened!" he stammered, the room seeming to reel about him.

"Yes! I heard! I listened and I found out how you have been deceiving me—you, whom I have trusted, whom I have loved as a friend of my heart, whom I have put my faith in, and come away with into this strange land. Oh! you have cheated and reviled me, and I believed in you. You have lied to me—lied, lied, *lied!* About my lover you have lied, about my country, about your patriotism—you have used me as a tool with which to accomplish your own dishonorable ambitions! Have you lied to me about my child? Answer me! Is she dead, even as you said? Why does she write no more? Tell me, do you know? Ah! I would not believe you even if you spoke, and yet, I must—I must— Where is my lover? Where? Tell me! You shall tell me! I will have the truth out of your lying throat!"

"Carmen!" he cried. "For the love of God be quiet! You are like a mad woman."

"Mad!" she screamed. "Would you not be mad? Tell me where he is, I say!"

"I will not!" he stormed. "Tell you—do you think *I* am mad also?"

"Then, if you do not tell me, I will leave you!" she said through her teeth.

His eyes were bloodshot as he glared at her furiously.

"You shall pay for this, you wild-cat!" he panted. "I will tell you nothing! And you are a prisoner from this moment!"

She gave a laugh, a terrible mirthless laugh, and clenched her hands at her sides, rigidly.

"Again you *lie!*" she flung at him. "I am no prisoner! I am going to find my lover!"

And turning swiftly, she flung open the door, stepped out and closed it after her, locking it as she did so.

"Carmen!" screamed Rowe, beating on the panels. "Carmen! I love you! Come back, and I will help you, Carmen!"

But Señora Carmen Daussa was gone, without money, without English, without the least knowledge of the city or of the way to turn—gone in search of her lover!

They were loudly applauding Old Nita's efforts.

CHAPTER XVIII

AND COUNTERPLOTS

WHEN Pedro and Sam Hill separated on the night of their Jersey adventure, the latter made straight for Jones Street, accompanied by Beau-Jean, and upon reaching the refuge of the rear tenement, tumbled into bed without more ado, and for seven hours slept the sleep of the just, his head upon an improvised pillow of quilting—beneath which his hand grasped the precious document that Iris, as he thought, had sent him.

Very possibly his repose would have continued for a much longer period, had it not been for the activity of Guneviere and Hermania in the room immediately below. These ladies, their household duties, as usual, entirely neglected, were loudly applauding Old Nita's efforts to instruct Koko in a new accomplishment; namely, to use as cymbals the lids of two fish-kettles strapped to his front paws.

Now the clash of cymbals, no matter how amateurish and uncertain the performer's efforts, is not conducive to slumber, to say the least of it; and, therefore, with a groan of protest, Sam returned to consciousness of all that had befallen him, and all that was yet to be undertaken. While he washed and shaved, he pondered deeply upon how he should set about getting the information that Iris desired. As he drew on his boots he still wondered, and uncertainty did not cease with the knotting of a silk bandanna about his throat. But at about this point, hunger began to distract his attention, and so, deciding that he would be able to think more collectively upon a full stomach, he descended to the flat below and demanded to be fed.

Koko dropped to his all fours at this intrusion, glad to be rid of the encumbering kettle-lids, which Old Nita untied, grumbling at the interruption of the lesson, but nevertheless delighted to see Hill. The other two women bustled about and prepared food for him, and soon he was munching ruminatively, oblivious of, and impervious to, the questions that they showered upon him. Upon a couch in the corner lay Anna, silent and pale, while Rico, who lounged upon the foot of the couch, bent over and whispered to her occasionally. For all the notice they took of the other occupants of the dirty little room, they might have been alone. At last, Hill's attention was arrested by them, however, and he inquired if Anna were ill.

"No," replied Nita. "She is going to have a baby in the spring, that is all, and she is getting so that she will not let Rico out of her sight; nor will she go out with him to dance the bear. How they will live, I do not know, what with bringing no money in, and such idleness! They are a pair of fools, those two. I am a very wicked woman, I am, but I really do think they should get married now."

"Are they not married?" said Hill, surprised. "Why not, do you suppose?"

Nita merely shrugged and turned away upon some matter of her own. Hill, cup in hand, arose and approached the lovers.

"*Bon jour*," said he abruptly. "Why the devil aren't you married?"

Rico looked up pleasantly, his smile ever ready and friendly for the beloved *Samhill*. Then, as the latter's words sank into the unknown depths of his slow mind, a cloud crossed his handsome face.

"Married? Why, I do not really know, *mon ami*," he responded slowly. "Anna—why are we not married?"

For a moment she looked as bewildered as Rico, and then a smile of understanding broke upon her lips.

"Why!" she said, "we love each other! We have been very, very busy loving each other, and dancing the bear. I do not believe we ever thought about getting *married*."

So serious and obviously sincere was this reply, that Hill scarcely knew whether to laugh or frown. But to refrain from making the patent suggestion was impossible.

"Why not do it, now that it occurs to you?" said he.

Rico looked at him earnestly.

"Do you advise it, *Samhill?*" he asked. "We could not love each other the more because of a few words said over us!"

"Very true," replied the painter gravely, "but there is the child to consider. You would like it to bear your name, would you not?"

"It shall be called Rico if it is a boy," said Anna's lover, "but a girl would be Anna, so what is to be gained in that case?"

"But your *last* name," insisted Hill.

"Last name? But I have none!" objected Rico.

AND COUNTERPLOTS 363

To gain time, Hill finished off his coffee.

"It would take a long while to explain just why it is a good plan to be married," said he at last. "But if you are willing to take my word for it, allow me to say, *that it is good!* In fact, I am contemplating doing it myself before very long."

"Well," said Rico, "if you say it is good, it must be so. We will find a priest if you agree, Anna."

"I've no objections," replied Anna; and so it was arranged.

Leaving them to discuss the idea, Hill again fell to planning how best to approach Vanderpool, that he might without unnecessary delay follow the advice that he had just offered to Rico.

In the midst of an "egg-and-lentils", the idea came to him. Why not go direct to Vanderpool at his office and put the matter frankly before him? Preposterous as the notion seemed at first, the more he thought upon it, the more plausible it appeared. Was there not as good a chance of finding out the truth in this manner as in any other? Vanderpool had agreed to his, Hill's, incarceration it was true, but the reasons for so doing were strong, and his objections had been overruled by the rest of the gang with whom the asphalt magnate had appeared to be associated. At any rate, it was worth trying. Vanderpool was aware of the knowledge which he, Hill, possessed, and under any circumstances the latter would be working under a search-light, so to speak, the moment his escape was discovered. On the whole, the notion seemed a good one, for by its execution, nothing could be lost, while much might be gained.

"And I think," he said aloud, "that I shall take Mr. Jones; he will make me more conspicuous and, consequently, safer."

"What's that?" queried Nita.

"Merely that I am going out now, mother," responded Hill, rising forthwith.

Out from the dimness and dirt of the back tenement, from the low-roofed houses, degraded mansions of an earlier day, out from the muck and squalor, the slush and grime of unswept Greenwich into the roaring cañon of commerce to the east, went Hill, the little brown bear tagging after, and joining with his master the river of humanity that swept between the towering cliffs of granite on either hand; the strange incomprehensible towers, which stretched up, up, higher than one at their feet could see, at a single glance, any more than he could grasp their significance with a single thought. Before one of these buildings Hill paused and assuring himself that it was that which he sought, began maneuvers to gain admittance.

At first there was difficulty with the door-keepers on Mr. Jones' account, but they were successfully persuaded, and he passed them only to be balked by the elevator man. There was more protest than that of the uniformed official to cope with, for Mr. Jones flatly refused to enter the car, and in the end Hill was obliged to leave him in charge of a half-delighted, half-frightened porter.

"Just as well," murmured the painter, as he was spirited upward. "If they have any clap-trap mysteries about that office, secret dungeons, etc., and I don't come down, they will get tired of holding the bear, and come up after me."

Even before he had come to this optimistic conclusion they reached the twenty-oddth floor, and the offices of United Asphalt Company.

However, difficulties were not at an end, and it was only after considerable argument and hauteur that Sam succeeded in having his name sent in to the president of the concern. The name, it seemed, was magical in its effect, for almost instantly the supercilious office boy who had condescended to take it in, returned briskly, and invited "Mr. Hill to please to step this way"—and so, without more ado, Sam found himself face to face with Iris' father.

As Hill entered the luxuriously appointed office, the distinguished man at the wide shining desk did not look up until he had finished addressing the letter upon which he was engaged. When he had done so, and secured the seal, he turned and faced Hill with the frank direct look that was known to be characteristic of him.

"Well, Samuel Hill!" he said, "so you have not only escaped, but felt it safest to beard the lion in his den—to seek out the conspirator in the midst of the market-place. Why?"

For an instant Hill wavered as to what course was best; and then, in view of the attitude with which he himself had come armed, decided to return frankness for frankness.

"I have come because of this," said he simply, taking Iris' manifesto from his pocket and spreading it upon the desk before her father. Vanderpool fumbled at the black silk ribbon that secured his eye-glasses, found and adjusted them, and began to read the little paper. When he had come to the

AND COUNTERPLOTS 367

end, he went back and read it for the second time; and then, spreading it upon his knee, sat looking at it in silence.

"Well?" said Hill, desiring, at any cost, to come to the point.

"You love my daughter?"

"Yes."

"And she?"

Hill merely pointed to the paper.

"She has been distressed about you for some time," said he, "and as you were unwilling to relieve her mind, she decided that you were being victimized in some manner, and so set Pe— me to find out the cause of the trouble."

"Hum!" said Vanderpool. "And why did you not come here this way, in the first place, instead of spying upon my activities disguised as a goodness-knows-what?"

"Because I knew you would be under no necessity to tell me anything unless I already possessed some knowledge," lied Hill with a readiness that surprised himself.

"Then this is a sort of blackmail?"

"Not at all!" cried Sam hotly. "I have no wish to use the power which the knowledge I have gives me over you—though that and the evidence of the friends who rescued me from that beastly hut would be a pretty strong weapon if I chose to use it. But I don't; to do so would be to defeat my own ends and those of Iris. What I want is nothing more than some statement from you, which will enable me to fulfil the conditions of that promise which your daughter has signed. Beyond reassuring her, I give you my word that I shall keep your confidence entirely: furthermore, if I can honestly do so, I shall even assist you in your enterprise!"

Vanderpool arose and began to pace up and down, silently, appearing to consider the proposition that the younger man had just made. Then he stopped abruptly, shooting a direct glance at Hill from under his fine brows. He was a man of quick decisions, and he had decided in Hill's favor.

"I believe you are sincere," he said slowly, "and therefore, I am going to trust you with the whole story. Sit down and smoke if you like—no, I prefer to walk."

The financier continued to pace in silence for a few moments, his white head bowed, his thin youthful figure alert and active as a boy's, his handsome cameo-like features contracted in thought. Then he spoke abruptly.

"You have surmised that a revolution was afoot? You are right—there is—in Venezuela. My asphalt interests are chiefly there. The export-tax, as it stands, would be a drain upon my profits, and ostensibly that is the reason for my backing this scheme to upset the present government. But there is another reason, a deeper one, known only to myself and one other—Rowe. It concerns a woman, who, he tells me, is kept a prisoner by the now president of that God-forsaken place. Let me tell you about her. When I first took up this business I went to Venezuela to make my contracts. I got good ones, and I made friends with the dictator—a fine old man. He had a very young wife—hardly more than a child. I fell in love with her and she with me. She had a child—a girl it was, but it was being brought up as a boy because the father had been so bitterly disappointed at having no son . . . and Carmen was faithful to her child and her husband . . . I am glad she was . . . I would not have had it otherwise. But we danced together a great deal . . . there was no harm in that . . . Then, one night the inevitable, or rather the usual revolution broke out. It broke out in the ballroom . . . where we were waltzing. The orchestra stopped abruptly: all was confusion. I was knocked unconscious while trying to save her husband. When I came to, I was aboard a ship bound for New York. The president was saved, as I learned afterward, but the revolution was successful and he was deposed. Carmen, I heard, was dead. Then, after a while, I married to please my family."

"Iris' mother?" said Hill.

"Yes," continued Vanderpool. "She died within a year, leaving the baby . . . I was fond of her, in a way, and sorry . . . but I never forgot Carmen. Recently, I came across Rowe, who had been prominent in the affairs of Venezuela during my visits there. He told me that Carmen was not dead. . . . Good God! that was all he needed to say, but he added that she was being kept a prisoner, to all intents and purposes, by the present government for fear that the country would rise in favor of her supposed son if she were left free. Now you will understand the situation. I have financed everything. The last boat sails on the early tide, before daylight to-morrow. I have here a letter to my daughter which I thought would sufficiently explain my absence."

"You are going with them—with the revolutionists!" exclaimed Hill.

"I am going to rescue Carmen," replied Vanderpool with a wistful smile.

"And you sail at dawn! Will you not come with me to the house at once, now, and tell Iris what you have told me," cried Hill excitedly. "By jove! it's a wonderful story! It will set everything right for me, if you'll only come along!"

"Impossible!" replied Vanderpool. "There are some vital details yet to be attended to. Besides, I prefer not to return to the house again. The servants have been told I have gone away for some time, and I do not now wish to do anything that will excite the slightest comment."

"But Great Scott!" exclaimed Hill in dismay, "will you write out a certificate for me to show her as the proof of what I shall tell her?"

"I heard the young lady giving instructions that you were not to be admitted," said Vanderpool with a twinkle. "Has the order been revoked?"

"I—I don't know," gasped Hill. Then an idea struck him, and he laughed aloud in relief.

"See here!" he said, "she is going to a costume dance at the Milligans to-night. Couldn't you go there with me just before you leave for the boat, and help me get things straightened out? I know it's a lot to ask, but—"

"But you're not above asking," finished Vanderpool with a laugh. "Yes, I think it could be managed. I'll have to go in these clothes, though. Will they let me in?"

"I'll take care of that!" cried Hill joyfully, "where shall I meet you?"

"Call for me at the Calumet Club, at about twelve," said Vanderpool.

"I—I don't quite know how to thank you," began Hill, but the other stopped him with a gesture.

"I have been twenty-five years without the thing I am helping you to get," said he. "Do you suppose I want you to wait? Then, too, I rather like the idea of having you for a son-in-law. You'll be good for Iris."

"Er—yes!" said Hill.

"And now, get out, I'm busy," said Vanderpool, tearing in half the letter that he had just written.

CHAPTER XIX

A MOMENTOUS EVENING

DE Bush dined at the Milligans on the night of the masquerade, and beside the great painter there were Edwards and little Berry Forest, who paints those fluffy landscapes. Blaume ate there, too, and Theodore Pell, who came in at salad-time, and absent-mindedly ate it all, while he told of seeing Pedro at Beer Peter's place, and of the splendid article which he, Pell, had made out of it. And as was the custom of the house, when the coffee-cups had been drained for the second time, Bell Milligan made them all help to clear up, and get the floor waxed, for it was nearly ten o'clock, and before long the guests would begin arriving.

Bell wore a yellow costume with sparkling things on it, and ornaments of the same sort across her forehead, and to it she added an all-enveloping gingham apron, while she superintended the arrangements, her frank chaff and the laughter which made her so well beloved by all these famous men, ringing clear.

The dim red lanterns were lighted, the cellar, with its two famous kegs of October brew, was arranged for those who chose to sit and drink to the accompaniment of dancing feet upon the studio floor above: the tiny kitchenette was crammed to its uttermost capacity with the good things for supper, and at half past ten precisely the musicians arrived: a thin flutist, a fat German cellist, a dapper dyspeptic pianist, and a temperamental hungry-looking violinist. These took up their places around the weather-beaten piano, and tucking their handkerchiefs under their chins, prepared for the strenuous time that was traditional of the Milligans' parties. Around the walls were couches, and between them, on the floor, cushions, to serve as seats.

"I wonder if there are enough?" said Don, and without waiting for an answer, darted across the alley to take from under the very head of a neighbor, the desired articles, with which he presently returned. Meanwhile, De Bush, gray-haired, dignified despite his pirate costume, was solemnly sliding over the wax he flung upon the floor, while on the balcony Blaume, the poet-model, and Pell, were giving each other illustrations of the latest Gotch-Hackenschmidt match, greatly to the detriment of their

A MOMENTOUS EVENING

costumes. Then the first "outside" guest arrived, a lady in the character of the Queen of Sheba. Instantly she was surrounded by an admiring, clamoring, teasing group.

"Am I the first?" asked the lady.

"No, indeed," said Bell comfortingly, with as much inanity as the question required. And then, just as the situation was becoming unbearably stupid, as such moments at the beginning of a party always are, the door opened to an Apache, full-painted for war. A wild whoop went up at once, and before it had subsided, the crowd began to stream in, many-colored, noisy, gorgeous or humorous, filling the dim studio with a dream-like throng, alive with movement, fraught with the delightful mystery of familiar friends in disguise. The air was full of chatter, of laughter, of delighted screams of recognition. "Good Lord! it's Bill! Look what Bill has on! Have you seen Mazie's tights!!! Kitty has on a blond wig!—yes, it is Ken Harris! Well! look at Mr. De Bush, will you! Hello, Pell, old boy, feel as great a fool as you look?" etc., etc. From the corner where the musicians sat, came an ungodly squeaking and scraping. The perfume of burning incense, of new-lit cigarettes, of heavy cosmetics and camphor, hung in the atmosphere. The hungry violinist readjusted his handkerchief and waved his bow; there was a blast of melody, maddening, enticing, and the crowd in the center of the room began to move rhythmically. The guests continued to pour in.

Among these came Leigh, clad in high boots, rough shirt, and trousers, carrying an ax, his coat thrown over his arm, this costume having been created to emulate the personal appearance of the great American for whom he had been named.

After a quick word of greeting to Don Milligan, he thrust his impedimenta into a corner, and began to search among the crowd for the face that had haunted him incessantly the eighteen hours past. But although many smiled at him, and beckoned him to join them, he shook his head in refusal, and continued to look for Pedro.

But Pedro was nowhere to be found, and instead, in a small room opening on to the balcony, he came upon Iris, who, seated upon a divan, was engaged in warding off the eager attentions of Pell, who was determined that she should dance with him.

"Hello, Iris!" said Leigh, coming up, and at once perceiving that she wished to be rid of the young reporter. "Hello, Pell! get out of this, will you? I've something particular I want to tell Miss Vanderpool."

"You brigand!" retorted Pell, making a wry face, "what right have you, boarding my ship this way? However, despite my newspaper instinct, I shall withdraw from ear-shot. But if you see a paragraph or two about yourselves, don't be surprised!"

With which witticism he was off.

"Fresh cub," muttered Leigh. Then to Iris, "May I sit down, or would you rather be left alone?"

"I—no, that is, yes!" said Iris confusedly. "Do sit here beside me, please. I—I feel rather unhappy to-night, and that boy bothered me. What is it that you have to tell me?"

"Absolutely nothing," said Leigh, sinking down beside her, "it was only a ruse. But I'll try and think up something if you like."

"Don't trouble!" replied Iris with a little laugh.

"Perhaps—that is, if you like to know—will you tell *me* something?" Leigh responded.

"That depends," said Iris, patting the shimmering skirt of her costume. "That depends on the nature of the question."

"I have no question to put," he told her. "It is

only that I can see you are unhappy, and there must be a reason for it. Now, if you told me that reason, the telling might help you to discern its real significance."

"You say such odd things," she replied, "and such true ones! In most cases your receipt might work, but, in this one, it won't. You see, my chief trouble is that I have made an awful fool of myself, and talking about it would only make me more fool than ever."

"Not necessarily," he responded. "For instance, you might have been misled in the first place. You are scarcely responsible for that, and all your foolishness might be subsequent and dependent upon such misleading, or deception."

"That's it exactly!" cried Iris. "Oh! Mr. Leigh, do you think it would be very terrible if I were to tell you something—something that involved a third person, I mean? It would ease my mind so, and I must have advice! My father has gone off somewhere, and there is no one else. Do you think I might?"

"I think you might," replied Leigh slowly. "I think it would do no harm to tell me if it concerned one particular person. I mean—Pedro!"

"So you know!" cried Iris, violently agitated. "You know! And I never even guessed, and went on making love to him . . . her, that is, and couldn't understand why he—she didn't like it. And oh! more than that, I did terrible things; that is, they would have been terrible if Pedro had been a man. I went there alone. The model told me I ought not to, and why; but I was mad—I did not really understand what she meant. And then, last night"—her voice sank to a whisper and she kept looking fixedly at the floor. "Last night I went to Pedro's studio again alone . . . I was desperate . . . I didn't clearly know what I was doing. And he (that was before I knew), Pedro, told me plainly, *right out plainly* . . . and I didn't care . . . and at last he had to confess he was a girl . . . and oh! Mr. Leigh, do you think Sam will ever forgive me for being such a wicked fool? And do you think he will ever come back so that I can tell him how sorry I am that I ever picked that silly wrong-headed quarrel with him? Oh! *do* you?"

Leigh's voice shook with emotion as he answered her, and he was glad that she did not look him in the face as he spoke, for he knew that at the moment its expression had got beyond his power of control.

"Yes," he said unsteadily, "it will all come right!"

He got to his feet, and took an uncertain step or two, the words she had just uttered concerning Pedro still ringing in his brain. The pace or two had, however, brought him facing the door. In it his eyes met a sight that would ordinarily have been sufficient to fill him with amazement, but Leigh was too much stunned by Iris' unconscious confirmation to feel any further emotion just then. But he managed to speak, and the words aroused Iris like magic.

"Yes," he said feebly, "I think you will have the opportunity of apologizing, for here comes Sam Hill now!"

Then they both stared hard at the door, where, sure enough, Sam was standing, disguised as a bear-trainer, every detail of his costume complete, down to the very bear itself. Iris gave a little cry. He was smiling at her, and behind him shadowed the tall figure of her father. She turned to her lover, her hands outstretched.

"Samuel!" she said brokenly, and was gathered into his arms.

"Samuel, beloved of the Lord!" muttered Leigh, as he reeled out on to the balcony like a drunken man. From the floor below came the rhythmic stamp of many heels, and the tinkling tune of the *Spanish*.

. . . . . .

In the little room a few explications were taking place.

"Sam, my son-to-be," said Vanderpool, "it seems to me that you needed neither my presence nor your document."

And Iris, still clinging to her lover, was sufficiently curious to ask:

"What document, father?"

"Why this!" explained Hill, taking her pledge from his breast pocket with his free hand, and showing it to her.

"*That?*" exclaimed Iris.

"Of course, dearest!" beamed Sam. "Your father here will explain everything and help me fulfil the conditions—but you seem surprised. Didn't you send it to me?"

With slow-dawning understanding, she looked from the document to his happy face.

"Of course I did, dear," said she, hereby uttering her first wifely fib. "And are you really safe, daddy?"

"I am in no danger of which I am aware," said Vanderpool. "Hill has the whole story, and I shall let him tell it."

"Then everything is all right!" cried Hill. "Come on, let's get out of this. Let's go to your house."

"Yes," assented Iris, wherewith the lovers went away, unheedful of the lonely man who bade them Godspeed, or of the bear, who had fallen asleep in a dark corner.

* * * * * *

Meanwhile, Leigh, his heart like to burst with a hundred culminated emotions, sat by the balcony rail, and scanned the crowd in eager search for Pedro. From this vantage-point he saw Iris and Samuel take their departure, and then the music stopped. There was a fluttering of hands, the ripple of applause died away, and the crowd broke up into groups, who laughed and ate with as little concern as though the world had not been changed forever for Leigh. Suddenly a strange thing happened.

The center of the floor was for the moment clear, and the musicians had retuned their instruments. Then, above the gay murmur of the human voices wailed the voice of the violin, the accompaniment throbbing softly below. For a moment or two no one danced, held back by that unwillingness to be the first which always follows the opening strains of a new measure. Then Leigh became conscious that a hush had fallen upon the crowd.

The street door had been thrown wide, and from the darkness without there emerged the figure of a woman. Her garments were of frail silks torn and mud-stained, and pitifully inadequate to protect her from the cold. Her golden head was uncovered, and disheveled, and from below its tumbled glory, her eyes shone bright and feverish from the dark-ringed sockets. But she seemed unconscious of her plight, and of the stares of wonderment that she invoked.

It was Carmen Daussa, tremulous with joy at finding the only house in the great cruel city where she possessed friends, where she might ask for help and shelter. At recognition of her, a breath of admiration went up from the audience, which swiftly changed to an expression of amazement as Vanderpool emerged from the extreme other end of the room. Then, as though drawn by an irresistible power, they advanced, seeing no one but each other, caring for no one else, totally unconscious of the existence of the crowd, speaking no word, uttering no cry, but coming nearer and nearer, swifter and swifter, as though impelled by a fate they had no thought to resist. And then, in the center of the gleaming floor they met, and, wordless still, he took her in his arms. And when the music stopped abruptly, she called his name, and he bent and kissed her on the mouth.

Once the spell which had held them snapped with the cessation of the waltz, the people crowded about the two, all talking, complimenting, explaining, laughing, pushing: and while this was at its height the studio door opened to admit the long sought for, slender figure, and Pedro was seen to inquire something of Bell Milligan. At her response, Pedro apparently thanked her, and disappearing among the crowd, quickly returned with the bear at heel, and vanished.

With a stifled cry Leigh sprang up, and hastily gaining the lower floor, crossed rapidly to Bell, who was deeply absorbed in explaining something to Pell, and who had to be shaken by the shoulder before she would answer Leigh's question.

"Where did Pedro go?"

"I—good gracious, such a performance! Did you ever—" gasped Bell—"where did Pedro go? He went home to pack."

"Home to *pack!*" shouted Leigh. "Good lord!" And without even waiting to find his hat, he rushed out into the alley and started madly off in the direction of Muldoon Place.

CHAPTER XX

THE BEGINNING

BY the light of a single candle, Pedro was packing a little knapsack with the meager belongings that his sojourn in the old studio had brought together. He went about the task with reluctance, but with the weary resignation of those who receive an unalterable decree from fate, and recognize it as such.

One by one his little personal things were tucked away in the ancient traveler's-kit—a book or two, some linen, brushes, a gay necktie, and a miniature plaster cast of Leigh's "sleeping bear". When these had been put in, and still a little room remained, he hesitated a moment, and then, going to the heap of sketches and small canvases with which the rack was filled, deliberated among them for a while; taking up first this one and then that, with loving hands, and throwing each in turn back upon the shelf from whence it came. Finally a sorrowful shake of the head dismissed them all.

"Of what use to take any?" said Pedro aloud. But nevertheless, he stood brooding over them for quite a time. . . .

By the fire lay Mr. Jones, blinking sympathetically. With a sigh Pedro turned at last from these children of his mind, and set about arranging the two rooms—the studio and bedroom—exactly as he had found them.

In the first place there were the pictures—*his pictures!* From the big easel the "Madonna Lady" smiled wanly upon her young creator—a beautiful, crude, unfinished thing, its possibilities beckoning enticingly from behind the haze of its incompleteness. Then there were the others. Significantly Pedro glanced from them in the direction of the fireplace, and heaved another sigh. No! that was impossible; infanticide! It could not be done! Yet, who would care for them. . . . Leigh? Perhaps. Piling them high, and topping them with the ever-smiling portrait of Iris, he stacked them neatly, near the door, and writing "For A. L. Leigh" on a folded bit of paper, left this message a-top the heap.

Next, he restored the furniture to its original arrangement as nearly as he could remember it, and bringing forth Hill's canvases from the cubby in which most of them had been reposing, set them around, even as he had found them, down to putting the unfinished portrait of the banker upon the throne from which the Madonna had just been taken. When this was done, the studio took on such an unfamiliar atmosphere that a lump arose in Pedro's throat. It seemed such a concrete representation of how completely his claim here had ended! With apparent irreverence he suddenly went over and knelt beside the bear, taking the creature's head between his hands, while tears started to his eyes.

"Poor fellow! Poor Mr. Jones!" said Pedro huskily, and then, having patted Mr. Jones upon the nose several times, arose slightly comforted.

The bedroom came next in order, and from press and bureau Hill's clothing, which had been laid away with so much care, was hauled out and hung in its accustomed place, each minor detail being attended to with care.

When all was accomplished, the worker came to the doorway where he had paused on that long-past autumn morning of his first awakening there, and stood gazing for the last time upon what had been the field of his labors these many months; and as he looked about, it seemed as though his heart would break at the thought of leaving it. But go he must.

Clenching his hands, he called himself a fool, speaking aloud in his pain. For a moment the wild hope came to him that he might, after all, stay on; or, at least, return; and then with renewed clearness the urgent reasons for departure came surging back. His secret, which Iris knew, was no longer safe. His mother, whose entreaties he dared not face, was living in the very same city, and might at any moment meet with him. Then there was Hill. He had found Iris, and all must be well between them, for had not Bell Milligan told how they had gone off together? This happy occurrence would end Hill's reasons for staying away. More, the painter had returned Mr. Jones, the only pledge Pedro had given him, thereby ending the bargain. Then, too, in a few weeks it would be spring, and the hedgerows would awaken, new-clad in green, and the broad highway would call and call. . . .

"But none of these is the great reason!" cried Pedro aloud. "Holy Mother! have mercy upon me! The real reason is Leigh! It is he, it is he whom I can not endure to leave! Yet go I must. Suppose he should suspect me! What would he say to such as

I—a wild hoiden thing who has defied and broken all the ties of womanhood? Holy Madonna! Have pity!"

His arms flew wide, as if to embrace the knees of the Virgin, and his face was drawn with anguish.

"I can never atone for my actions!" he thought. "If he discovers that I am a woman, he will always despise me! Better leave to him the memory of a boy friend whom he loved and who ran away!"

Then, gathering up his courage, he went a final round of the dearly loved workshop, caressing each object as he passed, as though it had been animate. Everywhere were things that reminded him of Leigh. There they had sat and talked on such a night; here he had perched while he showed some tricks of technique; together they had stood at this window looking over the roof-tops at the city which they had talked of beautifying, and beside this table he had often drawn a chair, when they sat down to share a scanty meal and an abundance of talk on subjects dear to them. Oh! it was too cruel, too full of poignant memories, this place! Nothing was to be gained by tarrying, but wounds, fresh wounds, added to that which he was doomed to carry forever! Since going was inevitable, best go quickly and be done. To run away down the dark stair, along the cold street—away, away, to the blossoming Southland and the search for forgetfulness.

With set lips he put on hat and coat, extinguished the candle, and by the dim glow of the banked fire, began to gather up the belt of the knapsack. Then a sound on the staircase caused his heart to give a great leap, after which it seemed to stop beating altogether. Nearer and nearer came the familiar step, and then, without pause it crossed the landing and the door was burst open to admit the towering figure of Abraham Lincoln Leigh.

. . . .

"Are you there?" the deep voice asked commandingly, as the man peered into the gloom.

"I—yes!" answered Pedro weakly.

"Thank God!" exclaimed Leigh. Then, as his eyes became accustomed to the darkness, he placed her.

"I was just going," began Pedro faintly, "I—"

"Sit down beside me," said Leigh gently but firmly, "I want to say several things to you."

"Yes, but—" protested the girl.

"Sit down, my dear," said Leigh, striking a light.

There was a tense silence while he lit the lamp,

the soft glow presently revealing them to each other. Then Pedro slowly obeyed the strangely put command, and they sat silently for a long moment, looking into each other's eyes with that perfect understanding that had been theirs from the first. Oh! how could she have doubted him for an instant? There was no misunderstanding the meaning of that "dear"—nor of the tone in which he had spoken it. A wild tingling sensation began to dance through her veins, and at the light in his eyes a deep flush began to creep over her face, feminine enough now, despite its frame of close-cut curls. At length she spoke, never taking her eyes from his.

"So you know," she said superfluously.

"Yes."

"How long have you known?"

"In my secret consciousness, from the beginning of time," he answered her. "Since last night, in actual realization. Why, I've been in love with you all these months, but I did not understand it, owing to—"

He indicated her clothing and again she blushed —a swift crimson this time.

"And you don't—don't despise me?" she asked, ashamed.

"No, I don't despise you: I want to marry you," he replied. "What is your name?"

"Pedro—I never had another, excepting Daussa y. St. Tron, of course. But . . . do you mean it?"

"That is the first utterly dull remark I ever heard you make," observed Leigh. "Now, when shall it be? To-morrow? It's a little late to-night!"

"No!" she cried, springing up. "Not to-night; not to-morrow; I must go away!"

"Why?"

"Iris knows about me; and think of the talk! what would your friends say? Oh! believe me, I must go away until I can come back as myself," she said distractedly.

His face was stern as he replied.

"I can usually see the reasons you put forth," said he; "but I can not feel that there is any need for you to go."

"Ah," she pleaded, "but *I* do! Let me come back as *myself*—as a *woman,* and as a woman should. I want to; can't you understand?"

"Yes—I think perhaps I do," said he slowly. "And in the meanwhile?"

"I shall be with Rico and Anna," she said, "until they have the baby. They can be together all the meantime, if I dance the bears and bring in the money for them; and then I shall slip away and bid the road farewell. . . ."

Then he did see. Saw all that the life of the road had meant to her, all that she would give up . . . for him . . . He got to his feet rather unsteadily, and at the look on his face she, too, sprang up, half-frightened, to escape him. But retreat was useless, and then, smothered in his mighty arms, Pedro received her first kiss. . . .

It was an hour later that they crept down the dark stairway and swung the door open to the faint glow of coming day. "When will you come back, Pedro—oh! when will you come back?" he whispered passionately.

"I shall come," said Pedro, "when the violets are in bloom; when it is full spring, I shall return."

Then she shifted the little knapsack into place across her shoulder and alone stepped off into the grayness, the little bear shuffling along at her heels.

The morning was bleak and chill, but Leigh stood quite motionless long after she had passed from sight; stood motionless until the housetops flamed with the coming sun, until the dawn was painted like unto the glory of love; and then he smiled, and, throwing back his head, sniffed the keen air as though he could already scent the unborn violets of that distant spring.

THE END